# HOW TO USE THIS BOOK

1. COME ON IN. HAVE A LOOK AROUND. Check out the Table of Contents to see if anything catches your eye. Bear in mind that **most of the lesson plans can be adapted for other grade levels,** so don't feel obligated to stick strictly to yours.

2. ALL OF OUR WORKSHOPS ARE DIFFERENT, SO ALL OF OUR LESSON PLANS ARE TOO. Generally, there's **an outline of the lesson** for you, and sometimes a **handout for the students**. We've tried to make them as user-friendly as possible.

3. TO HELP YOU PLAN YOUR CLASS, **WE'VE HEADED EACH LESSON PLAN WITH A TIME ESTIMATE.** This is how long the class generally runs. In your classroom it might go slower or faster, but we've tried to ballpark it for you.

4. AS MUCH AS WE'VE TRIED TO MAKE THINGS FUN, **WE'VE ALSO TRIED TO KEEP THINGS SIMPLE.** A three-ring writing circus with actual trained animals and cotton candy machines would be great fun for your students, but a great big headache for you, so **we've tried to keep the supplies and prep to a minimum.** We've headed each lesson plan and activity with the list of materials it requires. Most of the time this will consist of things you already have on hand. Fancier fixings are optional.

5. **WE ENCOURAGE YOU TO ADAPT THESE LESSONS TO SUIT YOU AND YOUR STUDENTS.** These lessons were taught in an after-school environment, with students who were there by choice, so we expect they'll need some tweaking to work for you. Make them yours.

6. SOMETIMES **YOU MIGHT HAVE EXTRA TIME AND WANT TO DO SOMETHING REALLY, REALLY SPECIAL.** When you do, look for the Superteacher bonus activity icon. It looks like this:

 ## SUPERTEACHER BONUS ACTIVITIES

Superteacher bonus activities are optional additions to the lesson plan that require a little more effort, but are guaranteed to dazzle your students.

---

7. IN THE APPENDIX YOU'LL FIND SOME OTHER TOOLS WE HOPE WILL MAKE YOUR LIFE EASIER: **evaluation rubrics to guide grading**, a **student self-assessment checklist,** and charts to **show you which Core Curriculum guidelines each lesson plan meets**.

8. WE'D LOVE TO HEAR HOW [...] ns? Comments? **You can contact us at** info@826national.org. Se[...]esson plan, or samples of your students' fabulous work. We'd [...]

DON'T FORGET to WRITE

for the ELEMENTARY GRADES

50 ENTHRALLING *and* EFFECTIVE WRITING LESSONS

AGES 5 TO 12

826 National | Edited by Jennifer Traig

JOSSEY-BASS
A Wiley Imprint
www.josseybass.com

Published by Jossey-Bass
A Wiley Imprint
989 Market Street, San Francisco, CA 94103-1741—www.josseybass.com

Jossey-Bass books and products are available through most bookstores. To contact Jossey-Bass directly call our Customer Care Department within the U.S. at 800-956-7739, outside the U.S. at 317-572-3986, or fax 317-572-4002.

Wiley also publishes its books in a variety of electronic formats and by print-on-demand. Not all content that is available in standard print versions of this book may appear or be packaged in all book formats. If you have purchased a version of this book that did not include media that is referenced by or accompanies a standard print version, you may request this media by visiting http://booksupport.wiley.com. For more information about Wiley products, visit us www.wiley.com.

Library of Congress Cataloging-in-Publication Data

Don't forget to write for the elementary grades : 50 enthralling and effective writing lessons (ages 5 to 12) / 826 National. -- 1st ed.

    p. cm.

  ISBN 978-1-118-02431-7 (pbk.)

  1. English language – Composition and exercises – Study and teaching (Elementary) – United States.
  2. Education, Elementary – Activity programs – United States. I. 826 National (Organization)

  LB1576.D6345 2011

  372.60973--dc23

                                                                      2011025956

Printed in the United States of America

FIRST EDITION

PB Printing   10 9 8 7 6 5 4 3 2 1

TABLE OF CONTENTS

LESSON PLANS

by JOAN KIM AND ROBERTO CARABEO

Just what it sounds like.

by JENNIFER TRAIG

Students gain confidence in their language skills by writing a short story
for a pet, then reading it to a pet audience. Ideal for very young writers,
kindergarten through fourth grade.

by MAGGIE HANKS

In this workshop, students build forts using tables, couches, sheets,
clamps, whatever you have around. They then go into the forts and do
writing exercises. Best for grades two and up.

by AMIE NENNINGER

Facts take a backseat to fiction in this incredibly inventive workshop.
Students compose their own wacky faux-science journal. A great way to
get more science-minded students interested in creative writing. Ideal
for students fifth grade and younger.

FOREWORD

THE FIRST INDICATION THAT THIS ISN'T YOUR NORMAL WRITING CENTER IS the storefront you have to pass through to get to the classroom. It might be a pirate shop, featuring a large selection of peg legs and eye patches, or it could be a robot repair lab, presided over by a burping automaton. It might be a time travel mart, offering dodo chow and 50-year calendars; or a superhero supply store with a phone-booth changing room. Past the shelves of student-authored books, zines, and newspapers, students slip through the secret door to the classroom. This doesn't look normal, either. There are plush couches inviting you to curl up and read, big mahogany tables begging you to hunker down and write, and some fixtures that make no sense at all, like portholes, or a fully functional grocer's scale. The teacher appears to be wearing a wig and a Viking helmet. Just what is going on here?

This is how we do things at the 826 National centers. From the time we opened our doors in San Francisco in 2002, our emphasis has been on fun, and there's been plenty of that. But something else happened: we helped students produce some great writing. Then we did it again. Students returned over and over and told their friends. Before long our workshops had long waiting lists.

We'd come up with a formula that worked. Soon we started hearing from people who wanted to bring our methods to their own hometowns. We expanded to eight centers across the country, each offering free after-school tutoring, in-class support for teachers and students, and workshops on topics ranging from spycraft to space exploration to screenwriting.

Word continued to spread. Teachers wrote, called, and came in, asking for ideas for their own classrooms. By 2005 we'd had so many requests we decided it was time to put all our best ideas in one place, so we published *Don't Forget to Write,* a collection of lesson plans from our best workshops and favorite authors. Six years and several hundred workshops later, it seemed high time to publish a new edition.

We ended up with so many lesson plans, in fact, that we had to publish two volumes, one for elementary grades, and one for middle and high school. In this volume, you'll find lessons on topics that appeal to elementary writers, both to those who like writing and reading (fairy tale do-overs, literary mash-ups, guerilla poetry) and those who don't (mad science, secret codes, Sasquatches, ice cream). There's a particular emphasis on fun, yes, but also on building blocks: the fundamentals of narrative, character development, self-expression. How do you communicate clearly? What makes a good story? What can words do? You'll learn how to interview a zombie; how to cook for Bigfoot; how to break through writer's block; and what onomatopoeia means. And, of course, you'll learn how to bring 826's methods to your own classroom.

What makes 826 workshops different? Well, first of all, they are often completely nuts. We think play is paramount, so we use lots of props, costumes, and drama. Our tutors are invited to teach courses on anything related to writing. Sometimes it's very practical, like a workshop on writing the perfect college application essay. Sometimes it's just silly, like

Writing for Pets (though this, too, has a pedagogical rationale: reading to a nonjudgmental listener, like a dog, is a great way to boost students' skills and confidence).

Whatever the topic, it's taught by a specialist in the field, from journalists to sportswriters to musicians. At 826LA, the first workshop was taught by filmmaker Spike Jonze. In San Francisco, when workshop teacher Michael Chabon told his colleague Stephen King that he was using his work in our Horror and Dark Fantasy class, Stephen decided to come to teach the lesson himself.

We would love to be able to dispatch pros like these to your classroom too. Instead, we've done the next best thing: we asked them to write lesson plans for you. A real scientist wrote the Science Club lesson. A professional cartoonist wrote the comic book lesson. An actual anthropologist wrote our lesson on the anthropology of garbage. Other contributors include classroom teachers (the most expert experts of all), college professors, working screenwriters, and even one former 826 student, who's gone on to become a writer himself. Our favorite authors pitched in, too. We think the end result is like having Jon Scieszka stop by to teach a class on fractured fairy tales, or Aimee Bender lead a workshop on magic realism.

The whole enterprise is the classroom equivalent of hiding the good-for-you vegetables under the potato chips in the secretly nutritious casserole. We've based our activities on proven pedagogy. The students think they're having fun, and of course they are, but they're also engaged in very academic endeavors. They are organizing their ideas, crafting arguments, revising their work, stating their point of view, peer-editing a friend's work, and generally learning an awful lot about the hard work and the craft of writing. They're playing, but they're also getting real experience. For two hours they're a food critic, a reporter, a mad scientist, getting an idea of what it's really like to do this for a living.

And they leave with concrete proof. All of our workshops are project-based. Everyone likes to have something to show for their time, so we strive to produce something in every class, be it a chapbook, a play, a newspaper, a short film, or a radio segment. We know that the process of making that product is the important part, but having something to hold on to at the end is the perfect punctuation to work well done. Also, making them is incredibly satisfying and enjoyable.

We hope you'll enjoy the process, too. Supporting teachers is our first priority, and we've tried to create a book that will make your job just a little bit easier and fun. We know that teachers are pressed for time trying to ensure content and skill requirements are met. To this end, we've made sure the lessons in this book meet the Common Core Curriculum standards. We created some charts to show you (see Appendix).

If you're nearby, come pay us a visit (see Appendix for a listing of all our centers). Workshops are only a part of what we do at 826. We also offer free after-school tutoring, free writing field trips, and free in-school support. You can learn more about our programs at www.826national.org. We'd love for you to come see all the excitement for yourself.

We hope you have as much fun as we have.

JENNIFER TRAIG, GERALD RICHARDS, *and* DAVE EGGERS

 # ACKNOWLEDGMENTS

LIKE ALL 826 NATIONAL PROJECTS, THIS BOOK WAS MADE POSSIBLE BY THE contributions of an incredibly creative and generous group of people who were kind enough to share their time and talents. We're especially grateful to 826 National cofounder Nínive Calegari for all her work putting the project together in the first place. Thanks, also, to the executive directors of all the chapters, and to the many staffers who helped and contributed, especially Amy Sumerton, Julius Diaz Panoriñgan, Joan Kim, Kait Steele, Chris Molnar, Ryan Smith, Maya Shugart, Lindsey Plait Jones, Karen Sama, Lauren Hall, and Mariama Lockington. Thanks to the wonderful volunteers who let us offer inventive workshops at all our chapters. Thanks to everyone at Jossey-Bass, especially Kate Gagnon, Tracy Gallagher, and Justin Frahm. Thanks to the very talented Tony Millionaire for his artwork, especially his Superteacher icon figure. Finally, thanks to our brilliant lesson plan contributors, some of them old friends, some of them new. We were blown away by their work and can't thank them enough.

THE AUTHORS

826 NATIONAL IS A NETWORK OF NONPROFIT ORGANIZATIONS DEDICATED TO helping students, ages 6 through 18, with expository and creative writing, and to helping teachers inspire their students to write. 826 chapters are located in San Francisco, Los Angeles, New York, Chicago, Ann Arbor, Seattle, Boston, and Washington, D.C. Our mission is based on the understanding that great leaps in learning can happen with one-on-one attention, and that strong writing skills are fundamental to future success. We offer innovative and dynamic project-based learning opportunities that build on students' classroom experience, and strengthen their ability to express ideas effectively, creatively, confidently, and in their own voices.

Each 826 chapter offers after-school tutoring, field trips, workshops, and in-school programs—all free of charge—for students, classes, and schools. We target students in public schools, particularly those with limited financial, educational, and community resources.

Jennifer Traig is the author of the memoirs *Devil in the Details* and *Well Enough Alone,* and the editor of *The Autobiographer's Handbook.* A longtime 826 volunteer, she has a PhD in literature and lives in Ann Arbor, where she serves on the board of directors for 826michigan.

826's History

826 Valencia opened its doors in 2002, growing out of a desire to partner the professional literary and arts community of San Francisco with local students in need of engaging learning opportunities. The tutoring and writing center was designed to be a vibrant setting for rigorous educational activities. Connecting students with local authors, artists, and college students while providing a space that is whimsical and fun proved to be an excellent model for achieving results, and the idea was replicated in seven additional cities.

Since 2004, 826 chapters have opened in Brooklyn, Los Angeles, Chicago, Seattle, Ann Arbor, Boston, and, most recently, Washington, D.C., each with a unique storefront as the gateway to the writing center. While the theme of each center is varied (in Los Angeles students are encouraged to dabble in time travel; in Chicago they may begin their careers as future spies), the 826 model always holds true: if you offer students rigorous and fun learning opportunities and one-on-one attention, they will make great strides in their writing skills and confidence.

As the 826 model spread, the flagship center became home to the nationwide support of the individual chapters, determining and encouraging the use of shared best practices, setting standards for program evaluations to ensure the quality of 826 programming, and framing the national dialogue about the work of teachers and the value of teaching writing. In 2004, the legal name of 826 Valencia was changed to 826 National, to reflect this bigger-picture work. Meanwhile, in San Francisco the programs continued to grow bigger and stronger. In 2008, we made the decision to

formally separate into two legal entities to reflect the different initiatives of the local San Francisco chapter and the national one. Since July 2008, 826 National has existed as its own legal entity, apart from 826 Valencia, and it supports the individual 826 chapters across the nation.

Pirette McKamey, the teacher with whom 826 Valencia worked at Mission High School last year, said this about our collaboration: "When students work with people one-on-one on their writing, the benefit is so great. It helps students begin to recognize the relationship between their writing and communication to other people—that writing actually has the power to do that. It's great to have outside people. I think the students feel less comfortable working with outside people, so they have to do some self-struggle and overcome barriers to figure out how to communicate their ideas to someone they don't assume is sympathetic. And it's good for them—very powerful, and good for them."

Our Student Programming

Each year, 826 is able to provide 22,000 students from low-income families and low-performing school districts with one-on-one tutoring, writing instruction, classroom support, and a wide variety of publishing opportunities. We give students high-quality, engaging, and hands-on literary programming. The result: better writing, improved grades, stronger community ties between young people and professional adults, and brighter futures.

ALL EIGHT 826 CHAPTERS OFFER THE FOLLOWING:

☞ AFTER-SCHOOL TUTORING: Neighborhood students receive free one-on-one tutoring five days a week in all subject areas at each center. 826 National's tutoring program is designed to inspire learning, foster creativity, and help students understand and complete their homework each day. We accomplish this by providing youth—particularly low-income youth, including those who live near our locations—free access to invaluable academic assistance.

☞ WORKSHOPS: Our free workshops foster creativity and strengthen writing skills in a variety of areas. All offerings directly support classroom curriculum while engaging students with imaginative and often playful themes. Workshops are project-based and taught by experienced, accomplished literary professionals. Examples of topics include: Writing for Pets (just what it sounds like!); Mad Science, in which students, wearing lab coats, isolate strings of their own DNA and then write stories about their DNA mutating in strange ways; How to Persuade Your Parents, Or: Whining Effectively; Spy Training; and How to Write a Comic Book, taught by a professional cartoonist.

☞ PUBLISHING: 826 publishes an array of student-authored literary quarterlies, newspapers, books, chapbooks, and anthologies, which are displayed and sold in the retail shops that front our writing centers and are distributed and sold nationwide. We use professional editors and designers to allow the students' work to shine. Our most significant student collaboration each year, the Young Authors' Book Project, partners a local high school classroom with professional writers and editors. The students spend three to four months crafting essays around a particular theme, continually collaborating with adult tutors through the editing and publishing process. When the project is complete, we celebrate the release with a festive party. The final book is a stunning reflection of months of hard work, engagement, and dedication on the part of the students and tutors.

☞ FIELD TRIPS: Up to four times a week, 826 chapters welcome an entire public school classroom for a morning of high-energy learning. In one field trip, Storytelling & Bookmaking, students write, illustrate, and bind their own books within a two-hour period.

☞ IN-SCHOOL PROGRAM: We dispatch teams of volunteers into local, high-need public schools to support teachers and provide one-on-one assistance to students as they tackle various writing projects, such as school newspapers, research papers, oral histories, and college entrance essays. We serve five thousand students annually through this deeply meaningful partnership with local schools and teachers.

Our five thousand volunteers make our work possible and our programs free of charge. They are local community residents, many of whom are professional writers, artists, college students, parents, bankers, lawyers, and retirees from a wide range of professions. These passionate individuals are found at our centers throughout the day, sitting side by side with our students after school, supporting morning field trips, and helping entire classrooms of students learn the art of writing. Our volunteers actively connect with youth every day.

If you would like to get involved in programs as a tutor or as a donor, please go to the 826 National Web site, www.826national.org, to find out more information or visit one of our chapter Web sites (the full list can be found at the end of the book).

THE CONTRIBUTORS

MEGHAN ADLER loves to teach writing, especially poetry, to the young and talented writers at 826 Valencia. When not volunteering at 826, she is an elementary educator and learning specialist for students in the Bay Area. You may learn more about her at www .meghanadler.com.

ELIZABETH ALEXANDER was born in Dallas but doesn't act like it. Her essays, short stories, and poems have appeared in *Archives of Neurology,* the *Journal of Feminist Studies in Religion, Golden Handcuffs Review,* and two literary magazines named after monkeys.

SCOTT BEAL'S poems have appeared in journals including *Indiana Review, cream city review,* and *Bellingham Review.* He teaches poetry and fiction workshops at the Neutral Zone teen center and 826michigan, and serves as Dzanc Writer-in-Residence at Ann Arbor Open School.

AIMEE BENDER is the author of *The Girl in the Flammable Skirt, An Invisible Sign of My Own, Willful Creatures, The Third Elevator,* and *The Particular Sadness of Lemon Cake.* Her short fiction has been published in *GQ, The Paris Review, Tin House, McSweeney's,* and more, and she has been teaching various forms of creative writing for the past 18 years to students from ages 4 to 75.

BRAD BRUBAKER is a musician (http://bradbrubaker.bandcamp.com), ice cream blogger/chef (http://icecreamuscream.blogspot.com), and arts educator (obviously). Not coincidentally, he is involved in both nonprofit fundraising and Chicago's vibrant clown community.

ERIC CANOSA is a writer and technologist living in Ann Arbor, Michigan. He is deeply grateful for Gary Snyder, Gary Larson, and Gary Gygax.

ROBERTO CARABEO designs buildings for a living. He is not an insect.

MOIRA CASSIDY is a senior at the University of Chicago, and she had the honor of working as an intern at 826CHI in summer 2010. Moira is a cyclist, a game designer, and a radio DJ, and it is her ardent hope to one day eat an entire birthday cake in one sitting.

NICHOLAS DECOULOS is a senior at Northeastern University studying English and cinema studies and plans to continue writing. He would like to thank his family, his friends, 826 Boston, and his English teachers for giving him the encouragement to write, and providing him with plenty of good writing material.

MARK DE LA VIÑA is part of the 826 Valencia tutoring corps that created the award-winning *Straight-Up News* at Everett Middle School in San Francisco in 2003. He has been an arts and entertainment reporter for the *San Jose Mercury News* and the *Philadelphia Daily News* as well as a contributor to the *Los Angeles Times,* the *Chicago Tribune, Latina,* and *In Style.*

JASON DEPASQUALE is a teacher, artist, and robot maker. He lives in Ann Arbor with his wife, Amy Sumerton.

AARON DEVINE is an MFA student in fiction writing at UMass-Boston. Originally from Minnesota, he can be found online at www.aarondevine.net.

SHANNON DIGREGORIO loves sharks, quilting, Scrabble, pretending she's a chef, and going on adventures with her friends. She volunteers at 826 Boston and loves telling the story of exactly how the Greater Boston Bigfoot Research Institute harvests its best-selling Unicorn Tears.

HOLLY M. DUNSWORTH is assistant professor of anthropology at the University of Rhode Island. She digs up fossils in Kenya and enjoys thinking like a caveman.

JULIET WELLER DUNSWORTH is an artist/writer living in Oviedo, Florida. She is currently mentoring and coaching middle school students in reading comprehension in preparation for state exams.

CHLOE DURKEE is a second grader who loves horses, kittens, bedtime stories (if not actually going to bed), and wearing multiple dresses simultaneously. She also has the good fortune of being the niece of 826michigan program director Amy Sumerton.

DAVE EGGERS is the cofounder of 826 Valencia and the founder of McSweeney's Publishing, LLC. He is also an author whose writings include *A Heartbreaking Work of Staggering Genius, You Shall Know Our Velocity, How We Are Hungry, What Is the What, Zeitoun, The Wild Things,* and *Teachers Have It Easy: The Big Sacrifices and Small Salaries of America's Teachers.*

BECKY EIDELMAN is a student at Wesleyan University who sometimes thinks of herself as an artist. When she is not searching for the lost city of Atlantis, she writes lesson plans and considers the most entertaining ways to teach grammar to fifth graders.

KATHERINE FISHER is a PhD student in English at the University of Michigan. She knew she'd made the right choice in moving to Ann Arbor when she learned it was home to 826michigan.

DAN GERSHMAN is a PhD student in space and planetary physics at the University of Michigan and has been volunteering at 826michigan for about a year.

KATHLEEN GOLDFARB recently served as director of programs at 826 Seattle.

LUCAS GONZALEZ is a New York City native, an English MA student, and a former 826NYC young author. His first novel, *Maple Machine,* appeared in the 2006 anthology "Nine Novels by Younger Americans." Lucas lives in New York where he continues to create works of poetry, fiction, drama, and nonfiction, as well as drawing, painting, cartoon, and mixed-media work.

SARAH GREEN is a PhD candidate in creative writing at Ohio University. Her poetry has won a Pushcart Prize.

MAGGIE HANKS is a poet, student, and mouthy broad from Ann Arbor, Michigan. When she's not leading Fort Society at 826michigan, she writes songs on her ukulele, glues stuff to other stuff, and plays with the jelly packets at diners.

ANGELA HERNANDEZ is a classroom teacher and resource specialist at a secondary school in Emeryville, California.

JENNY HOWARD lives in Ann Arbor, Michigan. When she was in third grade she wrote a letter to the president, and she's wanted to be in the White House ever since!

KATHERINE HUNT lives, writes, reads, and edits in Somerville, Massachusetts. She enjoys working with the talented staff and students at 826 Boston.

ABIGAIL JACOBS has volunteered at 826 Valencia since it opened in 2002, leading Sunday drop-in tutoring and serving on the development board. When she's not at 826, she's a public relations manager for Williams-Sonoma, Inc.

TAYLOR JACOBSON lives in Los Angeles where she works as an interior designer. She lives in Echo Park and enjoys stopping by her neighborhood Time Travel Mart on her days off.

JORY JOHN served as programs director at 826 Valencia for five years. He's the editor of *Thanks and Have Fun Running the Country: Kids' Letters to President Obama,* and coauthor of a children's book, *Pirate's Log,* and two humor books, *All My Friends Are Dead* and *I Feel Relatively Neutral About New York.* He works as a journalist and cartoonist in San Francisco. Visit him at www.bigstonehead.net.

LINDSEY PLAIT JONES is the program director at 826 Boston, where she embarks on new adventures regularly. In a recent past life, she was an unflappable public high school English teacher in Atlanta and Philadelphia. She lives in Cambridge with her husband and their dog.

ROBERT JURY is a screenwriter and director who lives in Iowa City with his wife and two kids. His screenplay, *Working Man,* was selected for the 2010 Film Independent (FIND) Screenwriters Lab as well as the 2011 FIND Directors Lab. Jury has written feature film screenplays for Twentieth Century Fox, Walt Disney Studios, and HBO Films. Jury is also a past winner of the Walt Disney Studios Writers Fellowship and a member of the Writers Guild of America, West.

TANIA KETENJIAN is editor-in-chief of *The [Un]Observed: A Radio Magazine.* She also is a journalist who has produced for NPR, PRI, the BBC, the BBC World Service, RTE in Ireland, and ABC in Australia.

JOAN KIM is the director of education at 826NYC.

MARGARET MASON is the author of *No One Cares What You Had for Lunch: 100 Ideas for Your Blog,* and publisher of Mighty Mighty Media. Her personal blog, Mighty Girl, was nominated for a SxSW Lifetime Achievement Award, and she was named one of Silicon Valley's Top 50 Influencers by Now Public.

MEGHAN McCOOK is a mom, artist, and art educator who loves art, music, movies, writing, cooking, yoga, gardening in her backyard, and dancing in her kitchen. She resides in Chicago with her husband, baby daughter, and two cats.

SUSAN MEYER studied English at Hendrix College in the rolling hills of central Arkansas. She currently works in educational publishing and resides in Astoria, New York, with her ever-loyal cat, Dinah.

CHRIS MOLNAR is a writer from New York City. During the day he manages 826NYC's Brooklyn Superhero Supply Store, where he tends to the kryptonite and cybernetic henchfish.

NICOLE MOORE is a Bay Area teacher who enjoys finding new ways to connect reading and writing to the outside world, even if it's a part of the world she doesn't know much about (yet). She is famous among her students for being horrible at math and science, but her respect for both leads her to try to write about those topics when she's feeling appropriately brave and/or caffeinated.

RYAN MOORE is a Bay Area writer and editor who wishes he were a classroom teacher, and may start figuring out how to change careers. If he were to become a teacher, he and his wife, Nicole, could be that cute teacher couple that you probably remember from high school, but even if he doesn't, he has an honorary title among Nicole's students as that funny, cool guy who helps make papers better.

JESSICA MORTON is a student at the University of Michigan Law School, and has volunteered at 826michigan for the past three years. She has always wanted to live out her secret(ish) dream of playing a life-size board game in the manner of Ron Weasley.

SUSIE NADLER writes about food and design. She lives in San Francisco with her husband, their twin babies, and their whippet.

AMIE NENNINGER loves reading, writing, and problem solving, and she puts these skills to use daily as a tutor and 826 volunteer. Her latest project is building a formidable San Francisco junior detective agency with her children, Beckett and Thea.

ELAINE PALUCKI holds a PhD in plant biology and is a science textbook editor as well as an adjunct professor at Brooklyn College. She regularly observes the science of superheroes as a volunteer at 826NYC.

JULIUS DIAZ PANORIŃGAN is director of education at 826LA, where he helps volunteers cook up madcap writing workshops and occasionally teaches his own. (For years, he's been reteaching and retweaking one of his babies: $8 - 2 = 6$, a math story workshop.) As far as he can recall, his atypical lesson planning started as a college senior, when he tasked his computer science section with programming a fictional robot to disrupt the always-annoying ProFro (prospective freshman) Weekend.

PARDIS PARSA is a performer, writer, bicoastal book club founder, and administrator for the arts. She enjoys expressive arts therapy, reading, baking, and making things up.

KATE PAVAO is a freelance writer and editor who lives with her family in Aptos, California. She recently taught a spy class at her daughter's elementary school that included code breaking, dusting for fingerprints, and—the most popular—finding clues by sorting through the trash.

GABRIELA PEREIRA has an MFA in writing for children from The New School, and currently works as a freelance writing teacher in New York City. A former toy designer, she loves developing activities that make writing fun and get kids (and grown-ups!) excited about writing.

MICAH PILKINGTON has worked as a Web editor and writer since 2000, with sporadic career digressions into film and theater. She lives in San Francisco.

TODD POUND is a San Francisco–based writer, illustrator, and designer who has had the good fortune of collaborating with some supremely talented people like Garry Trudeau and Mark Ryden. Right this very second, he is writing and designing a video game, which makes him popular with the kids.

GERALD RICHARDS is the CEO of 826 National, with more than 16 years of management and development experience in the nonprofit sector. Prior to joining 826, Gerald was the executive director for the Bay Area office of the Network for Teaching Entrepreneurship (NFTE). Gerald is currently a member of the Council of Chief State School Officers (CCSSO) and Ed Steps Curiosity and Creativity workgroup in Washington, D.C. He is an inaugural fellow in the California Leaders of Color Fellowship Program, a member of the 2009 class of Leadership San Francisco, and a 2008 award recipient of 101 African-American Champions for Youth in the Bay Area. He currently serves on the board of the Woodland School. Gerald has an MFA in writing from the School of the Art Institute of Chicago and a BA in film studies from Wesleyan University.

LINDSEY ROBINSON is a writer and teacher who is currently pursuing an MFA degree in writing for the screen and stage from Northwestern University. She taught the introductory screenwriting course at Northwestern and has worked at Lionsgate, Funny or Die, and Gary Sanchez Productions.

KAREN SAMA grew up in Queens, New York, earned a bachelor's degree in religion from Colorado College, and worked with preschoolers with special needs in Denver, Colorado. She is currently the Program Coordinator at 826 Boston in Roxbury, which puts her in the enviable position of having the incredible ideas of students, volunteers, and staff fly at her on a regular basis.

LAURA SCHOLES works as a copywriter and is principal of Story House Creative (www.storyhousecreative). She has an MFA in creative writing (fiction) from the University of Montana and has written one novel that's tucked away on an old hard drive.

JON SCIESZKA is the author of numerous children's books including *The True Story of the 3 Little Pigs! The Stinky Cheese Man, Math Curse, Baloney,* and *Sam Samurai.* He lives in Brooklyn and serves on the board of directors for 826NYC.

MAYA SHUGART is 826 Boston volunteer coordinator. She was born and raised in Denver, where she spent time Flamenco and Folklorico dancing. She relocated to Boston for school and graduated in May 2009 from Emerson College with a BA in writing, literature, and publishing and a minor in photography.

RYAN SMITH is 826 Boston's store and events coordinator, where he heads the Greater Boston Bigfoot Research Institute and orchestrates fundraising events. Ryan also volunteers as a writer for SmallCanBeBig, an online micro-charity. Ryan lives and writes poetry and prose in an apartment across from Boston's most thunderous trolley line.

REBECCA STERN taught in a "hard-to-staff" public school in Brooklyn before becoming a middle school language arts teacher in Palo Alto. Along with Brad Wolfe, she is the coeditor of a book of essays by notable authors aimed at the middle grades to be published by Roaring Brook Press/Macmillan in 2013.

SCARLETT STOPPA, when she's not reinventing the wheel, is a karma comedian. In 826 circles, she is best know for her outlandish wigs, obscure props, torrential brainstorms, cheerleader-level enthusiasm, and uncanny ability to inspire creative chaos.

J. RYAN STRADAL lives and writes in Los Angeles, where he sometimes works on TV shows. He has volunteered at 826LA since it opened in 2005 and helps make things for the Echo Park Time Travel Mart.

AMY SUMERTON is program director of 826michigan. She also manages the Liberty Street Robot Supply & Repair, a store she puts together with her husband, Jason DePasquale.

SUSAN VOELKER developed a healthy suspicion toward so-called adults by listening to Roald Dahl books on tape during family car trips from an early age. She got involved with 826NYC to join the youth resistance against dull, unimaginatve writing and goes to battle with mighty young armies one collection of stories at a time.

REBECCA WASLEY received a BA in creative writing from Miami University of Ohio. She lives in the Boston area and enjoys teaching workshops at 826 Boston.

BRAD WOLFE is the founder of Hopeful Media, an organization aimed at using various forms of media to cultivate inspiration, creativity, and mindfulness in education and business. He is also the president of the Sunbeam Foundation for rare pediatric cancer research and is the lead singer of Brad Wolfe and the Moon. Along with Rebecca Stern, he is the coeditor of a book of essays by notable authors aimed at the middle grades to be published by Roaring Brook Press/Macmillan in 2013.

JON ZACK is a feature screenwriter. He lives with his wife in Los Angeles.

MARCY ZIPKE, PHD, is an assistant professor in the Department of Elementary/Special Education at Providence College. She writes riddles and tells jokes for her 3-year-old daughter.

TRAGIC LOVE TALES (BY 6-YEAR-OLDS)

by JOAN KIM AND ROBERTO CARABEO

1 SESSION, 1 HOUR
MATERIALS: *Computer and/or computer projector to view short video (optional)*

SHREK AND FIONA LIVED HAPPILY EVER AFTER. SO DID SLEEPING BEAUTY AND Prince Charming. But who wants to read about happily ever after? Blech! In this lesson students learn the perfect recipe for not-so-happily-ever-after—a tragic story. Sometimes they're tragic love stories, and sometimes they're just plain tragic (6-year-olds, it turns out, aren't always too keen to write about love). But they are always, always, *very* sad.

We start with a word of caution. You are about to write a story that is *so* sad, *so* tragic, and *so* amazing, we tell our students, that the first thing they have to do is warn their readers. We distribute a warning form for the students to fill out, in which they answer the following questions: How will the reader feel by the end of your story? Who should avoid your story, at all costs? How many tissues will readers need to wipe the tears from their faces?

Next, we distribute the "Build Me Up, Buttercup" handout and discuss the steps of tragedy writing. The first thing you need to build an epic, tragic, amazing story: a great character who almost has it all—love, friends, money, power. Why? You raise your character up, so that he or she can fall (and fall hard).

At this point we like to watch this Wile E. Coyote video (www.youtube.com/watch?v=hz65AOjabtM) and think about the coyote's fall. Why do the writers put him up so high? So his fall can be especially spectacular.

So, we tell the students, you need to set your main character up. Ask yourself:

☞ How perfect is your character? And what is the *one flaw* that might bring him or her down?

☞ How perfect is this character's life? And what is the *one thing* that's missing?

Once students have introduced their characters, it's time to bring those characters down. As you continue your story, we say, your character has the *best idea ever* for how to get that thing he or she wants more than anything else in the world. We ask:

☞ What is that idea?

☞ And how is he or she going to make it work?

And then . . . the spectacular fall! We remind the students of their warning to the reader—this is going to be sadder than sad. Before they write the terrible end, we discuss the following:

☞ How will your character's flaw get in the way?

☞ How will things get worse, and worse, and worse, and worse?

☞ How will he or she get so close to his or her dream—only to lose everything?

The stories are finished and shared aloud, and then class ends. Unhappily, of course.

WARNING: SAD STORY

Warn your readers that your story is going to be TRAGIC. (Make sure you tell them just HOW tragic it will be!)

Dear Reader,

You are about to read a very sad story. After you finish it, you will feel like this:

_____

_____

_____

_____

You probably shouldn't read this story at all if you are:

_____

_____

_____

_____

You will need this many tissues to wipe away your tears: _____

Sincerely,

The Author

BUILD ME UP, BUTTERCUP
(JUST TO BRING ME DOWN)

Introduce your MAIN CHARACTER. Remember: He or she has an almost perfect life, except for that FLAW . . .

What is your character's name?

Where does your character live?

Can you think of two words to describe him or her?

    1. _____

    2. _____

How old is he or she?

What does your character look like?

What is his or her biggest FLAW?

What is the one thing he or she wants more than anything in the world? Pick one!

_____

_____

LOVE?

- Who will he or she fall in love with?
- Why will that cause problems?

POWER?

- What kind of power does he or she want?
- Who or what will stand in his or her way?

RICHES?

- What will he or she have to do to get rich?
- How will that cause a problem?

FRIENDS?

- Whom does he or she want to be friends with?
- What does he or she have to do to win that friendship?
- How will that cause problems?

Now, start your story by introducing your character and his or her practically perfect life.

Explain what your character wants and how he or she has tried all of his or her life to get it.

_____

_____

_____

_____

_____

_____

_____

_____

_____

_____

_____

_____

_____

_____

_____

_____

_____

_____

_____

_____

_____

_____

_____

_____

_____

WRITING FOR PETS

by JENNIFER TRAIG

1 SESSION, 90 MINUTES
MATERIALS: *1 pet*

THIS CLASS STARTED AS A LARK BUT quickly became one of our favorites for two good reasons: (1) anything involving pets is going to be fun; and (2) it's actually proven pedagogy. It turns out that reading to a nonjudgmental audience like a dog is a great way to boost students' confidence and skill levels.

This class couldn't be simpler. We learn about writing for animals, then we do it, then we bring a pet in to listen to what we've written. The students *really* get into it. And, my gosh, watching a 6-year-old solemnly read his story to a terrier is just about the cutest thing you'll ever see.

Because we keep getting interrupted by students who want to tell us what their dog did this one time—and because we want to hear—the discussion part takes about 40 minutes.

Class begins with a brief discussion about animals and language. We explain that pets know more English than you'd think. They probably already know these words: "No." "Down." "Heel." "Walk." "Treat." "Good girl/boy." "Bad girl/boy." They certainly know their name. They may even know whole sentences, like these:

"Go for a walk?"

"Who's a good girl?"

"If I told you once, I told you a thousand times: *don't drink out of the toilet.*"

We go on to say you could build a pretty great story from any of this stuff. Drinking out of the toilet alone is subject matter enough for a whole novel.

Next we explain that you need to be a little careful, because pets don't understand abstract representation. When we say "walk," we're talking about the *idea* of a walk. But for a dog, "walk" means "We're going for a walk right now." So if you write a story about a walk, and use the world "walk" 80 times, you are going to have a very excited dog on your hands. This is sort of funny, but also sort of mean, unless you really are going to take the dog for a walk. So we advise the students to choose their words carefully.

Next we explain that pets *do* understand tone. In fact, they pay more attention to tone than to the actual words. If you shout "GOOD KITTY!" in a scary tone, your cat will shirk and hiss. If you croon, "Stupid, stupid kitty!" in a loving tone, she'll purr and do her I'm-a-special-girl dance. Oh, what a stupid kitty. Ha-ha. Again, funny but kind of mean. The point is that tone matters most when you read to your pet, so we suggest students think about writing, and reading, in a tone that suits the material best.

Then we talk about writing for different species. Here is what we tell them. We are not sure if any of this is true, but it definitely inspires great writing:

CATS: Cats like literature more than any other species, and they enjoy it on several levels. Mostly, they enjoy napping on it. But they also enjoy being read to, especially if they can sit in your lap. They're sophisticated listeners who understand irony and dark humor. Lemony Snicket–type stories are ideal. They also like fanciful tales and stories about dictators. Most of all, cats like reading about themselves. Nothing will make your cat happier than an essay on her best qualities. Cats also enjoy writing. Put your cat on the keyboard and just see what she produces!

DOGS: Dogs generally like to read about dogs, and they like a lot of action. They do not understand metaphors or plays on words. They don't necessarily need a plot or a conclusion. A dog likes a story that's all "Go!"—all action and Frisbee chases. Dog stories are the most fun and the easiest to write. Odd as it may seem, dogs aren't too fond of shaggy dog stories—too long.

BIRDS: Birds only like one thing, and that's a good snack. If you want to hold a bird's interest write about potato chips or hazelnuts. They especially enjoying hearing recipes. Whatever you write, it has to be true. You can't fool a bird. Lie all you like to a fish, but a bird knows the facts. They can see everything from their eagle-eye view. Even birds that aren't allowed out are very well informed, because their cages are lined with newspapers.

FISH: Fish couldn't possibly be any more bored than they already are, so any story is a welcome diversion. But they especially like stories about the outside world. Since they've never been anywhere, you can make stuff up—they'll never know. Write a story about Bolivia or Sweden or Alaska. Write a fictional history of chewing gum or bicycles. Tell them what goes on, or what you wish went on, at your school. The only problem is getting them to hear what you write. But fish are expert lip-readers, so just get right in front of the glass and don't cover your mouth while you read.

VERMIN AND PESTS: Rats, fleas, spiders, and cockroaches may be smart and strong, but they are evil. The point of writing for vermin and pests is not to entertain, but to scare them off. Write them morality tales to show them the error of their ways. All stories for these creatures should end with them getting their wagons fixed but good.

MICE, HAMSTERS, AND GUINEA PIGS: Small household rodents enjoy fables, because they so often star in them. A country mouse/city mouse tale is sure to be a hit.

FOR THE ALLERGIC: Allergic to animals but love writing for pets? You can write for stuffed animals instead. They're not quite as responsive as real animals, but they have much longer attention spans. Write your stuffed animal an epic story of a thousand adventures.

Finally, we distribute the following handout and go over it. Then we break for 20 minutes or so and let the students write a fabulous story for a pet. By this point our pet audience has arrived, and we spend the last 30 minutes bringing the students over one by one to read their stories. Usually, the audience consists of a borrowed dog. Cats bore easily. Guinea pigs will do in a pinch, but once one lost control of his bowels *on a student's story* and since then we've been gun-shy.

TEN GREAT PET STORY IDEAS TO GET YOU STARTED

1. Write an extremely flattering poem about your cat. Describe her gorgeous coat, her glittering eyes, her many talents. Oh, she is a star, yes she is. She is a queen.

2. Write a heroic story featuring your dog. It could be made up (he saves a busload of kindergartners!) or true (he gets a flea shot and is very, very brave).

3. Write a movie for your pet to star in. Cats like historical dramas. Dogs like buddy pics.

4. Write your bird a research paper on the history of the doughnut.

5. Write a fairy tale in which your pet mouse/hamster/guinea pig is not the cute sidekick, but the hero.

6. Scare off the bugs and rats with a tragic story of their downfall. Perhaps they meet their ruin at the hands of a vacuum cleaner, or a skateboard. Either way, they've got it coming, for being such rude and messy houseguests.

7. Write a whole newspaper, just for your fish. She's probably dying for some current events. She won't know if you're lying, so you can just make up events you think she'll like.

8. Write a mystery that your pet gets to solve. If you're the coolest pet owner ever, you'll write *The Mystery of the Missing Treat.* At the end of the story, you can let your pet search for, then eat, the missing treat, based on the clues in the story. You might have to help him with the clues depending on how smart he is.

9. Write a science fiction story about a future world that is run by whatever species your pet is. This is a favorite fantasy of cats.

10. If you have several pets, write a play with parts for all of them, then dress them up and try to get them to act it out. Pets aren't so good at memorizing lines, so you'll want to keep the dialogue to a minimum.

DOES YOUR PET THINK HE'S PEOPLE? TAKE THIS EASY QUIZ AND FIND OUT!

1. Does your pet prefer people food? Even vegetables? Does he try to eat your nachos? Does he seem offended when you serve him kibble?

2. Does your pet stand on things to be eye-level with you?

3. Does your pet seem embarrassed when he does something kind of dumb, like walking into the sliding glass door?

4. Does your pet enjoy wearing hats, bandannas, and little sweaters?

5. Sometimes, when your pet meows or barks, does it sound like a word? Are you pretty sure he's trying to talk?

6. Does your pet get jealous when you're allowed to do something he's not, like sit on the couch or go outside?

If you answered "Yes!" to four or more questions, your pet thinks he's people! Be sure to include lots of people in your stories, because that's what your pet will relate to.

FORT PARTY!

by MAGGIE HANKS

1 SESSION, 90 MINUTES

MATERIALS: *A large space with tables and chairs*
At least one sheet or blanket per student, preferably more

SWEET EXTRAS: *Large binder clips for securing blankets*
Flashlights
Fancy scarves and shawls
Cushions
Cardboard tubes and such to construct a defensive perimeter

SO, SOMETIMES YOU HAVE A BABY SISTER. SOMETIMES SHE CRIES AND PUTS her sticky hands on your face while you're reading. Sometimes maybe you need someplace that is quiet and closed-in and smells a little like laundry detergent and a crisp new book. If you need some time by yourself, away from those pesky supervillains, LOOK NO FURTHER!

In this workshop, we're going to turn over chairs, stack up cushions, and convert your space into the coolest, coziest spot this side of the Mississippi!

Before the workshop begins, build an example fort and have building materials strategically placed around the room.

For the first 10 minutes or so, kids will start to trickle in and you'll hand everyone a worksheet as you direct them to sit near the fort you've already built. Anyone who is getting antsy should start drawing his or her dream fort. When you've got everyone seated, you can do a quick introduction by going around the room and sharing your ideal fort location. ("I would build my fort in the hot, molten core of the Earth!")

Now, take 5 or so minutes to talk about what kind of resources in the room can be used to build forts. Look to the sample fort for inspiration. Write suggestions on the board, shooting down dangerous ideas (you get a whole bunch of kids who want to build two-story forts), and encouraging creativity. Yes, use the chairs upside down! Yes, use binder clips to hold sheets together! Use this time to explain that everyone must have a separate, individual fort.

A quick aside about the importance of individual forts: Spaces like this are an awesome tool for team building and collaborative work. By which I mean to say, they quickly become a vortex of whispering and poking if there are not clear boundaries to enforce. More importantly, privacy is key in this workshop because its main goal is to give kids the tools to carve out a safe space for thinking and creating independently. No extra eyes. No red pens. No one watching if their lips move when they read.

Having informed them of the rules, **let the kids build for about 20 minutes**. Give them a 5-minute warning so that any sagging roofs can be spotted and tightened up before writing time. Make sure everyone has something to write on and something to write with.

Now, use about 10 minutes to transition from building to writing. Have everyone get in his or her forts and listen as you read something aloud. If everyone has a flashlight, dim the room lights. Inform kids that now, instead of calling out when they have questions, they need to stick their hands out of their forts and someone (probably you) will be around to help them. You can give them the writing prompts on the handout, or invent your own—these are just some ideas to get them started.

Use the remaining time to write, and about 15 minutes from the end of the workshop, have everyone come out and share. Sometimes it's nice for an adult to break the ice in the sharing portion if the kids are shy about reading. Encourage everyone to at least share his or her favorite sentence, or the idea behind what he or she wrote, but keep it light and fun—not everyone needs to read.

Deconstructing forts can be about as fun as building them. The forts all disappear fairly quickly after you model tearing down your own with proper Godzilla noises, form, and etiquette.

BEST FORT EVER!

Draw a picture of the best fort ever!

If you could invite anyone in the whole world into your fort, who would you pick? Why?

_____

_____

_____

_____

If you could have a fort anywhere in the world, where would it be? Why?

_____

_____

_____

_____

What must every awesome fort have?

_____

_____

_____

_____

WRITING IDEAS

Write a story that starts in your fort and ends at the North Pole.

_____

_____

_____

_____

_____

_____

Write a poem where every line begins with "Inside my fort . . ."

_____

_____

_____

_____

_____

_____

Write directions explaining how to find your fort. If you like, you can also draw a map.

_____

_____

_____

_____

_____

_____

_____

_____

MAKE-BELIEVE SCIENCE

by AMIE NENNINGER

1 SESSION, 90 MINUTES
MATERIALS: *Candy corn (or substitute)*
Dish of water
Items to test for floatability (toys, paper clips, and so on)
Chocolate kisses
1 copy of the handout packet for each student

DID YOU KNOW THAT SALT WATER AND salt combine to form cotton candy? Or that kittens, if fed the proper diet, can fly? Well, it's not true, but who cares? It's interesting! At 826, we believe the study of science shouldn't be bound by facts, formulas, and the laws of physics. If you agree, you'll love this lesson plan. First we learn some completely fictitious, but totally enthralling, scientific findings. Then we use our newfound knowledge to write some science stories, which we compile into a pseudo-scientific journal. Students leave with their own science journals, a head full of untruths, and, we hope, a new enthusiasm for creative play.

This is a great lesson plan for kids who think they don't like to write. Our version is designed for younger children, with lots of drawing and simple writing tasks, but it could easily be modified for an older crowd by asking for longer paragraphs and fewer pictures.

We start class by distributing the handout packets and telling the students they'll need to take a new name. No one named Bill Jones or Julie Smith ever won the Nobel. Adding the suffix -enschpreckenschpiel to your existing last name is certainly a good step toward scientific acclaim. Have your students write their new *nom de science* on the cover of their scientific journal.

Then we roll up our sleeves and start experimenting. Following the prompts in the handout packets, we learn some made-up chemistry, astronomy, physics, and anatomy and biology. We spend about 20 minutes on each subject, and this is what we do:

CHEMISTRY: The students learn that chemists are in charge of equations, a fancy word that explains how everything in the world adds up. The children volunteer equations they know (inevitably math, such as $2 + 3 = 5$). We discuss how equations can also use words, like when we describe color mixing we can say red + yellow = orange. We can also use our words to describe other combinations, and some of them are quite silly (a hummingbird + a book = reading really fast). Then we break to fill in the Chemistry page in our handbook.

ASTRONOMY: Sure, scientists use microscopes, binoculars, and telescopes, but there is an even easier way to catch a glimpse of the galaxies. Studies have shown that nibbling on candy corn improves your eyesight so much you can see life on other planets. Everyone enjoys a piece of candy and squints at light fixtures until the inner workings of Jupiter are revealed. Then we turn to the Astronomy page of our handbook, where students are asked to describe the setting and its inhabitants with words and pictures.

PHYSICS: Every good scientific think tank has an actual tank, and this class is no exception. Kids test a variety of objects (coins, toy cars, pompoms, corks, and erasers are great test samples) and record what happens when the object is tossed in a bucket of water. Then we turn to the Physics page of our handbook, where the junior scientists must record an observation and explain why this occurred. Was the object afraid of water? Why did it splash? Boats float, so the rule of rhyme explains that goats, coats, quarter notes, and sore throats will float too!

ANATOMY AND BIOLOGY: The human body is a mystifying organism that allows us to stand still with a running nose. No one really knows what happens inside the body, as it is actually quite dark in there. This is our best guess: after you chew up your food, it swings on a flying trapeze and splashes into a basin behind your lungs, where it is washed clean of any impurities like germs or lint. Then, tiny hairdryers blow it off. Once it's dry, the food falls backwards down a flight of stairs. You know how our bellies sometimes make noise? That's just the food falling down the stairs to the stomach! Once food is in the stomach, it is carried off by a well-trained pack of miniature squirrels that deliver nutrients to your cells. If kids don't believe this tour of the digestive system, they are encouraged to eat a chocolate kiss, then turn to the Anatomy and Biology page of the handbook and carefully record the morsel's path through the body.

For some extra science flavor, you may want to list and define some very scientific words for the students to include in their reports, like "ergo" or "QED" ("quad erat demonstrandum," which is Latin scientific-speak for "I proved it!").

And that's it! At the end of class, we teach all the students the secret scientist handshake (waggling fingers), and congratulate them on all their important work.

The Journal of
Parafictitious Scientific Inquiry

With Contributions by

Prof. _____enschpreckenschpiel, Ph.D.

CHEMISTRY

Chemists are in charge of EQUATIONS. Equations explain how everything in the world adds up. For example: yellow + blue = green or rain + mud = worms.

_____ + _____ = _____

_____ + _____ = _____

_____ + _____ = _____

_____ + _____ = _____

_____ + _____ = _____

_____ + _____ = _____

_____ + _____ = _____

_____ + _____ = _____

_____ + _____ = _____

_____ + _____ = _____

_____ + _____ = _____

_____ + _____ = _____

ASTRONOMY

Everybody knows that carrots are good for your eyes. But candy corn is even better. This one time, after we ate a whole bag, we could see Mars! We discovered Mars is made of butterscotch pudding, and ruled by kittens. Eat a piece of candy and then tell us what you see on Jupiter.

Describe Jupiter:

_____

_____

_____

_____

This is how it looks:

The creatures that live on it are . . .

_____

_____

_____

_____

And this is how they look:

_____

_____

_____

_____

PHYSICS

Recent research in our laboratory bathtub leads us to believe that some things, like marsh-mallows, cheese, and dump trucks, float because they are afraid of water. We've also discovered that all green things sink, because green things are lazy. Try placing a few items in water. Record whether they sink or float, and why.

ITEM #1: _____

SINK or FLOAT? _____

Why?

_____

_____

_____

ITEM #2: _____

SINK or FLOAT? _____

Why?

_____

_____

_____

ITEM #3: _____

SINK or FLOAT? _____

Why?

_____

_____

_____

ANATOMY & BIOLOGY

Did you know these anatomy fun facts?

- The knee bone is actually connected to the *cha cha cha* bone!
- Adult humans have 253 teeth!
- There's more hair in your nose than on your whole head!

WHAT HAPPENS TO THE FOOD YOU EAT?

We're not sure, but we think it's carried off by tiny squirrels who live inside your belly. What do you think? Eat a chocolate kiss and describe what happens.

First, the chocolate kiss goes to the _____,

where it _____.

Then, it goes to the _____,

where it _____.

Finally, it goes to the _____,

where it _____.

Here's a picture of what happens:

OH, YOU SHOULDN'T HAVE, REALLY . . .

(OR, HOW TO WRITE A JON SCIESZKA PICTURE BOOK)

by JON SCIESZKA

1 SESSION, 1 HOUR
MATERIALS: *1 Jon Scieszka book*
(the local library should have several)

IMITATION IS SAID TO BE THE MOST SINCERE FORM OF FLATTERY. IT'S ALSO a great way to start writing.

When I was a kid, I discovered Jack London's stories. All of my stories from that year featured brave dogs "bounding" through hazards of every sort. The "bounding" seemed vital. Later stories from my Edgar Allen Poe Phase were sure to include at least one misshapen dwarf, a surprise ending, and the word "dreary." My Kafka Period and my Mad Magazine Days seemed to have collided and fused to form my current style.

So the basic idea of the class is to show one of five Jon Scieszka picture books (listed below), read it, and then use it as a model for kids to imitate. It's a near foolproof plan because (1) it's nothing more than an organized version of what kids naturally do on their own, and (2) the writing challenge is easily adapted to fit the ability of each individual student. The concrete and literal writers can copy the story directly. The more sophisticated writers can write their own variations.

I would imagine starting the class by showing a Jon Scieszka picture book and announcing, "We have finally discovered how Jon Scieszka writes his books. Special agents learned that Mr. Scieszka is a sucker for flattery. He loves it when kids imitate his writing. So when the agents promised that kids would imitate his writing if he told them how he wrote his books . . . he spilled his guts. If you promise to imitate him, we can reveal his secrets."

This is the perfect time to bring up the aphorism, "Imitation is the most sincere form of flattery." Discuss.

Read the selected book. Choose from:

THE TRUE STORY OF THE 3 LITTLE PIGS! by Jon Scieszka

BALONEY, HENRY P. by Jon Scieszka

SQUIDS WILL BE SQUIDS by Jon Scieszka

MATH CURSE by Jon Scieszka

THE STINKY CHEESE MAN AND OTHER FAIRLY STUPID TALES by Jon Scieszka

Then distribute the corresponding handout, which explains how I wrote it. Remind the writers of their promise to flatter me with imitation, and brainstorm how they might write their own stories using the story that was just read as the model.

If you want to really keep imitating the Jon Scieszka writing model, explain to the students that I never draw the illustrations for my stories. I write them, then hand them off to someone else for the illustrations. I would be doubly flattered if they did the same, and drew some new pictures for the stories they read.

THE TRUE STORY BEHIND *THE TRUE STORY OF THE 3 LITTLE PIGS!*

HOW TO WRITE A FAIRY TALE FROM A NEW POINT OF VIEW
"It wasn't my fault."

That's what I was thinking the wolf would say if he got to tell his side of the three little pigs story. I thought about how the wolf would explain knocking down those pigs' houses, then I let him explain.

What would different characters in other fairy tales say if they got a chance to tell their own version of their story? Here are some thoughts to get you started:

I'll bet the witch had a perfectly good reason for fattening up Hansel and Gretel.

I wonder what the stepmom thought about goody-goody Cinderella?

The three bears must have some interesting opinions about Goldilocks that didn't make it into the official version.

What did the seven dwarves really think about Snow White?

_____

_____

_____

_____

_____

_____

_____

_____

_____

THE TRUE STORY BEHIND *BALONEY, HENRY P.*

HOW TO WRITE AN INTERGALACTIC TALL TALE

Tall tales are stories of wild exaggeration. The stories about Paul Bunyan and John Henry and Pecos Bill are tall tales.

Anybody can write a tall tale. It's a lot like making up a really outrageous bunch of lies. Say you are late for school one day and your teacher asks you why. You could say, "I was attacked by a gang of hungry sea lions." That would be an interesting beginning of a tall tale.

But if would be an even more interesting tall tale if you pretended you were from outer space and translated the words "sea lions" into another language. Then your tall tale would start, "I was attacked by a gang of hungry SEELOWEN." (German for SEA LION.)

Which is exactly what I did to write *Baloney, Henry P.*

So make up your wildest and craziest excuse why you were late for school. Translate some of the key words into other languages. Presto—you have an Intergalactic Tall Tale.

Internet translating dictionaries are great places to find your intergalactic words. Dictionaries and those funny little pocket travel books are good intergalactic word tools too. And for some reason, the most intergalactic-looking words seem to be Finnish or Dutch.

_____

_____

_____

_____

_____

_____

_____

_____

THE TRUE STORY BEHIND *MATH CURSE*

HOW TO WRITE A FUNNY MATH STORY

Anybody who has ever had to answer those math word problems can tell you where I got the idea to write *Math Curse*. I just wondered what would happen if one day everything turned into a math problem.

Use whatever math you are studying, and make up problems and answers about your life. Use addition, subtraction, multiplication, division, fractions . . . and don't forget True/False answers, multiple choice, and greater than and less than.

For extra credit, imagine and write what might happen if everything in your life turned into a science experiment, an art assignment, a history quiz.

_____

_____

_____

_____

_____

_____

_____

_____

_____

_____

_____

THE TRUE STORY BEHIND *SQUIDS WILL BE SQUIDS*

HOW TO WRITE A MODERN FABLE

Okay, I admit it. I took stories my daughter and son told me and turned them into fables. Is that so wrong? This guy named Aesop did it hundreds of years ago. So I thought I should too.

Fables are stories about people and the weird, annoying, funny things they do. But in fables the people are changed to animals, and there is usually a moral at the end. That way you can write about your friend Jessica who annoys you by always chewing your pencils, and not insult her because your fable is about a beaver.

Think of something annoying or funny or strange that a friend does.

Change his or her character into an animal, or breakfast cereal, a Madagascar hissing cockroach, or whatever you think is most like your friend.

Add the moral you would want that friend to learn from your fable.

Moral: Chew a pencil, lose a friend.

_____

_____

_____

_____

_____

_____

_____

_____

_____

THE TRUE STORY BEHIND *STINKY CHEESE MAN*

HOW TO WRITE YOUR OWN FAIRLY STUPID TALE

I already admitted how I thought it was fun to goof around with one fairy tale and turn it into *The True Story of the 3 Little Pigs!* So after I did that, it got me thinking—wouldn't it be even more fun to mess up a whole bunch of fairy tales?

And that's what I did.

Fairy tales usually have pretty obvious characters, plots, and action.

You've got your princesses, your princes, kings, queens, witches, trolls, giants, dragons, step mothers, and magical animals. You've got your magic spells. You know how most of the stories go.

So why not try to mess up the stories in as many ways as possible? Change one character. Reverse the plot. Twist the magic spell.

I started with thinking what would happen if the little old lady ran out of gingerbread and made the little man out of something else?

What if Rapunzel decided to do something different with her hair?

What if a not-very-smart giant told his tale?

What if Sleeping Beauty woke up early?

You would have your own Fairly Stupid Tale.

_____

_____

_____

_____

_____

_____

_____

SPACE EXPLORATION FOR BEGINNERS

WHAT TO DO WHEN YOU MEET AN ALIEN

by MOIRA CASSIDY

1 SESSION, 90 MINUTES
MATERIALS: *1 Starship Captain (Teacher)*
2 Space Lieutenants (TAs or other adult volunteers)
1 1:10 scale mock-up of a real live alien
1 space transit simulation device (hula hoop covered in streamers/string)
Official Space Explorer Logs (one for each student)
Assorted space junk (tin cans, Easter basket grass, googly eyes, pipe cleaners, yarn, and so on)
NASA-quality fixatives (Elmer's glue, duct tape)

THIS WORKSHOP IS INTENDED TO PROMPT YOUNG SPACE EXPLORERS TO imagine and record the events of their first cosmic journey.

As the intrepid explorers arrive, they should each be provided with one Official Space Explorer Log. These logs are of paramount importance to our mission, and the explorers should take care to note down what they expect to do on their journey into space while waiting for the lesson to begin.

Once these preliminary notes are complete and the entire crew is ready for Space Explorer Training to begin, explorers should share one activity they hope to try in zero gravity.

At this point, the Starship Captain should size up his or her crew in order to determine if they are ready to know what it is really like in space. They probably are. With the help of his or her Space Lieutenants, the Captain should tell the story of meeting his or her first inter-galactic friend (aliens are usually named things like Mrogalah, ♌, and Zorn). The Captain should then display the 1:10 scale model of Mrogalah, ♌, or Zorn they have constructed and brought for the edification of the class, and introduce the students to the mysterious and powerful Space Transit Simulation Device.

Starship Captains should take care to explain that although the Space Transit Simulation Device may *look* like a hula hoop covered in streamers, it is actually a highly experimental technology developed specifically for this training session. Once users enter the hula hoop and close their eyes, they will immediately be transported to the natural habitat of a previously undiscovered alien species. The Starship Captain and his or her Space Lieutenants should demonstrate this technology before the class, keeping in mind that the presence of realistic space sounds (for example, Symphonies of the Planets—NASA Voyager Recordings) will increase the potency of the device.

Each explorer must now wait for his or her turn with the Space Transit Simulation Device, which should be moved to another nearby room or nook so that the remaining explorers are not distracted by their fellow crew members' journeys. The Space Lieutenants should direct students to work on their log questionnaires while waiting for their turn. Directions for the operation of the Space Transit Simulation Device are as follows:

☞ The Starship Captain should direct the students each to stand in the middle of the Space Transit Simulation Device (which must begin its power-up cycle at rest on the floor) and close their eyes.

☞ The Captain should then raise the Space Transit Simulation Device off the floor to the full height of the student while rotating or swiveling the hoop. It may be necessary/prudent to produce powering-up sound effects or *whooshing* noises at this point.

☞ Rotation of the Space Transit Simulation Device should continue once it is fully powered up, and explorers should be notified that they have been transported to the habitat of an unknown alien in a remote corner of the cosmos.

☞ Explorers should then be asked to describe the creature they see (How big is it? Is it a boy or a girl or neither? What does it like to eat?) and give it a name, before the device powers down and they are returned to Earth.

☞ Once the device is fully powered down, explorers should be directed to return to their seats and complete the log questionnaire.

Once all explorers have completed their turns with the Space Transit Simulation Device, they can begin the construction of scale models of the alien beings they met/discovered. The Assorted Space Junk and NASA-quality fixatives will prove exceptionally useful for this task.

Finally, when the models are complete, all space explorers should use the information they recorded in their logs to write a pen pal letter to their new alien friends. Interesting topics broached in the first session of this class include: whether aliens like bagels, whether there are video games in space, and the extent to which Jupiter is covered in Jell-O. We at 826 are anxiously awaiting responses to these insightful inquiries.

SPACE EXPLORATION LOG QUESTIONNAIRE

SPACE EXPLORER'S NAME: _____

PRELIMINARY INQUIRIES

Name one thing you would like to try doing in anti-gravity:

_____

_____

What do you think space will be like?

_____

_____

What kind of alien would you like to meet?

_____

_____

POST—SPACE TRANSIT SIMULATION INQUIRIES

ALIEN'S NAME: _____

Describe your alien's natural habitat:

_____

_____

How big was your alien?

_____

_____

What color was it? Is it furry or scaly or slimy?

_____

_____

Is your alien a boy or a girl or neither?

_____

_____

What does your alien like to eat?

_____

_____

What doesn't your alien like to eat?

_____

_____

Can your alien talk?

_____

_____

What does your alien like to do for fun?

_____

_____

What should space explorers do if they meet your alien?

_____

_____

DRAW YOUR ALIEN HERE:

MAGIC REALISM

by AIMEE BENDER

WHAT'S MAGIC REALISM? IN *ONE HUNDRED Years of Solitude,* one of the major books of magical realism, one of Gabriel García Márquez's characters walks around surrounded by yellow butterflies. Nothing else is particularly magical about him—he's a living, breathing, regular person but just happens to have this extra magnetic butterfly ability. In magic realism, the world looks a whole lot like our daily world, it's proportionally our world, but some elements in it are magical and they are woven right into the realistic story line. People might fly. Something unexpected might rustle up from the ground. What's that unusual rabbit? What's the deal with John's right arm? In this class, students learn to create magic realist writing of their own. Writing with magical elements is fun, amazingly fun, because you can explore the consequences of one small but significant shift in the universe and the ripple effects can change the whole story line.

Begin with a short story: "The Very Old Man with Enormous Wings" by Gabriel García Márquez, or "Hirschel" by Judy Budnitz, or "Jon" by George Saunders (which is long).

Talk about what happens when this shift occurs. When a man shows up with wings, or when a baker makes people, or when there's teen demographic camp as in the story, "Jon."

Talk about the connection between the two words "magic" and "logic," which happen to share three letters but usually aren't thought of together. But they're so related! Magic relies on logic; we need to feel like the world makes sense, even if it's a different world. What are the consequences of one meaningful change in these stories?

Most of the exercises I have around this subject are building from the ground up, meaning the students can dive into a wild topic, and see what happens. Sometimes, this ends up as absolute realism, which is fine, too.

Exercise 1: Telling a Legend

Pass around two index cards for each student. On one, students write an element of nature. Brainstorm some elements of nature: waterfalls, carbon, palm trees, frogs.

On the second index card, students write a verb. Not a fancy verb, a fairly basic verb. Depending on the group, go over verbs for two seconds, too. Then, pass nature cards to the right, verb cards to the left. Each student ends up with an element of nature and a verb, from two different other students.

(Aside: I'm big on these index card passings because they really pop us out of our own mindsets,

34

which tend to get fixed. Getting "dirt" and "jump" suddenly forces the brain to rethink the rules.)

Once students each have their two cards, tell them about Rudyard Kipling's "Just So Stories" and how each chapter told a legend. "How the _____ Got Its _____." Here, they are writing a legend too: How the Cloud Got Its Balance. Some of them won't make sense—How Fire Got Its Laugh—but in a way, that can be even better. Go around the circle, hear everyone's title. Then, let them write it out, see what they discover. Share a few after about 15–20 minutes of writing time, depending on the group and age.

Exercise 2: Creating a World

This one is more calculated, more about creating a world of magical realism from scratch. It works well for more logically minded students, but can cramp the style of those who don't want to think things through much in advance. Still, worth a try.

Have the students write down five small changes in the physical world: Rain is made of metal! Or people grow two heads!

For older kids, and adults, have them also write down five customs, altered slightly: We shake hands when we are hungry, or when someone sneezes, you feel blessed.

Have the group go around, and each student reads one of his or her their altered rules in the physical world, and one custom. These are fun to hear, and usually spark the imaginations of students who feel stuck.

Then: consequences. Back to magic and logic. Have them pick one to write about. The writers have a chance here to build their own new universe, one that exists with this one rule changed. What's the impact? On people, on religion, on money, on Los Angeles, on roses, on love, on everything and anything they can think of. They can make a list here, or just start describing the world and seeing if a story begins to develop. Maybe they find a character who doesn't fit in this world, for whatever reason, and see what happens. This is another good point to refer to the stories at the beginning again, as a way to see how other authors have done this.

Write and share!

RECYCLED ELVES

FAIRY TALE DO-OVERS

by LUCAS GONZALEZ AND CHRIS MOLNAR

2 SESSIONS, 2 HOURS EACH

WE'VE HEARD THE SAME OLD FAIRY tales for too long! What about the original version of the story, before it was changed, when Little Red Riding Hood gets eaten by the Wolf? And what if the Wolf's belly actually turned out to be a portal into an alternate universe, where you are a talking recycling bin who drives a Mister Softee truck?

When we found ourselves at 826NYC as interns in fall 2010, director Joan Kim was eager to give us the opportunity to work with the young writers who find inspiration in the writing lab behind the swinging shelf of 826's Superhero Supply Co. As we flipped through the pages of a past edition of 826 National's writing workshop manual, we came across one lesson plan that we thought would be perfect for the young learners we had been working with: writing your own fairy tales. This format (that of the fantastical precautionary tale with a moral bent), would be a perfect vehicle for the imagination of our young writers. Our hope was that this workshop would open the door to some fun, wild, strange, and inventive stories by reimagining fairy tales, recycling their format, and learning how such stories have evolved over many centuries.

Our journey began with a discussion of some familiar quirks and tropes: the vital elements to fairy tales. So we started by asking our students about some fairy tales they knew. We talked heroes, we talked villains, we talked pigs, fairies, and wolves, and we talked elves. We knew we needed to have a mission, and we knew that mission needed to be interrupted by some sort of dilemma: monsters, aliens, or what would eventually turn out to be a trio of evil space dictators in one student's story. Whoever he or she or it would be, our hero would need to find a way out of this situation and teach us all a lesson. But, as we learned in our workshop, fairy tales haven't always had happy endings!

Staying mindful of kids' attachment and long relationship to the versions of modern fairy tales, we began to discuss famous fairy tales as they once existed in a primitive form, stories that are not without their sense of shock value to the wholesome and Disneyfied tales we are used to.

LITTLE RED RIDING HOOD
In the original version of this story, there is no Grandma! There is no valiant woodsman who saves LRRH from the belly of the

wolf! There is only a little girl with a riding cape and deceitful wolf with a full belly.

SNOW WHITE

The witch wants the heroine's liver and lungs! That's right! For dinner! No magical kiss here, either, sadly. Just a righteous downfall for the evil witch . . . the brothers Grimm condemn her to dance to death in red-hot iron shoes.

GOLDILOCKS AND THE THREE BEARS

We all know this heartwarming tale about a pretty little girl who stumbles into the abode of the three bears. There are purportedly two version of the original tale. In the first, Goldilocks, upon realizing that the bears are returning, jumps out the window, breaks either her legs or her neck, and is sent to prison for trespassing. In the second version, the story is all too short! Upon the bears' arrival home, our little heroine is immediately devoured.

The list, as you will find from some research on the Web, goes on and on! Fairy tales have never seemed more strange than they do now, when we can look back on their evolution over time and see how different stories send the same message in a very different way. The enslavement of children, the threat of man-eating beasts, and the deeds of wicked witches and demons have never seemed so tame as they have today!

Leave it up to the students to decide what kind of tale they want to tell. The only goal is to tell a story that serves as a spellbinding tale of caution! The characters are theirs to shape. The elements of the plot, the twists and turns, are theirs to shuffle and reinvent. Let's recycle some old stories and begin creating the next generation of fairy tales and whimsical warnings.

One way we decided to start writing was by doing a fairy tale together, Mad-Libs–style (next page).

Working through these Mad Libs will give students an idea of the format they can take on. It will give students a chance to get warmed up, talk about some characters and some elements of the stories, and open up the possibilities of their own tales.

In the first session, we did the intro just described and got started with our stories. In our second workshop, we finished the stories and took some time to illustrate them with collages and drawings. The workshop concluded with some amazing storytelling, with our writers reading their new fairy tales to an audience of parents and staff!

THE REALLY COOL PARTY

A _____ hosts a _____ and
(royal figure or celebrity)   (kind of party)

_____ and _____ evil
(hero or heroine)   (his/her)

_____ are invited to come. A fairy _____
(relatives)   (noun)

turns _____'s lame _____ into
(hero or heroine)   (article of clothing)

_____. But the fairy _____ has made
(better article of clothing)   (noun)

it so that _____ will lose their _____
(hero or heroine)   (better article of clothing)

at midnight. The _____ falls in love with
(royal figure or celebrity)

_____, but _____ forgets about
(hero or heroine)   (hero or heroine)

time and rushes out at midnight before telling _____ who
(royal figure or celebrity)

they are. However, _____ goes over the guest list to the
(royal figure or celebrity)

_____ and goes to find the person who fits the
(kind of party)

_____. Definitely not the evil _____!
(better article of clothing)   (relatives)

Eventually, _____ finds _____,
(royal figure or celebrity)   (hero or heroine)

and they live _____ ever after.
(adverb)

THE BREAKFAST BANDIT

A family of _____ (creature #1, plural) live in a _____ (dwelling) in

the woods. They each have their own _____ (container)

of _____ (food). One day, they go for a walk while their

_____ (same food) cools. A young _____ (creature #2) is

walking through the woods and spies the _____ (same dwelling). The papa

_____ (creature #1)'s _____ (same food) is too hot, the

mama _____ (creature #1)'s _____ (same food) is too cold,

but the baby _____ (creature #1)'s _____ (same food) is

just right, and the _____ (creature #2) eats it right up.

When the family of _____ (creature #1, plural) come back, they

find _____ (creature #2) asleep and

chase _____ (creature #2) away!

CREATING A GUIDE TO MODERN GIRLHOOD

by MEGHAN ADLER

20 SESSIONS, ABOUT 20 MINUTES EACH
MATERIALS: *Chart paper, lots and lots of best-selling books for girls
(so students can study them), good attitudes, open minds, senses of humor,
honesty, sharp pencils, colored pencils, lined paper, ink pads*

GIRLHOOD DOESN'T HAVE A HOW-TO MANUAL. IN THIS WORKSHOP, WE AIMED to remedy that. In a series of 20 mini-lessons conducted over eight sessions, our all-girl class doodled and drew; wrote poetry, letters, journal entries, and lists; drafted autobiographies; shared our work; discussed how to be responsible; mused on the meaning of friendship; and figured this whole girlhood thing out once and for all.

Please note: you are welcome to follow these lessons in order day-by-day, or feel free to pick and choose any of the following lessons and teach them whenever you want.

Session 1: Deconstructing Best-Selling Books for Girls

Students will be given copies of advertisements for best-selling books for girls (from book catalogs—ask your librarian or call publishing houses), actual best-selling books for girls, and lists of book titles from best-selling books for girls. (Go to www.lisiharrison.com, Web site of the author of the popular *The Clique* series, to get a complete list of her books/book titles. Also, try www.megcabot.com, Web site of the author of the popular *Princess Diaries* series, to get a complete list of her books.)

Students will then create a master list of what attributes make up this kind of book genre. The teacher will record the information on large chart paper (so that students can refer to the list throughout the upcoming weeks). The list tends to include things like this:

☞ Catchy covers—bright, pink, sparkly.

☞ Purposeful misspellings—to make us feel better when we misspell (which is normal).

☞ Light reading—not lengthy books.

- Perfect, thin girls; lots of makeup.
- Cliques.
- A lot of these books come in a series.
- Fashion labels.
- It's okay to be spoiled (not really).
- May not touch on bad moods—or other emotions we all feel.
- Mostly Caucasian girls.
- Guys—girls want guys to like them in these books.
- Diary-like format.
- Fairy-tale endings (or not).
- How to . . . (be popular, be cool, and so on).

Now, discuss the pros and cons of these attributes. Invite students to reflect in written form.

Session 2: Self-Portraits/Doodles/Diagrams

Students will be given time to draw themselves. Using the techniques in best-selling books for girls, students can exaggerate their features (or not), label themselves, and tell stories. Examples might include: "This is a scar on my right cheek that I am embarrassed about." "There are my blue eyes." "I love my long eyelashes." "I get my curly red hair from my grandma." Students also have the option of using only the colors that are most apparent in this book genre (pink and purple).

Session 3: One-Minute Autobiography

For one minute (yes, sixty seconds), have your students write the story of their lives—in bulleted or list form. (Speed means less self-censoring.) Suggest that students include both big moments (broke left wrist, won first place in a swim meet, grandpa died) and small ones (found a blue piece of sea glass, went to Disney World).

Session 4: Thumbprint

Share Eve Merriam's poem "Thumbprint" (a Web search should turn it up). Have your students write their own "thumbprint poem" about their futures. Ask your students: How will they imprint the world? Use the ink pads, so students can make their own thumbprints on their poems.

Session 5: Exploring Shame

Share my poem "Brief Autobiography." Have your students write their own poem or prose entry about shame—something they did when they were younger that they now feel bad about.

BRIEF AUTOBIOGRAPHY

Your first memory of sin goes like this: You and your kindergarten friend, Elizabeth, shove more than your allotted Oreos into the deep plastic pockets of your painting smocks. You hide with her in one bathroom stall, devouring them atop a toilet seat, you two, small as dimes. Your second sin is debatable: Four years later at Woolworth's, Pond's Cold Cream costs a buck more than you managed to save, and after skillfully palming the porcelain jar into your jean jacket pocket, that night you rubbed your hands soft, wrists perfumed like your dead grandmother's, you returned it the next day. But maybe, it's this sin that keeps coming back to haunt you—details still fuzzy, not sure really if this is part of your so-called story or your best friend's—the time someone did this to Galina, the new Polish immigrant. She enters your sixth-grade class midyear not speaking a word of English. Hasn't yet learned the rituals of grooming, and nobody wants to sit near her because she smells of cabbage. Brown hair greased to her scalp, dandruff flakes scattered on the back of the black sweater she wears every day, overweight with yellow teeth. You feel you want to save her. You know you do. So you place a bottle of honeysuckle Suave shampoo and cinnamon Aquafresh in her locker. You can still hear faded laughter from the boys as they watched Galina find these shiny new American products, and, unsure of their use, thinking of them as welcoming gifts, asks the other girls in the hallway what they're for. You or your best friend knew she needed help, needed presents. You understand this at last now as sin. Don't you?

—Meghan Adler

Session 6: Hair

Share the short story "Hairs" from *The House on Mango Street* by Sandra Cisneros. Have your students write their own entry, short story, or poem about their hair.

Session 7: Character Description

Share the character descriptions on the backs of *The Clique* books. Ask students to write their own character description—in a deeper, kinder way.

Session 8: Manifestos

Discuss the definition of a manifesto—a public declaration of intentions, opinions, objectives, or motives, or a statement of rules to live by, purpose for life, and so on.

Ask your students to create their own manifesto statement for their life. Create a manifesto collage or poster.

Here's the one our class created:

Created by the writers of
the workshop "Tween/Teen
Autobiographies: Write About
Your Life (So Far)" [illegible]
Audre · Emma · Hadiyah
Hannah · Jillian · Lupe
Meghan · Melissa · Robin
Sarah · Tahirah · Tatiana
Tessa · Zoe
826 [illegible] artwork by melissa chevalier
copyright © 2007
All Rights Reserved Worldwide

RELAX
STAY CALM
FLY!
MAKE NEW friends and keep the old one is SILVER and the other GOLD.

Everyone has a story and it takes courage to tell it.
DON'T WORRY ABOUT BEING AROUND PEOPLE Who don't want you Around
autobiography
LET GO
BELIEVE
Better [YOU] than right.

be heard NOW
Carpe Diem
How's the weather inside?
inspire hope
live and love!
AWAKEN

thrive play
CREATIVE MANIFESTATIONS
Every time you CONCENTRATE ON SOMEONE WHO DOESN'T LIKE YOU—YOU MISS OUT ON SOMEONE WHO DOES LIKE YOU.
SCREAM

KEEP GOING...

Session 9: Princess Lessons

Share samples from Meg Cabot's best-selling book *Princess Lessons: A Princess Diaries Book*. Encourage your students to create their own "Princess Essentials List" and "Princess Beauty Regimen." As always, with all of these activities, lists can be tongue-in-cheek or serious and empowering.

Session 10: Ins and Outs

Share samples of "In and Out" lists from Lisi Harrison's *The Clique* books. Ask your students to make their own "In and Out," Pro/Con, Can/Can't, Fact/Fiction lists.

Session 11: Quick Questionnaires

Have the students fill out quick questionnaires about their characteristics, likes, dislikes, and so forth. Some examples:

NAME: _____

_____

NICKNAME: _____

_____

MY STYLE: _____

_____

FAVORITE BAND: _____

_____

FAVORITE COLOR: _____

_____

BIGGEST FEAR: _____

_____

BIGGEST DREAM: _____

_____

FAVORITE FOOD: _____

_____

MOST HATED FOOD: _____

_____

. . . AND SO ON. _____

_____

Session 12: Defining Friendship

Share the "Ten Ways to Lose a Friend" list from the book *The Witch: Friends*. Ask your students to create their own list.

Session 13: Bug Off!

Read the excerpt titled "Bug Off" from *Amelia's Notebook* by Marissa Moss. Discuss with your students times when they have been angry, furious, upset, and overwhelmed. Have them choose one specific time and write about it. Invite your students to use Marissa Moss's technique of using large fonts, ALL CAPS, and different colors to portray their feelings of anger or confusion.

Session 14: Today, I Will Not . . .

Share Jean Little's poem "Today" (a Web search should turn it up). Ask your students to make their own list of things they will not do today.

Session 15: Two Friends

Share Nikki Giovanni's poem "Two Friends" (a Web search should turn it up). Ask your students to write about their experiences with a friend. Encourage your students to mimic

Ms. Giovanni's style of writing like a math equation ("two pierced ears, five pigtails, one good friendship").

Session 16: Hyphen Talk

Share the poem "Perfect Blend" by Andrew Fusek and Polly Peters (a Web search should turn it up). Have your students notice how the combination of adjectives and hyphens creates better descriptions and a poetic sound ("talk-for-hours-non-sleeper, hold-head-high-whatever-walker"). Encourage them to try this technique.

Session 17: Pop Quiz

Have your students create their own multiple-choice pop quiz. Encourage your students to respond to the themes they see in best-selling books for girls by poking fun at them, mimicking them, or taking a more serious route.

Feel free to use these examples as inspiration:

1. Who is your hero?

   A. Leonardo DiCaprio

   B. Paris Hilton

   C. Spongebob

   D. Me

2. Where do you buy your clothes?

   A. Old Navy

   B. Neiman Marcus

   C. J. Crew

   D. Target

   E. Who cares?

3. You put the "H" in . . .

   A. Hairy

   B. Hard-headed

   C. Hybrid

   D. Humanity

4. What brings you happiness?

   A. Straight hair

   B. Designer clothing

   C. Money

   D. Being yourself

Session 18: Beauty

Share the poem "Beauty" by Grace Nichols (a Web search should turn it up). Invite your students to decide what "beauty" means to them. Have them define "true beauty" and then write about it.

Session 19: Fortune Cookies

Have your students create their own fortunes to help determine or predict the futures they want. Use small white pieces of paper to emulate the look and feel of a real fortune cookie. Lucky numbers written on the other side are optional, but they make it even more fun.

Some examples:

You will do fine in ninth-grade math.

Your sister will not always be so mean to you.

Session 20: Pink Is . . .

Pink signifies a wide range of meanings, symbols, and stereotypes. Ask your students to explain what the color "pink" means to them or to the world.

HOW TO WRITE A HOW-TO

by JORY JOHN

1 SESSION, 1 HOUR
MATERIALS: *Handouts, paper, pens*

EVERYBODY EVERYWHERE HAS A HIDDEN TALENT, ABILITY, OR WEALTH OF knowledge. Yes, *you* do too. If I had to take a guess, I would say that you, gentle reader, are passionate about chess, making mix tapes, and parallel parking. In fact, you could probably teach a comprehensive course about these three things. I could be wrong. You know yourself better than I do. But you get the idea. (The idea is: you have areas of interest that other people don't.)

Your students, of course, have plenty of different talents and interests, and now you're going to help them harness all of it into a fun series of how-tos. The key to this exercise is to get your class thinking about what lesson, exactly, they can share with their peers and the world at large. Today, *they* will be the teachers, and their lessons should reflect the variety of interests in your class. Encourage your students to come up with something from their lives outside school. Maybe somebody has a parent who's a chef and that student can offer up some acquired cooking tips. Maybe there's a sports star in your midst, or a video-game conqueror. What about somebody who can do long division in her head, or a three-ball juggler? There are no wrong answers when it comes to what you know or what you can teach.

The end product of this how-to lesson will be a small pocket-size book of collective knowledge, one page per student (a how-to diagram), that the kids get to take home with them.

Preparation

The first step of the lesson is to review the "How to Avoid a Shower or Bath for as Long as Possible, or Even Longer" handout. Let your students know that it's OK to use humor in their approach. Additionally, it's OK to be a bit *scheme-y* in their lesson, as long as it's legal. These how-tos can absolutely be lessons on how to get away with fun stuff.

As a warm-up, open the topic for classwide discussion. Ask the students to offer up some of their hidden talents or secret knowledge. Get five kids to share out loud. Simply ask them: "What are you really good at? What can you do? Any hidden talents?" Open up with one of your own hidden talents. What about that thing about parallel parking?

Next, have the students individually make a list of 25 things that they know how to do well. These lists will be all over the place. Let them know that the more specific, the better. For instance, "How to Be Really Quiet" is fine, but "How to Tiptoe Across the Living Room and into the Kitchen at Midnight to Get a Late-Night Snack" is way better. "How to Kick a Goal in Soccer"? Pretty good. But "How to Kick a Goal in Soccer During the Championships in Double Overtime" is simply great.

Give your students 20 minutes for this. However, if any students are struggling, hand them the list of suggested how-to ideas. These will help get the ideas rolling. In fact, they can even "borrow" from that list if they see anything that jumps out at them.
After the students have written their 25 items, have them review them and circle their three favorites. (These should be things that the students think they can expand into six instructional points.)

Go around the class and have each student read his or her three favorites out loud. After each student has read, ask the class for input. What's the most original item that that student has on his or her list? (Talking about the items beforehand will also ensure that there are no duplicate how-tos in your eventual book.)

Now, with the class's input, the student should select his or her ultimate "how-to" category. Students will need to come up with a list of instructions explaining how to employ their talent. Have them refer back to the "Shower or Bath" handout as a reference. Get the students to boil their instructions down to six main points, which they will write on the handout. Once the students have their six steps, have them draw small illustrations to go with each instruction.

Have students stand up and read their how-tos out loud. Collect them at the end. Let the students know that you'll be making copies and turning them into books for everybody to use.

In the final moments, take suggestions for book titles. A silent vote should indicate the winner. And now you have a book of knowledge, written by your students, useful to everyone.

HOW TO AVOID A SHOWER OR BATH FOR AS LONG AS POSSIBLE, OR EVEN LONGER

1. DON'T FIGHT IT: The more you protest a bath or shower, the greater the suspicion when you try to *fake* one. When Mom suggests getting in the water, get in that bathroom, Buster. Give somebody a "thumbs up" on the way there, even.

2. GET THAT WATER RUNNING: Too often, bath dodgers forget to turn on the water. Big mistake, friend! That's the surest sign of shower fakery! (You will, however, have to "sacrifice" your arm. Place it under the water every 45 seconds for occasional splishy-splashy noises.)

3. SINK IT: It's impossible to get away with avoiding a shower or bath without getting your hair a little moist and floral-scented. Solution? Plug the sink, run some water, and mix in a hint of shampoo. Swirl it around and flick a little on your head. Repeat until damp.

4. MOVE STUFF: If you were taking a *real* shower or bath, you probably wouldn't put the soap or shampoo in the exact same place you found it, would you? Answer: Probably not.

5. EMERGE: With a towel wrapped around your neck, say these words: "Wow, I feel refreshed! G'night!" Get out of sight.

6. BONUS: Rubbing some Epsom salt under your armpits will help with the advancing odors.

SUGGESTED HOW-TO IDEAS

How to Make the Best-Ever Bowl of Cereal

How to Draw a Cartoon Character

How to Open a Bag of Chips Without Making Any Noise

How to Get Tree Sap off Your Hands

How to Hold Your Breath for as Long as Possible, and Maybe Even Longer

How to Stay Awake at a Slumber Party, or at Least Not Be the First Person Asleep

How to Make a Three-Pointer, Just About Every Time

How to Run a Quick Mile, or at Least a *Not-Slow* Mile

How to Tell a Really Funny Joke

How to Cure the Hiccups Every Time

How to Get Your Parents to Let You Do What You Want to Do

How to Get More Allowance This Week

How to Hide Something That Can't Be Found

How to Hit a Baseball That's Flying Past You

How to Tell a Lie Without Getting Caught

How to Make My Favorite Snack, Which Is _____

How to Watch Three Different Television Shows at Once and Know What's Happening in All of Them

How to Fake a Cell Phone Call When You Don't Want to Be Bothered

How to Stay Up Later Than Your Bedtime on a Weekday

How to Disguise Yourself So That You're Unrecognizable

How to Get an Animal to Like You Every Time

How to Ride a Bicycle with No Hands

How to Make Your Parents Breakfast in Bed

How to Cure the Common Cold

How to Throw a Party Without Anybody Knowing

TALKING TRASH!

by HOLLY M. DUNSWORTH AND JULIET WELLER DUNSWORTH

1 SESSION, 2–2½ HOURS
MATERIALS: *See each activity's instructions*

TRASH HAS LOTS OF INTERESTING THINGS TO SAY. TRASH IS ESPECIALLY GOOD at talking to archaeologists, cavemen, and inventors who are absolutely fascinated with the stuff that people just throw away! In this activity, students will become archaeologists, cavemen, and inventors, and they will marvel at, mull over, and modify a piece of ordinary garbage into something magnificent.

This lesson has all sorts of nooks and crannies that are guaranteed to light up your students. But it also challenges them to think in ways that may be very new to them. They're asked to see a common object and not only to write about it scientifically and objectively, but to engage their imagination and invent a use for it.

Examples of trash/artifacts that we've used with great success include a number of clean household items like hair dryer attachments, vacuum attachments, odd kitchen tools, a motherboard from a dead computer, a tube from a guitar amp, a beaded necklace, a feather duster, a toothbrush (never used), a dog leash, a compact disc, an audio tape, a VHS tape, a plastic water bottle, an empty egg carton, and so forth.

Watch out, though, because students will often exclaim, "This isn't trash!" Apparently they haven't seen the great stuff that people toss out. Plus, they may not be aware that not all artifacts studied by archaeologists are prehistoric waste; the objects could have been tossed, lost, stored, buried (like in a grave), or simply left behind by the people who used them. As long as water (like a river or a flooded lake), wind, or a volcano deposits sediment over the site, it will be preserved long enough for archaeologists to find it.

Another thing to watch out for is that students may become so attached to their trash that they will want to take it home. An extension for a vacuum hose? Really? Of course they want to keep it because now it's a magic-super-crazy-poisonous-frog-arrow-machine-for-mindreading®. We didn't allow students to keep their trash/artifacts because, well, imagine what the parents would say. But the way to get around this problem best was to ask them to store their artifacts in the "museum" at the end of the activity. This way you can reuse the objects again and again.

Part 1. Archaeologists

MATERIALS: *Pictures of excavations; archaeologists at work at their dig sites; and artifacts from books, the Internet, and so on*
"Archaeology site" = Labeled/decorated box or bin of clean, interesting trash items, which are your artifacts
National History Museum Catalog Information handouts
Measuring devices (rulers, calipers, measuring tape ...)

To Do:

1. Hold a discussion

   What is an archaeologist? What kinds of things do archaeologists find? What would these things tell you about people of the past?

2. Transport the students

   It's the year 3689, and you're now in New [Your town name here] where the students are archaeologists who study the artifacts left behind by the ancient civilization of Old [Your town name here] way back in the year [the current year here]. Have them "dig up" one artifact each from the site by reaching into the "archaeology site" box and pulling one "artifact" out.

3. Scientific description of the artifact (with handout)

   Students make their discovery official. Remind them how to approach their artifact objectively, like a scientist would—which is very much like how an alien would. They need to observe it as a completely foreign object. They can create fictitious details where necessary (for example, site name, GPS coordinates, and the like). The last part of the handout challenges them to think creatively. Many will know what their artifact is in "real life," but it's important that they go beyond that. For instance, a toothbrush isn't just for polishing the teeth of a number of species, it could also be used for removing the proost particles that build up every other light year in the refurberator of a Sporg's intergalactic refrigination system.

Part 2. Cavemen

MATERIALS: *Pictures of cavemen and cave art from books, the Internet, and so on*
(Brown construction) paper taped to the underside of the tables or desks
Chalk and/or pastels

To Do:

1. Hold a discussion

   What was life like before cities and towns, and even before farming? What was it like for people who foraged and hunted for food? What were cavemen and cavewomen like way back in the Stone Age? What was their typical day like? What kinds of things did they build? Prepare yourself for the possibility of some pretty macabre and even gory assumptions about cavemen. The expected student response (that is, that cavemen were stupid) is a good launching point to discuss how technology has to start somewhere and that it increases in complexity through time. Prehistoric humans had essentially the same brains and bodies as us. It's thanks to their getting things started that we have cell phones today.

2. Transport the students

   They're no longer future archaeologists. In fact, they're going back in time where they are ancient people in the year 32,734 BCE. They live simple hunting-and-gathering lifestyles, and one day, while tracking a wooly rhinoceros, they stumble across these futuristic objects that must have fallen through a crack in the universe. (These are their same objects from Part 1.)

3. Cavespeak

   Have the students pair up and discuss their objects with one another like cavemen. Would they use English? Would they use body language? Would they be curious or excited?

4. Cave drawings

   Prehistoric people didn't write with words, but they did etch, carve, and draw symbols all over the walls and ceilings of caves. When they were really excited about bulls and horses, they drew a bunch of bulls and horses (for example, at Lascaux Cave, France). The students, as cavemen, are really excited about these objects that they found, so they will draw them the way cavemen did. Have them look under their desks where you've previously, secretly attached paper to the underside. Have them go down there, into their "caves," and draw their ode to their object on their cave ceiling. They can draw their peers' objects too. Dim the lights if you want to create a more cavelike atmosphere. We placed a few jack-o-lantern lights (those battery-operated candles that flicker yellow) on the cave floors for an even more authentic feel.

Part 3. Inventors

MATERIALS: *U.S. patent application (This official document is freely available at the U.S. Department of Trade and Commerce Patent and Trademark Office Web site, or use the provided handout.) Patent award certificate*

To Do:

1. Transport the students

   Students are present-day inventors who are searching for ways to reuse common crapola.

2. Hybrid inventions

   Instruct students to make a quick sketch of their object (same object from Parts 1 and 2), then cut their drawing in half, and trade one piece of it with their neighbor. Now, they should tape their two halves together; this is the raw material for the invention they will create. It needs a name and a use or purpose. They will now fill out a patent application. They can make up any of the details as necessary. They should also write a paragraph that describes their invention and what it's used for.

3. Patent awards

   Have students each present their invention and their application in hopes of being awarded a U.S. patent! Of course, everyone gets a patent, but they must explain things well first. We attached gold seals and red ribbons to the certificates to make them look even more distinguished.

Part 4. Art Collage

MATERIALS: *Oversized paper or posters*
Scrap paper and old magazines
Archaeology, caveman, and inventor/invention
pictures printed from the Internet

To Do:

Students glue their work (museum catalog information, description of artifact, cave drawings, hybrid invention sketch, patent application, invention paragraph, and patent award) to a poster and use the additional materials provided to arrange them in an artistic collage.

At the End...

Students archive their objects in the "museum," which is just the "archaeology site" box turned around with its other side labeled "Museum."

SUPERTEACHER BONUS ACTIVITIES

- Hats: We wore imaginary hats for each section, putting on our archaeologist hats to do Part 1, taking them off and putting on our caveman hats for Part 2, and then putting on our inventor hats for Part 3. This helped separate the different roles that students were asked to fill. It also served as a springboard for discussion because what their imaginary hats looked like had lots to do with what they already knew about archaeologists, cavemen, and inventors.

- Teacher's artifact: It works wonders if the teacher has his or her own artifact. That way everyone can work on the teacher's artifact together as part of the discussion. Then they are better prepared to go and work on their own artifacts.

- Conch: We used a big colorful faux feather duster as our teacher's artifact (or, as we described it, a wooly rhino's ear cleaner), and it doubled as "the conch." During discussions, students holding this artifact had the floor and the others knew to be quiet and listen until they got to hold it.

Natural History Museum Catalog Information

Specimen #: _____

Date: _____

Time: _____

Collector's Name: _____

Locality/Region: _____

Site (Name or #): _____

GPS Coordinates: _____

Brief Description: _____

Artifact Description, Analysis, and Interpretation

Include a drawing of the artifact inside this box.

What color is it?

_____

_____

What is it made of?

_____

_____

How big is it compared to your hand?

_____

_____

What are its measurements?

How long and how wide? *Write these near the drawing. Be sure to include the units (centimeters, inches, and so on).*

Who or what used this artifact? To do what and how? How many different uses can you think of?

_____

_____

_____

_____

_____

U.S. Patent Application

Inventor Name:

_____

Invention Name:

_____

_____

Description:

_____

_____

_____

_____

_____

_____

_____

_____

_____

_____

_____

_____

_____

826CHI

Wicker Park

Chicago

Illinois

The Midwest

The United States Of America

North America

The Western Hemisphere

The Earth

The Solar System

The Milky Way Galaxy

The Local Group

The Virgo Cluster

The Virgo Supercluster

The Universe

The Commissioner of Patents and Trademarks

Has received an application for a patent for a new and useful invention. The title and description of the invention are enclosed. The requirements of the law have been complied with, and it has been determined that a patent on the invention shall be granted under the law.

No. _____

Invention: _____

Inventor: _____

This _____

day of _____, 20___

WHY DID THE CHICKEN CROSS THE LESSON PLAN?

WRITING JOKES AND RIDDLES

by MARCY ZIPKE

1 SESSION, 2 HOURS

AS YOU'VE PROBABLY NOTICED, ELEMENTARY STUDENTS ARE STAND-UP COMEDIANS in the making. Their inventory of jokes (such as riddles or knock-knock jokes) is impressive. In this lesson, we put these comedic skills to work, aiding the development of metalinguistic awareness (a working understanding of the constraints posed by our language). Puzzling over—and writing your own—riddles is a fun way to learn about language as well as an important step in achieving fluent writing and reading comprehension. All we need to have handy for this lesson are a few joke books and a children's dictionary or thesaurus.

Start by telling a few jokes in which the humor depends on language manipulation. The riddles can turn on a word with more than one meaning:

Q: What kind of bed never sleeps?

A: A river bed.

Q: How do you stop a skunk from smelling?

A: You hold his nose.

Or the riddles can depend on the way you arrange the words in a sentence:

Q: What did the boy say when he was told that his dog had been chasing a man on a bicycle?

A: Don't be silly! My dog can't ride a bicycle.

Ask if any of the kids have riddles to share. When everyone is sufficiently hooked, explain that it is easy to write your own riddles—all you have to know are some words that go with a favorite sport or activity.

As an example, have the kids choose an activity to write riddles about (baseball works really well). Brainstorm a list of words associated with the activity.

Example. Baseball:

Bat

Ball

Bases

Plate

Umpire

Player

Outfielder

Shortstop

Catcher

Coach

Diamond

Uniform

Now explain to the kids that a homonym is a word with more than one meaning. Homonyms make the best riddles because you can ask a question that seems to be about one thing, but really turns out to be about another. Have the kids find and explain the homonyms in your list.

Example. Baseball homonyms:

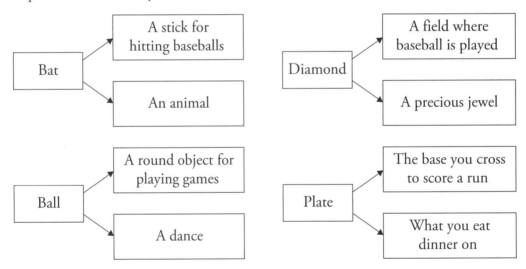

Now's it time to make up the riddles! Remember that only the question or the answer will really be about baseball. Here are some real third graders' baseball riddles:

Why was Cinderella the worst player on the Yankees? Because she couldn't go to the ball.

Why is a catcher such a good dinner guest? Because he is always cleaning the plate.

Why are the Red Sox the coolest people on a hot summer day? Because they have lots of fans.

Why does it take longer to run from second base to third base than from first base to second base? Because there's a shortstop in the middle.

Why do frogs make the best outfielders? Because they are good at catching flies.

Where is the biggest diamond in Chicago? Wrigley Field!

Why did the policeman run out onto the baseball field? Someone was stealing second.

Homophones (words that sound alike, but are spelled differently and mean different things) work really well for writing riddles too. Start by brainstorming some pairs:

Hare → Hair

Bare → Bear

Dear → Deer

Meet → Meat

From here, the kids can write riddles that resolve both of the definitions:

What do you call rabbit fur? Hare hair.

Older kids can make up riddles from expressions or idioms:

What did the calculator say to the student? You can count on me!

When the kids have written riddles they like, encourage them to record the riddles in a small notebook or on folded pieces of paper, with the riddle on one side of the page and the answer on the other. Illustrating the answers with a funny drawing is always fun too.

The kids will each leave with their very own personalized riddle book!

Want more? The following two books are excellent for aspiring comic writers:

Fiddle with a Riddle by Joanne E. Bernstein

Funny Side Up! by Mike Thaler

SPY SCHOOL

by KATE PAVAO AND JENNIFER TRAIG

1 SESSION, 90 MINUTES
MATERIALS: *1 copy of the handout packet for each student*
Costumes
Lemon juice
Toothpicks
Fruit
Index cards

MOST PEOPLE HAVE NO IDEA HOW MUCH WRITING SPIES ACTUALLY DO. Everyone thinks spying is all martinis and high-speed boat chases. The fact is spies have to write all the time. There are cases to file, forms to fill out, memoirs to pen, and more paperwork than you can imagine. This class prepares students for future careers as highly literate covert operatives. It also gives them lots of practice observing and describing. And boy, do they have fun.

This lesson does require a fair amount of prep. You'll need to make a copy of the training manual handout for each student. You'll definitely need a whole bunch of fruit and some index cards. Yes, we said fruit. And if you happen to have some items for disguises to bring in—like hats, scarves, or sunglasses—that would be great. Bonus points for lemon juice and toothpicks (for invisible ink). And if you can find a volunteer to dress up strangely and pay your class a visit, you'll have a lesson your students will never forget.

Here's how class works: we distribute the handouts and welcome our recruits to Spy School. All students are encouraged to take an alias, so we spend a few minutes going around the room and asking everyone what his or her new code name is. Then we get down to work.

The first thing we learn about are the tools of the trade. We spend about 10 minutes going over "The Spy's Toolbox" in the handbook. This is a lot more interesting if there are actual items on hand for the students to check out, so we usually show things like funny hats and goofy glasses. We ask a few brave students to model them, showing how easy it is to completely transform your look with just a few small accessories.

Next we move on to cryptology. We turn to the "Codes" section of the handbook, and learn all the different codes: the Mason Cipher, the Number Code, the Caesar Cipher, the Magic Five, and the Da Vinci Code. This takes 10 minutes or so. When time permits we mix up a batch of lemon juice for invisible ink as well. Then we give the students an assignment. Using the prompts on the "Spy School Needs You!" page of the handout, they have 10 minutes to write a coded message for our agent in Brazil. The students trade papers with their neighbors and try to crack each other's code.

Next we bring out the fruit. We turn to the "Gathering Intelligence" section of the handbook and give each student a piece of fruit (usually an apple or an orange). Their assignment: for the next 10 minutes, they have to observe every little thing they can about their fruit, taking notes and making a sketch. What makes this apple different from all other apples? Is there a bruise? A black spot? A hole? Does it have a stem? A sticker? What's the color like? Is it uniform or mottled? When the 10 minutes are up, the students all hand over their fruit, and the teacher places each piece of fruit on a card with the student's name on the other side. Then, one by one, the students come up to see if they can pick out their piece of fruit.

Next, we eat the evidence.

Finally, it's time to put all our new spy skills to the test. We turn to Spy School Case File #1 in the training manual. All of a sudden, a mysterious person (usually a cooperative colleague, friend, or parent) comes into class dressed strangely and behaving even more strangely. She may mutter or drop things. All of these things are clues. For the next 15 minutes, the students fill out Case File #1, observing as much as they can about this mysterious visitor. Who is this crazy person? And what is she doing here? Is she a double agent? A fellow spy trying to send you a message? Or is she just plain crazy?

Spy School is almost done. Only one thing remains: the debriefing. We go around the room, asking each student to share their theories on the identity of the mysterious visitor. Then we turn to the "Debriefing" section in the training manual, and invite the students to make up a cover story. They certainly can't tell their parents they were spying all morning. They've been practicing their nonfiction writing; now they'll get a chance to practice writing fiction, making up a convincing tale about the nice, safe, non-spy-like things they did instead.

CLASSIFIED

Training Manual

This top-secret manual belongs to _____.

If that's not you, put the book down right now and back away, or we will find you! You have been warned!

Why are you still reading this? Put it down! And by all means, don't open it!

THE SPY'S TOOLBOX

DISGUISES

You definitely need a disguise. In general, it's better to blend in with an outfit that doesn't draw too much attention, but that's not much fun, so if your spy uniform involves a cowboy hat and a feather boa, that's just fine with us. Here are some basic incognito supplies that provide instant camouflage:

Glasses: The bigger and the darker, the better.

Scarves: Provide instant coverage. Also, they prevent sunburns.

Hats: Easy and portable.

Wigs and false moustaches: Not very subtle, but fun.

Funny teeth: Change your whole look instantly! Buckteeth are especially good.

HARDWARE

Yes, yes, it would be wonderful to have a shoe phone and a lipstick camera, but the clever spy doesn't need to rely on high-tech gadgetry. That stuff is for amateurs! You can make your own spy supplies from stuff you already have at home. Here are some useful materials:

Scotch tape: Want to know if anyone has been snooping in your room? Place some scotch tape on the door, high up or low down, where no one will notice. If it's torn when you get home, you'll know someone was snooping.

Dixie cups: The classic listening device. Place it against a door or wall and you can hear what's happening on the other side. If you have two cups and some string, you can make a low-tech spy phone to communicate with your fellow agents.

Hair: Drape a hair over your journal before you leave. If the hair has moved when you return, you'll know someone was peeking.

Milk cartons: Make your own periscope from an empty milk carton and a hand mirror. You can see what's going on around corners!

RESOURCES AND FURTHER READING

You might enjoy these books:

Harriet the Spy by Louise Fitzhugh

Stormbreaker by Anthony Horowitz

Encyclopedia Brown by Donald J. Sobol

From the Mixed-up Files of Mrs. Basil E. Frankweiler by E. L. Konigsburg

Spy Science: 40 Secret-Sleuthing, Code-Cracking, Spy-Catching Activities for Kids by Jim Wiese and Ed Shems

Crime Scene Investigations: Real-Life Science Activities for the Elementary Grades by Pam Walker and Elaine Wood

Codes

MASON CIPHER

This code was used in the Civil War. It was very popular with the Masons, who gave it its name. It's also known as the Pig Pen Cipher, because the symbols look like little pig pens.

Use the key to decipher this sentence:

NUMBER CODE

Assign every letter a number. You can use a simple formula, like A=1, B=2, or something more complicated, like A=1, B=4, C=9, D=16, and so forth. Then write your message in numbers instead of letters. What does this say? *Hint:* 20=T and 15=O.

20 15 1 19 20   9 19   20 1 19 20 25

CAESAR CIPHER

This code was used by Julius Caesar. Simply substitute the letter three places down the alphabet for the letter you actually mean. So, A=D; B=E; C=F; and so on. What does this say?

EULWQHB VSHDUV

MAGIC FIVE

To decipher this code, circle every fifth letter and ignore the rest. What does this say?

STSRMHTGHYDRJUFIOKMEPUJHESDLKTDRPOSNJDRMKOBGELPVCLSRBVL

DA VINCI CODE

This code is simple: just write backwards. Write from right to left and flip all the letters. Use a mirror to read it. This is how Leonardo da Vinci wrote everything! What does this say?

INVISIBLE INK

Write your message using a toothpick dipped in lemon juice. It will dry invisibly. To read it, have an adult help you iron the letter on a low setting (be careful not to singe the paper). The heat will make the letters appear.

Spy School Needs You!

Spy School needs to get a very, very, VERY important message regarding our bubblegum supply to our agent in Brazil. However, if the message fell into the wrong hands, the results would be devastating! Catastrophic! An international bubblegum disaster! Imagine how messy that would be!

We need you to write the message in code. You can use one of our crackerjack cryptology methods or make up your own. Write your message here. When you're done, give it to a fellow agent and see if she or he can solve it.

_____

_____

_____

_____

_____

_____

_____

_____

_____

_____

_____

Gathering Intelligenc

To be a good spy, you need to be a good observer. You need to be able to look at a suspicious person or at a crime scene and quickly make a mental note of all the important details: Does he have freckles? Eyeglasses? Tattoos? A funny walk?

You need to be able to describe these valuable pieces of information accurately so that your bosses back at headquarters can read your report and understand exactly what you saw, what you heard, what you smelled, what you felt with your fingers—perhaps even what you tasted.

Prepare for an on-the-spot test! Pencils down! Spend some time really sniffing, measuring, comparing, inspecting, tapping, and staring at the object your instructor gives you before you begin writing and drawing.

_____

_____

_____

_____

It looks like (go ahead and draw a picture here):

Official Spy School Case File #1

On _____, 20_____, I, Agent _____, was dispatched on a top-secret mission of the highest importance. It was something, all right. Here is what I observed:

The subject(s) looked like this:

_____

_____

_____

Here's a picture:

_____

Here's what the subject(s) did:

_____

_____

_____

Here's what I overheard the subject(s) say:

_____

_____

_____

Putting it all together, I draw the following conclusions about the subject(s)' identity and mission:

_____

_____

_____

_____

Debriefing

The final phase of any spy mission is the debriefing. This is where you lie about what you actually did. You can't tell your family you were chasing international double agents all day! They would go crazy! Instead, make up a nice boring story about spending your day organizing the sock drawer, or sweeping.

It was a beautiful day, perfect for calm tidy activities in which no one gets hurt, like…

_____

_____

_____

_____

So that's what we did, all day. Boring? No! Who could get bored spending the day in such a safe manner? Let me tell you a little more about this exciting activity!

_____

_____

_____

_____

Yes, it was very exciting indeed, and we worked up quite an appetite. We had a nice nutritious snack of milk and…

_____

_____

_____

And then we took a nice quiet nap. It was all very nice and perfectly safe. And if you're wondering how I got that little hole in my shirt, it's quite simple. I...

_____

_____

_____

_____

_____

_____

_____

_____

_____

_____

_____

_____

_____

_____

LITERARY MASH-UPS

by SUSAN VOELKER AND SUSAN MEYER

3 SESSIONS, 90 MINUTES EACH

MANY STUDENTS ARE AWARE OF THE CONCEPT OF A "MASH-UP" AS IT RELATES to music: combining two seemingly different songs that complement each other to create an exciting new work. However, they might not have thought about how this concept could be applied to stories. This workshop is intended to help students gain an understanding of the basics of different literary genres and use that knowledge to shake up their creative writing. By combining the elements of two (or more!) popular genres of literature, students can create something truly unique.

Once the group is gathered, ask the students if they know what a "genre" is. Explain the concept and ask the students for examples of different genres they may be familiar with from books they've read or movies they've seen. You can distribute the student handout on genres to foster discussion or make suggestions. Once a student suggests a genre, ask the other students for characters, plotlines, settings, or themes they might expect to see within that genre.

For example, if the genre suggested is "horror," suggestions could be:

☛ Ghosts

☛ Haunted houses

☛ Vampires

☛ Ancient Indian burial grounds

☛ Werewolves

☛ A car that won't start or a blocked escape route

Once the students have a firm idea of several common genres, hand out the prewriting worksheet. Tell them that they will be writing a story that intertwines the elements of two distinctly different genres. Explain that the prewriting sheet has two different columns, so that they will be able to separate the elements from each genre while formulating their ideas; however, they will only be writing one story that will combine all of these elements.

Ask them to start by choosing the two genres they would like to combine and writing them at the top of the two columns of their prewriting sheet. Help the students fill out the rest of the worksheet, making sure that they understand how they will be integrating the two genres in their story.

Once the worksheets are filled out, have the students use them to begin writing their stories. The workshop ends with the students finishing their stories and sharing them with the class.

LITERARY MASH-UPS

GENRE: A category of artistic composition, as in music or literature,
marked by a distinctive style, form, or content

- **Romances** tend to be stories that principally focus on love and relationships, and may take as a subject a single love relationship, or an individual looking for love.

- **Westerns** can be a branch of historical fiction but may more loosely deal with life in the American Wild West, as it was settled.

- **Mysteries** often have characters that investigate crimes or various puzzles.

- **Science fiction** tends to use some scientific data as the basis for stories, and might focus on things like apocalypse scenarios, future worlds, or space travel, to name just a few.

- **Fantasy** may deal with various "unreal" or magical things, or things not possible in the real world, and may contain alternate worlds or mythical and made-up creatures or peoples.

- **Thrillers** are sometimes called spy thrillers and may have themes in which spies are involved in investigating various events, often on a global scale.

- **Horror** may rely on elements like the supernatural, apocalyptic events, or, in some cases, gruesome events caused by humans or other sources.

- **Historical fiction** invents characters or events for a specific time period and may tell the story of that time period through fictional or fictionalized real historical characters. A variation of this is the period novel, written either during or after a certain time period and particularly emphasizing what it was like to live in that era, with perhaps fictional characters as examples.

- **Nonfiction** includes historical accounts or true accounts or descriptions of phenomena, places, people, or things.

PREWRITING WORKSHEET: MY MASH-UPS

	GENRE 1	GENRE 2

Character(s):

_____

_____

Setting:

_____

_____

Where?

_____

_____

When?

_____

_____

Action:

_____

_____

Conflict or obstacles:

_____

_____

Resolution or conclusion:

_____

_____

BRAIN SPELUNKING

by SCOTT BEAL

2 TO 4 HOURS (DEPENDING ON WHICH ACTIVITIES ARE USED)
MATERIALS: *See each activity's instructions*

OVER A HUNDRED YEARS AGO, A GUY named Sigmund Freud pointed out that our brains are not as smart and orderly as we like to think. Instead, there's a ton of weird stuff swirling below the surface—which we see shades of in our dreams about dinosaur dentists and flying bananas and going to school in scuba gear. The crazy ideas we see in our dreams are always right there inside us, but they mostly try to hide during the daytime.

Suppose your brain is like the Earth. On top is the crust, which is the part we can see, that has trees and skyscrapers and giraffes on it. But that's just a small fraction of the planet. Below that there's roiling magma and tectonic plates and a molten iron core. And that deep-down hidden stuff causes major happenings on the surface—like volcanoes and earthquakes and gravity—even though we never see it directly. Sigmund Freud suggested that our brains are like that. He called the top layer the Conscious, and the underneath layer the Unconscious (or Subconscious), but the principle is the same: all that hidden stuff we glimpse in our dreams has a big effect on who we are, even though we can't always see the connections.

One way to find amazing material for writing is to trick that stuff into coming out when we're awake—to dive below the surface (like brain spelunkers!) and dig out the sparkling buried nuggets. That's what this workshop is about.

Note: The sequence of activities here is flexible—none of them depends on the others to work, so you can mix and match, or leave things out for a shorter workshop.

Spelunking Trick #1: Augmented Automatic Writing

First, have each student make a small deck of random item cards, as follows:

Take a clean sheet of paper and fold it in half three times, then unfold to show a page divided into eight boxes, like this:

1. In row #1, write two animals

2. In row #2, write two machines

3. In row #3, write two things that taste good

4. In row #4, write two things that hurt

For example:

worm	ocelot
stapler	F-16
cheddar	mango
rug burn	thorn

Tear the sheet along the folds, leaving you with eight scraps of paper. Put them in a pile, shuffle, and place face down.

At this point, I read the students a surrealist or pseudo-surrealist poem—usually Andre Breton's "The Verb to Be" or James Tate's "My Private Tasmania" (a Web search should turn them up). We discuss what parts of the poem stick out for them and what kind of sense (if any) the poem makes. You can skip this part to save time or if you don't have a suitable poem handy.

Then I ask them to pick the name of a powerful emotion or a faraway place (such as Loneliness or Jealousy or Zanzibar or East St. Louis), and to write down a first line in one of the following constructions:

"I know the general outline of _____ [emotion or place]."

— following Breton

"My private _____ [emotion or place] has never been . . ."

— following Tate

Then I ask them to write, as follows:

1. Once I say "go" you must start writing immediately, and you must not stop until I say "stop." Whatever pops into your head, write it down. Even if it's "la la la la la" or "I don't know what to write." Don't worry about whether it's any good or makes any sense.

2. Whenever you get stuck or need a jolt, turn over a card from your stack, and whatever is on that card, put it in the poem immediately. Then keep going. You don't have to go through all your cards—use as many or as few as you want or need.

I give them about ten or twelve minutes to write. If they complain that their hands are cramping, that means they're doing it right.

Rationale: The purpose of automatic writing is to keep writing so quickly that the brain doesn't have a chance to filter anything out, so that weird stuff happening in the subconscious can make it onto the page. The use of the random object cards is meant to surprise the brain into making unusual connections that it wouldn't otherwise (consciously) make.

Spelunking Trick #2: Question Chains

Have each student write down three questions beginning with "Why" and three answers beginning with "Because." The answers do not necessarily have to go with the questions.

Pair up. One student reads his or her first question, and the other reads his or her first answer, with (presumably) absurd and amusing results. They take turns reading questions and answers until they get through their lists. If time permits, have each pair present their best question/answer combination to the whole group. What are their favorites, and why?

Now that they have the idea, give them 5–10 minutes to write a quick poem (or script) consisting of questions and answers. Logic is neither required nor encouraged. (As an alternative, you can just have each student pick a favorite question/answer combo and use it as the starting point for some free-form writing.)

Rationale: The randomness of the pairings circumvents the strict cause/effect logic built into the structure of the why/because questions, which forces the brain into confronting nonsense as logic.

Spelunking Trick #3: Technicolor Rorschach Blots

MATERIALS: *White or colored cardstock, 1 or 2 sheets per student (regular or construction paper will NOT work) Food coloring, various colors*

Give each student a sheet of cardstock and set a few droppers of food coloring at each table. (*Note:* It's not a bad idea to cover each table with newspaper first, assuming that newspaper still exists.) Each student should sprinkle a few drops (not too much) of food coloring on his or her cardstock. Then fold the cardstock quickly down the center and press the two halves together. After a few seconds, unfold the cardstock and see a symmetrical abstract design—like a classic Rorschach inkblot, but in color.

Have students make a quick brainstorming list (3 minutes) of all the shapes and images they can see inside their inkblots. Then ask them to write a story or poem (10–15 minutes) focusing on the one image that is most interesting to them, or else trying to combine all the various images together.

Making inkblots is fun, so they may want to do more than one. If you have time and cardstock to spare, you may want to let them do two or three each, and then pick their favorite to write about.

Rationale: Free association of images seen in a Rorschach inkblot was a classic psychoanalytic technique to reveal hidden obsessions or traumas at the heart of patients' problems. The way our brains assemble random blobs of color into images, it is presumed, reveals something about our makeup.

Spelunking Trick #4: Mystical Image Delving

MATERIALS: *One set of interesting images (postcards, storybook illustrations, magazine photos, and so on)*

You can use any set of images for this exercise to work. Once every student has a card or image, ask them each to write a three-sentence description of what they see happening. Who is doing what? How are things positioned, and how are they moving or changing? (The sentences can be straightforward, and they don't have to cover everything, but if they write, "I see a tree. I see a man. I see some water," then the exercise won't go anywhere.)

Now, have students perform the following steps:

1. Take the description you've just written and draw a box around every noun.

2. Circle every verb.

3. Underline every adjective or adverb.

4. On a separate sheet of paper, make a list of all the nouns you've boxed.

5. Below that, make a list of all the verbs you've circled.

6. Below that, make a list of all the adjectives and adverbs you've underlined.

7. Put away your image and your original description, so you are looking only at your lists.

8. Do a quick free association for every word on your three lists. That is, look at each word, and then next to it, write down the *first thing* that it makes you think of. For example, if your first noun is "key" and that makes you think of "palm tree," then write "palm tree" next to the word "key" on your list. Do this for every noun, verb, adjective, and adverb. Go quickly and don't think a lot about it.

9. Get back out your original description.

10. Rewrite the original three sentences, but substitute in all the new words for the original words. (So, in the example above, where the word "key" appeared in the original sentence, now you will write "palm tree.")

The new three sentences can be considered a complete piece—congratulations, you're done!

Isn't it weird? Alternatively, students can keep adding sentences that try to continue the weird mojo of the first three, or that try to explain the first three.

Rationale: As odd as the resulting sentences may be, they are a reflection of the students' own brain. Their original descriptions come from the details that they have observed from their image (whereas another person may have picked up on completely different details), and the replacement words all come from their own associations. So the new bizarre writing is a reflection, on some level, of the way their brain works.

PJ PARTY

by AMY SUMERTON, JASON DEPASQUALE, AND CHLOE DURKEE

1 SESSION, 90 MINUTES
MATERIALS: *2 storybooks*
Computer and LCD projector, overhead projector and transparencies, or chalkboard

MOST KIDS ARE EXPERT STORYTELLERS. THEY LIVE IN A WORLD THAT IS EQUALLY populated by the adults who guide and mentor them as it is by Disney characters, pet ants, and grass that grows inexplicably *backwards*. At that young age, students are still surrounded and delighted by the all the magic in the world—and they are eager to hear and tell new stories about that magic. It's always been Really Strange to me that so many 6- to 8-year-olds are *such* eager storytellers, but they rarely have their stories recorded. Also strange is the fact that kids are so often told bedtime stories, but so few bedtime stories are told *by* kids. What gives? This lesson is an attempt to address these contradictions.

Preparation

The bare-bones preparation for this lesson is fairly minimal: simply find two storybooks that are appropriate for your audience. One of them should be action-packed and perhaps filled with onomatopoeia. The other story should be relaxed and bedtime appropriate. Of course, more can always be done. This lesson results in each student creating a unique story. To enhance this lesson, you might prepare materials to bind the students' resulting stories into small volumes.

Procedure

If at all possible, I recommend wearing pajamas on the day you do this lesson. If you can get away with it, ask your students to wear pajamas, too! It will emphasize the atmosphere of the lesson and help delineate it from your other curriculum, making it special and encouraging the students to DIVE IN to their zones of proximal development. Select two students to be readers during the first portion of the lesson. Have the first student read the appropriate bedtime story. While the student reads, pretend to get all relaxed and sleepy. Then, switch to the other student with the loud, action-packed story (something about trucks, maybe). During THAT story, act disturbed and alert. Alternate between the readings a couple times, responding appropriately, and allow the students to enjoy the presentation. Next, begin a discussion with your students about elements of a good bedtime story. You'll want to cover the cornerstones: characters, setting, types of conflicts (for example, Princess Brunhilde can't find her cake), and duration. Remind the students that adjectives (we call them "sparkle words") and dialogue help turn a good story into a great story.

Now, help the students work as a group to write the beginning of their own, original bedtime story. The ideal technology for this would be a computer screen and a projector, but you could also use overhead transparencies or a chalkboard depending on what's available to you. If you plan to bind a volume of the story for each of the students, you'll at least need to record what the students are saying and be prepared to make enough copies for each student to have all the pages.

Finally, have the students work individually or in small groups to finish the story they started as a class. It might be a good idea to have paper and drawing materials on hand for students to make illustrations if they finish early. Once everyone is finished, bring the class back together and ask for volunteers to share the endings they wrote. Then, drink a nice mug of chamomile and go to sleep!

ANY WHICH WAY

CHOOSING YOUR OWN ADVENTURE

by LINDSEY PLAIT JONES

4 SESSIONS, 1 HOUR EACH

CHOOSE YOUR OWN ADVENTURE (CYOA) books allow the reader to become a central character on an adventure through space, a jungle, historical periods. Readers are asked to make choices for that character along the journey, with direct, immediate results to the character's fate.

This lesson is divided into four sessions, but it can easily be lengthened to give students more time, to research the settings students choose, to create more beautiful books, or to allow for students to work in pairs.

Session 1: Introduction to CYOA and Character Development

I begin by reading a CYOA book aloud to my students during story time. If you don't have a book on hand and cannot order one through your library or online, you can begin by creating a story with your students using a flow chart (see the student handouts for an example) or by narrating one you've made up in advance. You can take a character to the moon and get into some trouble with aliens and competitive space explorers, or journey back in time to a pirate ship bound for Spain where your character is a stowaway. Your story should involve a few choices where your students vote to tell you which way to go.

Once we've finished reading together, we brainstorm a list of elements of the story we just read, like characters, setting, genre, a title, plot, choices, problems, and solutions. At this point, I go over the literary elements carefully to make sure everyone understands the elements our stories will contain. The parts of a story that we will use in this project should stay posted where students can refer to them and where I can add concepts as they are introduced.

Then I ask students what they hoped would happen to the character along the way. We discuss the benefits and drawbacks (if any) of having choices in a story. Did they like having choices? Could the story have been improved? What does reading a story with choices remind them of? Some will say the concept is like a video game or even like the dreams they have while sleeping. These familiar experiences will help them relate to this kind of story writing.

I prompt the students to tell me what they remember about the character in the story we just read. Then we make a list of all the attributes we might know about a character in a story (characterization), using all the senses. For example: What he/she/it eats, what it wears, its physical features, what it dislikes doing, where it lives, how it moves, what it smells like.

Then the students get to work! They must independently create unique, original characters for their own stories by listing at least ten attributes of that character on a blank sheet of paper. Characters must be named!

If students have trouble thinking of characters, they might start by choosing a setting (as described in Session 2). Students can also be prescribed a time period or location for their stories and told to think of a character who might belong in that setting or who might be in danger in that setting. As a last resort, students can fashion their characters after themselves!

I wrap up this session by having students introduce their characters to the class, acting as the character him/her/itself, or by having students write down one idea for an adventure this character might have and handing it to me on their way out the door. I want to make sure all students have developed their characters and have an idea of what the characters will be able to do in a CYOA story.

Session 2: Determining a Setting and Beginning a Plot

To begin this lesson, I ask students to brainstorm places and times their character(s) might visit on an adventure. I jot down some of their setting ideas on the board to get their minds racing and give everyone somewhere to start. Remember— these stories are a chance to get out and explore! (*Note:* Studying settings is a neat place to insert some ecological, historical, or astronomical research into the writing curriculum to make sure the students' settings are accurate and lifelike.)

Once students have chosen a setting, they should write it down on the back of the characterization page they created in the last session, and record plants, creatures, sights, sounds, or objects that might be in their settings. They'll use this list for illustration ideas later, and can also incorporate settings into their stories as imagery or as possible sources of conflict (for example, a river could flood and wash a character away, a desert could be home to quicksand).

Once all students have chosen and described their settings, I ask students what we need to do to make the story move. If our characters stayed in their settings and everything was great and nothing happened, would they want to read on? Most likely, the answer is no! Plot is driven by conflict and problems, because they make new and exciting (or disastrous) things happen. I ask them to name one conflict the character faced in the story we read together in the previous session. What other choices could the character(s) have made to solve that problem? What else could have gone wrong? There are many possibilities!

Before we start creating a plot for our stories, I ask the students to think of the first problem their characters will have. They should come up with some big conflict that will drive the story at first. They can talk this over with classmates or me to make sure it's juicy.

Then I give the students the "Plot Worksheet" handouts, on which they will brainstorm the events in their stories. I show them how to fill in the first box with narration, using the story we read at the start of the project as material for my own worksheet. They should write in shorthand or incomplete sentences here to save space and get the ideas out on the page quickly. Students start by writing their introduction and first problem into the first box.

Each box for text should have an accompanying set of choices for the reader. Students must write the choices their characters can make in those spaces. Then, following the arrows, they fill in new text boxes to show what happens after the reader/character makes each choice. They keep doing this until they finish out a full plot. Then they can move around the page, making new options for their reader and character. I model these steps and then check in with each student to check for comprehension. If they need help, I may go step-by-step, showing them what to fill in and then giving them time to work on that one step before proceeding.

Each plot may have several endings. All plots will not be the same length—some choices might lead to an early demise for the character, and others allow the story to continue longer. We'll talk about those in the next lesson. Also, space is provided on the worksheets to fill in page numbers so that students know what text to put on each page and to make sure that the directions they give the reader are correct. This should be done later, once all the plots are completed on the worksheets.

We use the rest of the time in this class to brainstorm the plot of our stories. This may take a while! I move around the room, answering questions and helping students get situated. If they finish early, they can work on illustrations for their story. It's really important at this step to make sure all my students grasp the concept and the format and to be very encouraging! These students are trying something new and very complex. Praise the heck out of them.

Session 3: Brainstorming Plot and Creative Conclusions

I will give students more time to finish their plot maps during this session, but first I want to show them where we're going. I write down four types of endings on the board:

1. Hollywood Ending: Character gets all he ever wanted, everything ends up great.

2. Switcheroo Ending: There's a surprise twist at the ending.

3. Tragic Ending: Everything ends badly. Characters might die or be badly hurt.

4. Mystery Ending: Ending is unclear. Readers are able to make up their own minds.

I ask the students to look at their story maps. Their main characters have gotten into a lot of trouble at this point, and they have many plots for

readers to explore. We must end each of these plots in unique ways. We go over each of the endings and give some examples. I mention that students must end all their plots today. Students will need to use some ending types more than once, because there will be lots of conclusions in their stories, but I ask them to try writing each type of ending.

Then we get back to brainstorming! I continue to move around the room, monitoring their work and helping students who may get confused. I ask the students to show me their stories, and I follow the choices to make sure they grasp the format and are on track. Watching the stories materialize is a lot of fun, and this is a great time to provide individual encouragement.

As soon as students are finished with their brainstorming worksheets, I check their work and help them mark out page numbers for the finished book. One number is assigned to each page and each number should be assigned to only one page.

I hand out book pages for them to use or let them work on the computer. Alternately, we could use notebooks that are prebound and number the pages before starting. To help them keep track of things, I distribute the "Page Types" handout and introduce the items that belong on each page—text, illustration, directions, and page number—by drawing a sample page on the board with labels for each item.

Students should write in the text for each page, leaving space for illustrations on the top and directions on the bottom. As they write, they use the plot worksheet for ideas, but add detail and beautiful language to their narration. Each page contains only one step in the story, and each page must be numbered. The page number can go at the very bottom of the page or on the outside top corner.

I check with students along the way, reading through their stories as they're being written to ensure that the directions can be followed. I also provide lots of encouragement because this work can be tricky.

At the end of the session, students should have a finished plot worksheet, complete with many endings, and should be creating pages for their book.

Session 4: Creating and Sharing Choose Your Own Adventure Books

For the majority of this session, students should finish writing their stories. This is the time to lengthen the text on their pages and make the story come to life with description and suspense. This step takes the most time, and we plan accordingly.

They should ask a classmate or two to read through their books and check the pagination for all plots once they get the text down but before they start illustrating. If the directions they give the reader lead to the wrong page, they must fix the numbers in those directions now to make the story flow correctly. It helps to lay pages out on a table and check the pagination visually.

Once students finish writing and adding directions, they should put their pages in order and illustrate! Then they add front and back covers. All covers should include an illustration, the author and illustrator's name, and an original book title.

Their books can be bound with staples or thread. If time permits, they can write author biographies for their back covers and write reviews that they attribute to famous authors and icons.

The finished books are best enjoyed when shared with others. I have students read to each other and sometimes invite teachers, family, or younger students to visit us and hear our stories.

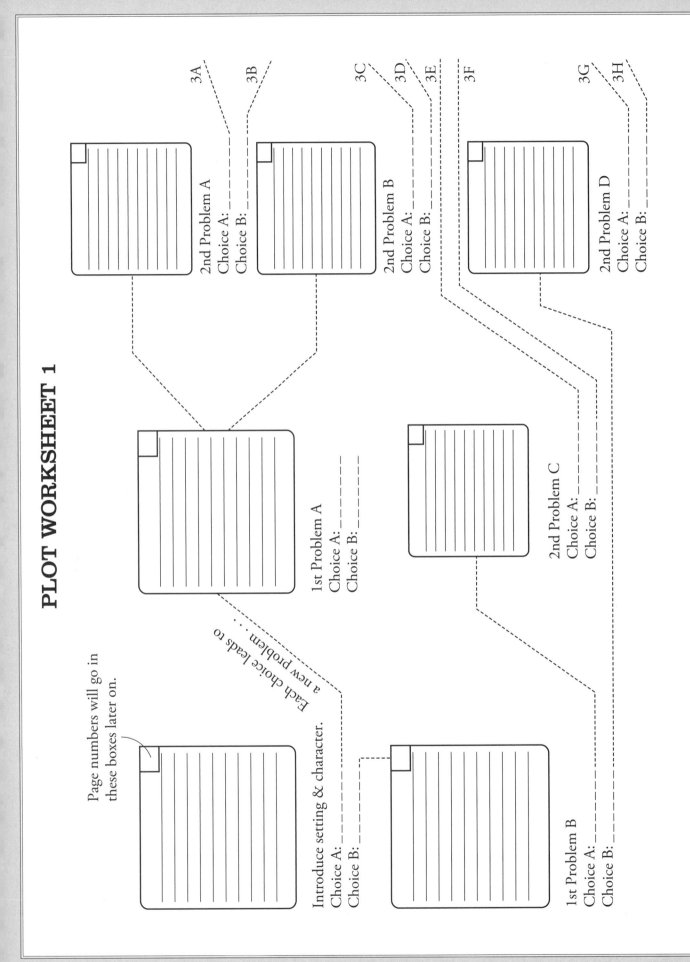

PLOT WORKSHEET 1

Page numbers will go in these boxes later on.

Introduce setting & character.
Choice A: _ _ _ _ _ _
Choice B: _ _ _ _ _ _

Each choice leads to a new problem . . .

1st Problem A
Choice A: _ _ _ _ _ _
Choice B: _ _ _ _ _ _

1st Problem B
Choice A: _ _ _ _ _ _
Choice B: _ _ _ _ _ _

2nd Problem A
Choice A: _ _ _ _ _ _ 3A
Choice B: _ _ _ _ _ _ 3B

2nd Problem B
Choice A: _ _ _ _ _ _ 3C
Choice B: _ _ _ _ _ _ 3D
                      3E

2nd Problem C
Choice A: _ _ _ _ _ _
Choice B: _ _ _ _ _ _   3F

2nd Problem D
Choice A: _ _ _ _ _ _ 3G
Choice B: _ _ _ _ _ _ 3H

Note: Thanks to Julian Glander for designing this diagram.

PLOT WORKSHEET 2

When you write a choose your own adventure story, you don't go in order from one beginning to many ends! Make a diagram like the one below to show your teacher how your story will read. Start with one introduction. Then give your readers a choice. Depending on the choices, take them to see what comes next! Some choices will continue the story—others will end it.

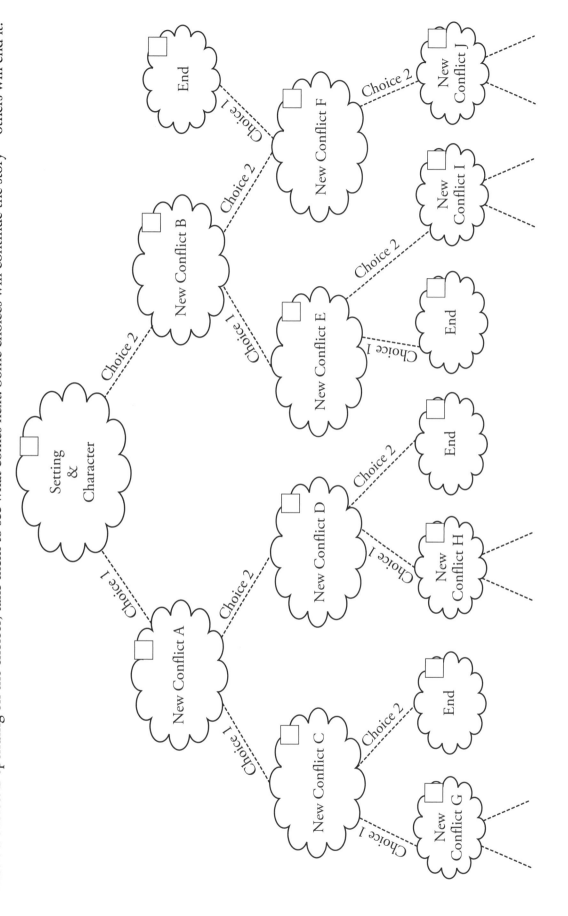

Note: Thanks to Julian Glander for designing this diagram

PAGE TYPES

Page # ____

Illustration

Plot

Choices: ____ ____

Page # ____

Plot

Choices: ____ ____

Page # ____

Plot

Illustration

Page # ____

Illustration

Ending

Note: Thanks to Julian Glander for designing this diagram

LIFE-SIZE BOARD GAME!

by KATHERINE FISHER AND JESSICA MORTON

1 SESSION, 75 MINUTES
MATERIALS: *Poster board for game board squares*
Cardboard die
Index cards
Masking tape
A few adult facilitators to help out

SOMETIMES THE HARDEST PART OF WRITING IS KNOWING WHERE TO BEGIN. Sometimes the luxury of time for reflection, thought, and prewriting (though we don't want to discount these!) can be a recipe for hours of staring, blankly and frustrated, at a continuously empty page.

How, you may ask, does one get students to jump right into even the most ridiculous writing prompts? By turning those students into pieces in a life-size board game, naturally.

This workshop gives students the opportunity to collaboratively create a plethora of short writing assignments that can be shared or expanded at a later time. Most importantly, it gets them writing, right away, and turns what is often a solitary activity into a group effort.

Before the workshop begins, take some time to create the physical squares for the board game. We cut out posterboard in five different colors and wildly varying shapes, each about a foot in diameter. When the time comes, use masking tape to lay them out, in a random order and an interesting shape, around the room you're using. You also need to make a cardboard die. Our die was about eight inches tall, and we labeled the sides with: 1, 2, 3, 4, Roll Again, and Switch. You should also get some index cards and write random words and phrases (pinecone; Frisbee; "That was when everything changed," she said; especially; walking) on about two-thirds of them. If you're playing with younger kids, it's also important to enlist help, preferably one adult for every two to three participants.

Ready?

READY.

To start, ask all the students to write one of their favorite words on a blank index card and add it to your pile. Then take about ten minutes to brainstorm different writing genres. Our brilliant, amazing students came up with: acrostic poem, short story, cartoon, wild card, recipe, haiku, limerick, free verse poem, short play or skit, six-word biography, road sign, news article, advertisement, song, and Twitter-length story.

By either democratic or totalitarian means, narrow the list down to five, and assign each genre a color. Organize students into pairs or groups of three, and assign each team a facilitator.

Each team will roll the die, telling them where to move on the game board. They'll also choose one of the index cards at random. They then have to write something in the genre that corresponds to the color they landed on, using the word on the index card as their topic. This is where the facilitators are extremely helpful, making sure that the teams stay on track and that everyone gets to participate. When the team completes that exercise, they can roll the die again and move on. The first team to reach the end of the board is the "winningest" in a group of winners.

The trick of this game is that no one ever gets bored, because everyone's playing simultaneously. Learning to wait your turn is a good lesson, but it's hardly the most exciting part of board games. Or of writing. This means that from the outside, the game can look like organized chaos, but from within, it's a maelstrom of joy and creation. Give into it.

BRAINS! OR, WRITING WITH ZOMBIES

by BRAD BRUBAKER

2 SESSIONS, 90 MINUTES EACH
MATERIALS: *Zombie DVD (optional) or zombie pictures*
Zombie music
Zombie (or a human posing as one)

IN THIS WORKSHOP I INTRODUCE MYSELF AS A ZOMBIE EXPERT, BUT THE course is structured to demonstrate that it is the students who are the experts. The workshop starts with a simple question, "What are some things zombies can do?" and from that moment the zombie concept is under the ownership of the students.

Session 1

As the students enter, a DVD is playing showcasing not-too-spooky zombies, with a certain Michael Jackson song serving as the soundtrack. If you don't have time to put together a best zombie hits DVD, some pictures pulled from the Internet and posted on the board will do. This transforms the space into a place of spectacle, grabs their attention, and gives those unfamiliar with zombies a visual to pull from. Believe it or not, some elementary school students are not immersed in zombie folklore.

Once the mood is set, we stop the DVD and the music and begin with an **icebreaker**: we ask everyone to do their best impression of a zombie from the "Thriller" video. This simple physical activity is a great way to get the energy up, energy that later shifts from kinetic movement to kinetic thought and imagination.

Having warmed up, we are 20 minutes into the workshop and only now will we begin discussing zombies. Casually sitting in a circle on the floor, I ask who is familiar with zombies and let any eager hands expound upon their knowledge for everyone's benefit. This is how we segue into the **group activity**.

The students are asked to work together to create a list of activities zombies can and cannot do, what they can and cannot be, where they can and cannot go, and so on. Some hands shoot straight up and help get the ideas flowing for the others—one student informed us with extreme urgency that a zombie cannot operate a parachute. When a student is so moved by the subject as to dominate the conversation, I inform the group that I will only call on "quiet hands." Especially shy students are asked about their daily routine and whether zombies perform the same routine activities, like brushing their teeth. As with any group of scholars, disagreements can occur (for example, do zombies play video games?); at this point list-making turns to public forum as each side is respectively listened to and given consideration. Though ultimately the majority decision is what makes the list, it is fine-tuned to be more inclusive of everyone's ideas. (Zombies play video games, but are offended by zombie-themed games like *Left 4 Dead*.)

All of the findings from the group brainstorm, which have been documented on the board, are considered and used in the **individual assignment** that ends the first session. Students return to their desks where they are asked to compose a story in which a zombie attempts to do something that our lists indicate cannot be done by his or her species. One girl started with the idea that zombies cannot do cartwheels; she took this information and turned it into the story of a zombie cheerleader who loses her limbs when attempting acrobatics until all that is left is "dust and nothing more."

Session 2

As before, students enter with the DVD and music playing. The **warm-up** is reviewing the list of things zombies can and cannot do. New ideas are added to the list.

Starting in a circle on the floor, I inform the students that a special guest will be joining us: a REAL LIVE ZOMBIE! Our task is to collaborate and decide on some interview questions for Dave the Zombie. I write on the board furiously as the kids shout out dozens of questions ranging from factual (Do you have zombie pets?) to theological (When you become a zombie, do you go to a special place?), preferences related (What is your favorite way to eat brains?), and conversational (How's the wife?). If we end up with far more questions than we can actually ask, we vote on our favorites.

Finally, it is time to bring out Dave the Zombie (a volunteer in full costume and zombie makeup). After some brief introductions and an explanation of how I came to befriend a zombie, the James Lipton–style interview begins. I make sure to hit each of the students' favorite questions, while adding other questions that feel appropriate based on the direction of Dave's improvised responses. This **performance** is down-to-earth and moves past one-note stereotypes, leaning toward silly before it leads toward scary. (A transcript can be read on the following pages.)

After the interview, which would feel too short no matter how much time it is allotted, Dave the Zombie leaves. All of the new information from the interview serves as mental kindling for the **individual assignment**: write a zombie story of your own creation. I suggest a few ideas (What if a celebrity were actually a zombie? What would happen if a zombie went to school . . . or were your teacher?), but most students have already started frantically writing. Success!

DAVE THE ZOMBIE*

The Interview

The following is the transcript of our students' interview with a real-life (sort of) zombie. As far as we know no students were transformed into zombies themselves following the encounter, but we cannot guarantee it.

WHAT IS YOUR FAVORITE WAY TO EAT BRAINS?

Shish-ka-bobs. I like my brains crispy.

ON A DIFFERENT NOTE, HOW'S THE WIFE?

(Pointing at empty ring finger) I'm not married. But I have a lovely girlfriend with purple skin and one green eye. We met in a graveyard. I was playing zombie music and she started dancing. We went bowling. It's good.

DO YOU FEEL HAPPINESS?

I . . . feel . . . hungriness. *(Looks hungrily at his interviewer, specifically in the cranial area)*

I'M GOING TO GET SERIOUS FOR A MINUTE AND ASK YOU A PERSONAL QUESTION THAT I HOPE YOU DON'T FIND UPSETTING. HOW DID YOU DIE?

I went to a party. My friends said, "Don't go to that party. It's going to be dead." I didn't realize they meant the living dead. I got bit.

ARE ZOMBIES PLANNING TO TAKE OVER THE WORLD? IT'S OKAY, YOU CAN TELL US.

No, we're not planning to take over the world. We would like to buy Antarctica. You aren't using it and we could because zombies don't freeze to death. It would be a good place. We could eat penguins and hang out with seals.

WHAT'S THE BEST PART ABOUT BEING A ZOMBIE?

No one bothers you. They just scream and run away. I always get a seat on the bus!

---

*Chicago actor and Oracle Theatre company member David Boren in full costume and zombie makeup.

DO YOU THINK YOU HAVE BRAINS?

(Looks at his bloody shirt) I have brains.

YES, I CAN SEE. BUT DO YOU THINK YOU HAVE BRAINS IN YOUR HEAD?

(Knocking loudly on his own head) Probably not, or I would have eaten them.

WHAT IS YOUR JOB?

I don't have a job. It is hard to get one.

(The interview is interrupted by an audience member who farts.)

I do a lot of that. But even though I don't have money, I go to the zombie market to buy brains, helmets, and other necessities.

HOW TO WRITE A COMIC

by TODD POUND AND JENNIFER TRAIG

3 SESSIONS, 90 MINUTES EACH
MATERIALS: *Artist (optional)*
Costume supplies (optional)

THIS CLASS IS GREAT FOR STUDENTS who think they don't like to write, because it lets them tell stories through pictures. It's a grand tradition. Visual storytelling has been around forever—just take a gander at some hieroglyphics or cave paintings. Before you know it, a few words creep in, and boom, you're telling a story using both text and pictures, like a true *artiste*. Of course, text and pictures need to coexist peacefully on the page. This class shows students how they can work together to produce great stories.

We'll be honest: the part of this class everyone likes best is the drawing. It works best if you have a real-life artist (amateur or pro) to illustrate points on the board. The plot diagram really comes alive when it's being sketched out right before your eyes using atomic alligators and nuclear fish. Character development becomes very engrossing when you have an artist right there, sketching out exactly what the class dictates: "A miniature giraffe! With a Mohawk! And earrings! Wearing a tutu, with flames shooting out of its nose!" If no artist is available, take a deep breath and do it yourself. We bet you're a better artist than you think.

Session 1: Character

We start by asking for a volunteer. This hapless student is then outfitted with a couple accessories—maybe just a hat and glasses, or maybe a wig and feather boa. We ask the class to describe the character they see before them. "Librarian!" they shout. "Movie star!" "Crazy lady!" We ask why. "Because she is wearing glasses, so she must be smart." "She's dressed like a celebrity." "Normal people wouldn't wear that."

We use this to illustrate a point: they were able to get all this information from just two little accessories. In comics, you have to keep the text brief, so you need to communicate things like character using a visual shorthand. How they look, how they talk, their name—all these things will let us know who characters are. The Character Design! handout goes over this in detail, so we distribute that and go over it with the class. As for drawing characters, we remind them that simplest is generally best. They're going to have to draw this character over and over, and penciling in a hundred legs or a thousand freckles gets tiresome. The most famous characters are generally pretty basic. We start to sketch a few characters on the board and ask the class the shout out the answer when the recognize them: Batman, Mickey Mouse, Bart Simpson. Usually, they can guess from just one or two strokes, from the hairline or the ears alone, which is why these are such great characters.

SUPERTEACHER BONUS ACTIVITY

Have the whole class design a character together. It can be anything: a rhino with dreadlocks and a tutu, a lion-gator hybrid with braces and roller skates, a talking banana. To keep things fair, you may want to have the students write character features (like "braces," "sunglasses," "braids," "funky boots," and so on) on scraps of paper, then place them in a bowl. Sketch the character on the board, adding features you've picked from the bowl. As you're drawing, invite the class to come up with the character's backstory. How did this crazy creature come to be? What are its likes and dislikes? Fears and loves? What's its name? What does it do for fun?

After 40 minutes of discussion the students are usually pretty eager to get to work, so we turn them loose to create their own characters. First, they draw them using the "Illustrated Model Sheet." This is what the pros use, to make sure the character stays consistent from frame to frame. Students are instructed to draw their character from a few different angles, for example, from the front, side, and back. The notched lines will help you make sure the character stays the same height, with the same length arms. We talk about the concept of "heads high," basing your character's height on the measurement of his or her head. Superheroes are generally about eight heads high; normal people are about five; Calvin of *Calvin and Hobbes* is about two. If they finish early, they can practice drawing their character in different moods: happy, angry, excited, scared.

Next we distribute the "Written Model Sheet." Here, the students list all their character's qualities. It helps them flesh out the character's personality and keep track of things, so if we learn on page one that he's allergic to chocolate, we don't see him eating a candy bar with impunity on page six.

Session 2: Story

In the next class we discuss story. We go over the "Structuring the Story" plot chart handout. We talk about the concept of "backstory"—how did

your character get to be the way he or she is? We discuss the backstory of Superman, Batman, and Spider-Man as examples. We limit the lecture to 30 minutes, because the students are eager to work. We hand out some blank panels and they spend the next hour working on a first draft.

Session 3: Composition

In the final class we discuss composition, in both senses of the word—composing objects in a frame, and composing words on a page. We go through comic books to see how other artists compose. Is the POV (point of view) looking down, like a bird in the sky? Looking up, like a worm? What's big? What's small? What's in shadow? What's barely sketched out, and what's really detailed?

Then we teach them the cardinal rule of writing for comics: KEEP IT BRIEF. The reader gets bored if there's a big chunk of text, so you have to be concise and find other ways of telling the story—through art and dialogue, for instance. We talk about using satisfying words instead of wishy-washy ones. Brainstorm a few good ones and write them on the board. And we define the most important comic writing technique, onomatopoeia. We practice: What is the sound of a skateboarder crashing into metal trash cans? Of slipping on a banana? Of a mirror breaking?

Finally, we distribute more blank panels, and the students show us everything they've learned. We are always blown away. When they've finished and time permits, we photocopy everyone's work and bind it into a class comic book with a blank cover the students can decorate themselves. It's usually so good we could charge money for it.

CHARACTER DESIGN!

Creating characters is the most important part of writing a comic book. It's also the most fun! Here's how to do it in four easy steps:

1. Decide what your character will be: a man, a woman, a child, an adult, an animal, an alien, an ice cream scooper … anything at all. You can base your character on a friend, a family member, a pet, a famous athlete, or even a fictional character from a story you like. Once you've got your hero, you'll also want some supporting characters like sidekicks and mortal enemies. Look around you to find examples of characters you might want in your story. Remember, your characters will drive the plot, so it's important you really understand what makes them tick.

2. Think about your character's backstory. If she's a cranky field mouse, figure out why she's in such a bad mood. Is it because she hates the country and longs to live in the glamorous, glittering big city? If your character's a mutant, figure out what caused the mutation. Was it a nuclear accident? A food allergy? Think about all your character's likes and dislikes, strengths and weaknesses. Is he super-strong but afraid of bunnies? Is he addicted to sardines? These little details will make the character feel rounded and real. Broad, one-dimensional characters are fine in some comics, but it can be interesting to have more complicated characters too. Give your character some personality traits we might not expect. Maybe your superhero's hobby is pottery. Maybe your archvillain wears frilly ankle socks under his combat boots. Surprises are good.

3. Give your character a really cool name. Pick a superhero name like Surpasso or a really normal name like Al. You could let us know that your hero is a good guy by naming him Valiant P. Whitehat, or you could play off our expectations by, say, making Angelica Goodchild an evil brat.

4. Sketch your brand new characters. The way the characters look will tell us a lot about who they are, so put some thought into their features, their figures, their clothes, even their haircuts. That doesn't mean you have to dress a nerdy character in plaid highwaters and goggles, but you can. You can also play against our expectations by making the seven-foot square-jawed giant a fraidycat. Use your characters to define the "tone" or "mood" of your story. Is it dark and scary or light and funny? The tone is created not merely by what your characters say and do, but also by what they look like.

Here are some things to remember:

* We have to care about the characters, but we don't have to like them. We can love to hate them, too.

* You have to feel comfortable drawing your characters. Select a drawing style you feel confident about. Remember your characters are all just a collection of geometric shapes.

* Draw them from every angle. Create a model sheet for reference. What do your characters look like from the front? From the side? Draw them over and over.

* Study other characters. What makes Snoopy so cool? Wolverine? Wonder Woman? What characters do you like? Why?

ILLUSTRATED MODEL SHEET

ILLUSTRATED MODEL SHEET

Written Model Sheet

Character's name:

_____

_____

Home:

_____

_____

Personality traits:

_____

_____

Greatest strength:

_____

_____

Greatest weakness:

_____

_____

Sidekick:

_____

_____

Other pals:

_____

_____

Archenemy:

_____

_____

Love interest:

_____

_____

Backstory—How did this character become who he or she is?

_____

_____

Mission in life:

_____

_____

When he or she gets angry . . .

_____

_____

When he or she is happy . . .

_____

_____

What's in his or her refrigerator?

_____

_____

If this character went to a karaoke club, what song would he or she perform?

_____

_____

STRUCTURING THE STORY

A HANDY-DANDY CHART!

3. Climax

Archenemies battle! The clock is ticking... can the hero save the day before it's too late? We're on the edge of our seats!

2. The plot thickens...

The villain enters. Something fishy is going here...

Tidy Wave has Litter Bug where he wants him ...but can he bear to touch the filthy fiend?

1. Introduction

We meet the characters and explore the setting. On the surface, everything looks perfect... but is it?

Tidy Wave and his sidekick Squeaky Clean keep the streets of Sparkle City safe and spotless.

Who is turning Sparkle City into his own personal dumpster? Could it be that vile varlet, Litter Bug? And why does Tidy keep washing his hands?

4. Denouement

The action wraps up. Things begin to fall into place. Loose ends are tied into neat little bows.

Tidy & Squeaky mop up.

5. Conclusion

The bad guys are caught, the heroes celebrate. Show's over! Now get your coat and go home!

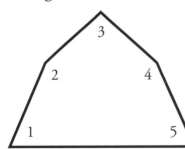

HEY! You don't have to tell the story in order. You could tell it backwards or chop it up. Arsty-fartsy!

Tidy slips on some fresh gloves and slaps Squeaky Clean a well-earned high-five.

HERE ARE SOME IDEAS TO GET YOU STARTED

You could base your comic book on a fairy tale, and tweak it to make it your own. Turn Goldilocks into a foul-mouthed hillbilly and the three bears into super-intelligent, genetically altered animals who teach at the local junior college. Juuuust right.

Ghosts. Ghosts are great because they are ooky, kooky, spooky, and easy to draw. Your comic book could be very serious and suspenseful (what does this phantom specter want?) or goofy. Maybe your ghosts are simply spiteful, doing no actual harm but annoying the living by replacing the shampoo with Miracle Whip.

Talking animals. Talking super-intelligent genetically altered animals!

Talking food. Here's a great idea: "the secret life of groceries." Do a comic book about what happens in your refrigerator when the door is closed. Do the carrots and celery stalks fence? Is the head cheese bossy? Does the salad dressing try to stage a coup?

You could go the super-realistic route and do a story about an everyday event, like cleaning the bathroom. All kinds of magical, exciting things can occur while cleaning a bathroom.

Superheroes! Is anything better? They have powers! And such fashion sense! They're classic! You could play with the usual format by making your superhero very, very stupid, lazy, or cowardly. Here are some superhero guidelines to follow or subvert:

- They must wear tights (boots are good, too).
- Also, cheekbones. Prominent ones.
- They are haunted by dark secrets.
- They make witty puns while beating the daylights out of pesky villians.

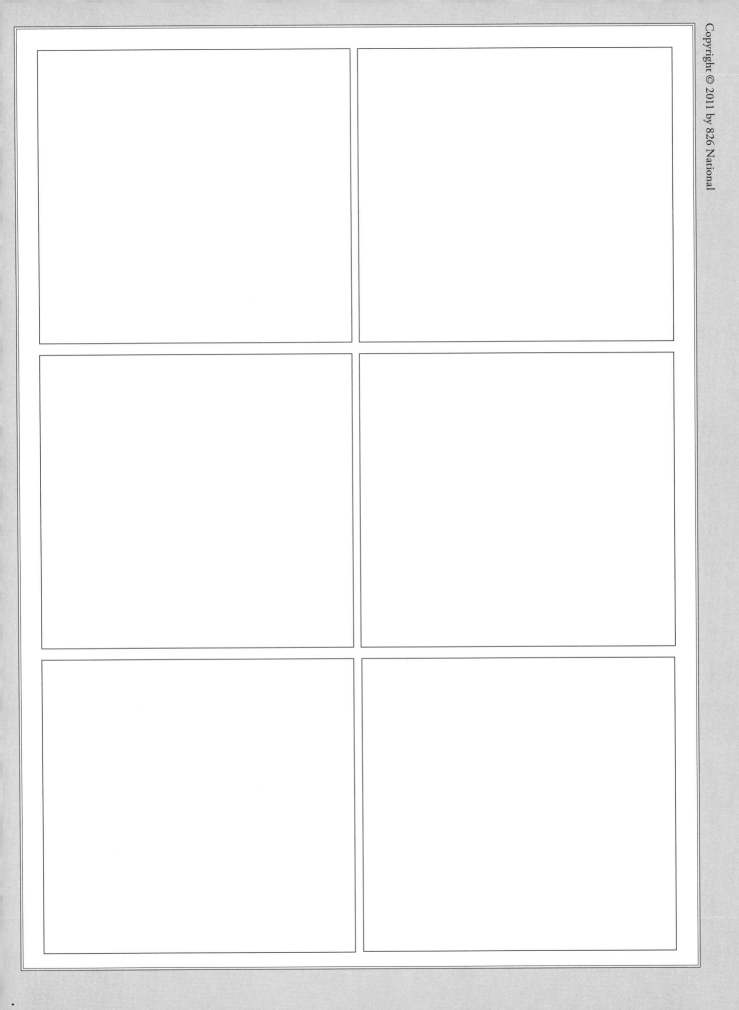

THE MEANING OF LIFE (THE SHORT ANSWER)

WRITING BIG, LARGE, AND SMALL!

by ELIZABETH ALEXANDER AND KATHLEEN GOLDFARB

"IT HAS RECENTLY COME TO MY ATTENTION," SAID PLUCKY PURCELL, "THAT CHARLES IV (CHARLES THE BLAND) ONCE SAID THAT LIFE IS A PICKLE FACTORY. I CANNOT ACCEPT THAT, AS I FIND IT IMPOSSIBLE TO DETERMINE WHETHER LIFE IS SWEET OR SOUR."

—TOM ROBBINS, *ANOTHER ROADSIDE ATTRACTION*

2 SESSIONS, 2 HOURS EACH
(APPROXIMATE TIMES FOR EACH TOPIC ARE PROVIDED)

WHAT ARE SOME FUN WAYS TO TREAT BIG QUESTIONS (LIKE WHETHER LIFE IS sweet or sour, lovely or awful)? In this workshop, we identify our own big questions and explore them in stories that are both goofy and serious. In Session 2, we brainstorm questions, hatch a grand plan, and write a first draft. In Session 2, we give and receive feedback, revise the old Brand X (a.k.a first draft), and read our grand finales.

Session 1 is mainly instructional. Session 2 is devoted to receiving personal feedback on first drafts and completing and sharing stories.

Session 1

As students arrive, they each receive a note card on which they are asked to draw a picture of an animal or object that they have strong feelings about. (Perhaps they love gorillas or have a terror of golden-winged dragonflies. Perhaps they're alarmed by hot pink kitchen sponges.) These animals or objects will become the main characters; in students' stories. We then go around the room and we explain why we chose a particular animal or object. [10 minutes]

Assuring students that even "adults" like us enjoy a good picture book, we display and read aloud one or two picture books that treat big questions in simple, engaging ways. (We've used *Joseph Had a Little Overcoat* by Simms Taback, which treats loss, and *Bad Dog, Marley!*, by John Grogan, which explores the incompatibility of love and control.) Students have many comments about the books; after letting the discussion flow freely for a little while, we focus their attention on themes using questions such as: "What is this book about?" "What problem does the main character face?" and "Has someone you know faced a problem like the main character's?" [20 minutes]

Now comes the most conceptually challenging part of the workshop: identifying our own big questions to write about. We begin by asking students to name some issues that kids they know face and listing their responses on an easel or whiteboard. "Being popular" is a common response, along with "adults fighting," "parents getting divorced," "bullying," "death [of a pet, grandparent, or sometimes parent]," and "cancer." We group similar responses, go back over the list, and invite students to say more about each problem, throwing in our own two cents from time to time. [15 minutes]

This is a good juncture for a stretching break. [5 minutes]

Returning to the list of issues kids face, for the next 15–25 minutes, we:

1. Elicit from students how to rewrite each issue in the form of a big question, for example:

   Being popular: Who says it's important to be popular?

   Parents fighting: What should kids do when parents fight?

   Death: What happens to people after they die?

2. Ask students to choose one big question for their stories to address and then imagine their animal or object confronting that big question. For example:

   ☞ An ordinary housefly feels bad because the prettier, more popular dragonflies make fun of her.

   ☞ A house cat learns to deal with his ADHD.

   ☞ A beloved granddad, who has died, reappears to his grandson as a gorilla.

At this point, students know enough about their stories to start writing and may be raring to go. We extend the instruction a tad longer to talk about story beginnings. (This can help student writers avert the pitfall of a tedious preamble.) We read aloud the first few paragraphs of a story or novel with a riveting beginning (we especially recommend the beginning of *Harry Potter and the Deathly Hallows*).

We ask, "How does the author engage readers, so they want to keep reading?" We deliberately choose a selection in which the author uses dialogue, action, or both, and encourage students to begin their stories in a similar fashion.

For the remainder of the session (approximately 45 minutes), students write. We work individually with students who need extra help formulating their stories, want personal feedback on their plans before they start writing, or have trouble staying focused.

Session 2

We tell students how great they're doing, that we love their stories, and that we'll be giving them individual feedback before they begin finishing and revising their drafts. We invite one or two students who have written fabulous beginnings to read them aloud. [10 minutes]

Next we make a few general comments about where students are in the story-writing process, observing that most are beginning the long slog through the middle. To keep students engaged and help them with plot and character development, we read aloud and discuss several excerpts from a story that exudes oomph: P. L. Travers's "Miss Andrew's Lark" (Chapter Two in *Mary Poppins Comes Back*).

We briefly review the meaning of figurative language and have students raise their hands when they hear it (for example, "*Chir-up!*"; "with a thundering rush she dashed towards the cage"; "*Tramp-tramp. Tramp-tramp*"). We point out modifiers that enhance the writing, rather than sink it ("a bumping, jumping, thumping voice sounded overhead"). We talk about what readers learn about the characters from what they say, how they say it, and how the narrator comments on it. Students have great fun with this story and want us to read more of it, but we don't have time. [10–20 minutes]

—◆—

We distribute students' drafts from Session 1, which they will now expand on. Students seat themselves at a Silent Table or a Whispering Table and resume writing. Instructors circulate, answering questions and working with individuals as needed. [50–60 minutes]

We stop writing 20 minutes or so before the end of class, allowing time for all students to read their stories aloud. Instructors comment, briefly and enthusiastically, after each reading:

☞ "Hank's kitten shows me how hard life can be for people who 'have trouble organizing their thoughts and can go drifting off even when they're trying not to.'"

☞ "Malia's dog feels so bad when the humans yell at him that *I* want to cry."

We could go on and on about the meaning of life, but we say good-bye.

HOW TO SURVIVE ANYTHING

by REBECCA WASLEY

1 SESSION, 2 HOURS

WHAT DO YOU TELL YOUR TEACHER WHEN YOU FORGOT YOUR HOMEWORK? How do you defend yourself against a vampire? How can you get out of doing your chores? How do you stop aliens from taking over the planet?

This lesson plan has kids come up with ideas of sticky situations, from the mundane to the ridiculous, and then create the perfect solutions. Students will each pick a problem they need to survive and write the solution. All of these pieces will be combined into one large book that everyone gets to take home. This lesson can be used for any age group, and the difficulty and humor of the pieces will range. It's also a good exercise for beginning writers who need some structure to their pieces.

Introduction and Explanation

Start by explaining what a survival guide is and look at some real examples. I like to use *The Common Sense Survival Guide* and *The Worst Case Scenario Survival Guide,* but there are plenty of examples out there depending on the age group and interest of the kids.

Next, talk about what makes a good survival guide and writing style. Then list some possible problems on the board.

EXAMPLES:

- How to talk to an alien from another planet
- How to get out of cleaning your room
- How to make your mom think you ate your vegetables
- How to survive a bear attack
- How to live on the moon
- How to escape quicksand

- ☞ How to wrestle an alligator
- ☞ How to survive a bad haircut
- ☞ How to get rid of vampires

The problems can be serious or funny, and this can set the *tone*. What tone do they want their survival how-to to have? Should it be serious and straightforward or funny and tongue-in-cheek? Help the kids define and understand tone and discuss how to use humor in writing and what makes things funny (that is, taking something ridiculous but creating real steps you can follow to solve it). Use an example like the following to show one way things can have different meanings depending on how you say it and have the kids think about what they want their own tone to be: serious, sarcastic, funny?

EXAMPLE:

TONE is used to show feeling and emotion and can set the mood:

- ☞ Sincere: She rose from her chair when I came in and exclaimed with a smile: "Wow! Nice outfit!"
- ☞ Sarcastic: She gave me one look and said, with a short laugh, "Yeah, right! Nice outfit!"
- ☞ Envious: She glanced at me quickly and muttered reluctantly, "Um, yeah . . . nice outfit."
- ☞ Insulting: She looked at me incredulously and said, "Eww! Nice outfit!"

To make it funny: Put these examples up on the board to help illustrate different techniques to use to show humor in a piece:

- ☞ Using a "surprise ending"
- ☞ Exaggerating
- ☞ Using opposites
- ☞ Putting your idea in an unusual place
- ☞ Using funny words
- ☞ A special type of wordplay known as a "pun"
- ☞ A combination of the above

Pick a problem to do together as an example. To give the kids a guideline, have each problem use five steps to reach a solution. Talk about using words that move along the explanation: first, next, then, finally, and so on.

EXAMPLE:

How to talk to an alien: When an alien from another planet lands in your hometown you'll have a lot to talk about. However, you might not be able to understand each other. Here's how to talk to an alien so you can become fast friends.

First, smile and give the alien a high-five so it knows you are friendly.

Next, motion for the alien to come inside and watch your favorite TV show with you. Since aliens are really smart, by the end of the show the alien will be able to speak and understand English.

After the alien knows how to speak English ask it about its planet and tell it about Earth. Describe your family, your friends, your school, and what you like to do for fun.

Then, invite the alien to play a game with you. Aliens are very good at playing games and do not like to lose, so you might want to let it win.

Finally, when you are tired and hungry from playing, ask the alien to eat pizza with you. Aliens love pizza, so make sure you have a lot. Once the alien is full it will be happy and want to be your friend forever. You can take the alien to school so it learns everything you do and helps you with your homework.

Finally, refer to the list of possible scenarios written on the board (and other new ones you forgot) and have each student pick one to write the survival steps for.

Writing and Sharing

Now have the kids break off and work on creating their own survival instructions. If students need help organizing their piece they can use the handout, or they can just be as free-form and creative as they like. Allow at least half an hour, and if they need a break you can stop and share in the middle. Sometimes this helps other kids see if they are on the right track.

Once kids start finishing up have them create a cover for their own copy of the book. I usually create some extra ones for any students who don't have enough time to make one. Once all the survival scenarios are complete, make copies of all them for everyone in the class and put them together for a take-home finished project. Let the kids volunteer to read their sections aloud to the group.

HOW TO _____

Description: _____

_____

_____

First, _____

_____

_____

_____

Next, _____

_____

_____

_____

After, _____

_____

_____

_____

Then, _____

_____

_____

_____

And finally, _____

_____

_____

_____

VINDICATED VILLAINS

by NICHOLAS DECOULOS

1 SESSION, 2 HOURS

NO ONE HAS ANY SYMPATHY FOR THE villains anymore! What if the "heroes" of our favorite tales were lying? Or perhaps left out other important information? Help us rectify the injustices of these well-known villains by uncovering the truth!

This workshop is meant to teach elementary-level students about perspective writing and writing things from new points of view.

The workshop begins with a short discussion of some favorite or perhaps interesting (fairy-tale) villains. (Fairy-tale villains are a good start because they are often very recognizable.)

A great example of this is *The True Story of the 3 Little Pigs!* by Jon Scieszka. The story presents the well-known tale of the "Three Little Pigs" but told from the wolf's perspective. The wolf tries to validate and explain what "really" happened, suggesting he isn't to blame (see Lesson Five for more Scieszka fun).

To make sure students are on the right track, it's good to test their comprehension of the story by asking a few questions. How was the wolf wrongly accused? How are the three little pigs presented? How does the wolf justify his accusations?

After that, it makes for an easy transition to discuss different perspectives and subjectivity in writing, whether it is first-person or third-person narrative.

Ask the students to pick personal stories in which they were wrongly accused of something, and map out both sides of the story. For example, a brother and sister get in trouble over who broke a lamp—both blame the other sibling, but what are their separate stories? Then, have the students find the differences in the two stories.

Next, have students discuss these types of scenarios in fairy tales that they're familiar with, such as Captain Hook and Peter Pan. Was Hook perhaps wrongly accused of something? Was it Peter Pan who was the instigator and just down-right mean?

Once each student has picked a familiar hero and villain pair, have the students again map out what they know about the plot. But this time, students will discover there are holes in the story. Now they can get creative and fill in those plot holes to tell the story through the villain's eyes (much like the wolf asking for a cup of sugar). It's best to drive the students away from having either character "get revenge" in order to avoid violence and to branch their creativity. The best suggestions come from those that try to defend the innocence of the villain as much as possible.

About an hour into the session, students can share how their villains are actually innocent. Then, as a class, we help provide ideas on how to put fault on the hero. What vile characteristics might the hero have that can prove the villain's innocence?

Finally, the students rewrite their story from the villain's perspective using the innocent details for their villain and the more mean and vile characteristics for their hero. Make the villain seem like an angel! Everything bad that happened was really just the hero's fault!

Students may write their stories in any format. But a fun suggestion is to write in the form of a newspaper headline and article. They can draw a picture of the villain looking innocent, or the hero looking mean (much like the art on the cover of *The True Story of the 3 Little Pigs!*).

Then, if time permits, students may share their stories.

ONO-MATO-WHAT-NOW?

by KATHERINE HUNT AND PARDIS PARSA

1 SESSION, 2 HOURS

MATERIALS: *Noisemakers (box of pasta, measuring spoons, paper fan, or just about anything)*
Extra adults to help (optional)

WE ALL KNOW KIDS CAN *MAKE* A LOT OF NOISE, BUT HOW ARE THEY AT SPELLING noise? We think this is something that young writers—natural noisemakers, all—should be just as good at. After all, it's tough to write a thrilling adventure story without spelling the sound a dragon's talons make while he's walking across a parquet floor, or the sound of an evil frog's menacing cry echoing through the woods. In this workshop, we encourage kids to find ways to spell the noises that everyday objects make, then we take these spelled-out noises and create an adventure story together that incorporates them. In our adventure story, of course, those noises play more interesting parts than they do in real life—for example, the *cchhhkk cchhhkk* of a box of pasta being shaken might turn into the sound of bones rattling down in a castle's basement.

To begin, we tell the kids that, while spelling sounds might seem really hard, they have actually all done it or seen it done before. We write a few well-known sounds on the board, and ask them to identify the well-known sources of these sounds:

whooosh	the wind
boom	something heavy falling, a gun, an elephant walking over your head
hissss	a snake
bzzzzzzz	a bee

We reveal the news that there's a word for these spelled-out sounds—they are all examples of onomatopoeia! Onomatopoeia, we tell them, is what we call words that imitate the sound of actions, animals, machines, and anything else they can think of that makes a noise. We ask if they can think of any other examples, and write them on the board.

Then the real work starts. We lead the kids to a table covered with all sorts of noisemaking items, things that make noise when you shake them, or tap them, or clink them, or open and shut them. Things that are designed to make noise, like maracas and bells, work well, but so do many ordinary objects: boxes from the pantry, bowls, silverware, rocks. Really, almost anything can work. Each student chooses an item (you can also pass them out so there are no squabbles about who gets what). We try to bring in many more items than we anticipate having students, so they can each get something they are at least mildly interested in or swap out if they are uninspired by the object they've chosen.

Once everyone has an object, we return to our work area and do a "group listen." One at a time, the students shake, tap, clink, beat, or ring their respective items, and we talk about the sounds. Do the students hear any particular letter or groups of letters in the sound? In what part of the sound? Is it a long sound or a short sound? Would you need lots of letters to spell it out?

After this discussion, the kids are on their way to spelling out their first sound. On the "Ono-Mato-What-Now? Practice Sounds!" worksheet they write the name of the object they have in front of them, and then write what it sounds like. Then, they pick a new item from the table, or trade with someone else, and come up with sounds for two more items. Extra grown-ups help a lot here—they can circulate and work with kids who need some direction in coming up with words for their sounds.

In 10–15 minutes we ask them to put their noisemakers down, and then share the sounds they came up with for each item. We collect them all by writing them on the board.

After we have added all of the sounds to the board, we begin to get some inspiration for writing our story. Brainstorm about who the main character of the story might be. We've had a lot of suggestions, so it may be best to limit the number of main character suggestions and then take a vote for who the main character should be.

Next, we start with some basic story structure. You can either use the "story spine" structure or simply ask "what comes next" as you are getting each sentence. We found that many of our sentences started with one of the new sounds.

STORY SPINE

Once upon a time . . . (or something along these lines)

And every day . . . (incorporate an action and sound to model how they will write the rest of the story)

Until one day . . . (incorporate another sound)

And because of that . . .

And because of that . . . (this can go on until there are no more chain reactions)

Until finally . . .

And ever since that day . . .

Story Example

Once upon a time there lived a turtle named Jack and his sidekick Mr. Man. They were a spy team. "Squick squack." They walked up to an abandoned castle with a drawbridge over the moat. "Crck," said the alligators. "Qsss," said the snakes, who were swimming in the moat.

If the kids are having a hard time figuring out how to use the sounds, you can brainstorm how the sounds might come up in the context of the story. They can even brainstorm new sounds as they begin to develop the idea.

As we write collaboratively, one of our extra adult helpers transcribes the sentences while another, who has great artistic ability, illustrates each sound in the sentence (this is not necessary but it is lots of fun). At the end of class we read the story out loud to hear all of the wonderful sounds that have come up throughout the workshop. If there is extra time, students can work on their own illustrations for the story. If you have an advanced group they can also work on their own to create entire stories and share them at the end of the session.

ONO-MATO-WHAT-NOW? PRACTICE SOUNDS!

Onomatopoeia: the formation of words whose sound imitates the sound of a noise or action, such as *hiss, buzz,* and *bang.*

Write down your own ways to spell noises:

OBJECT 1: _____

Your best idea for how to spell the sound:

_____

_____

_____

OBJECT 2: _____

Your best idea for how to spell the sound:

_____

_____

_____

OBJECT 3: _____

Your best idea for how to spell the sound:

_____

_____

_____

ONO-MATO-WHAT-NOW?: THE STORY

(25) ALL-STAR SPORTS STORIES

by AARON DEVINE AND KAREN SAMA

1 SESSION, 2 HOURS

SPORTS AND GAMES ARE A NATURAL source for storytelling. They feature heroes and villains, underdogs and world champions. Writing about sports is not only fun, it's also instructive for storytelling elements like character, conflict, and conclusion.

The goal of this workshop is to encourage students to write their own exciting, detailed sports stories by focusing on three key components:

1. Setting the scene

2. The dramatic moment

3. The achievement (or, the result)

To warm up, students brainstorm and share sports stories. These can be personal experiences, professional games seen on TV, or games featured in books and movies. As you listen to each other, ask: What information does the storyteller include, and what does he or she leave out? Compile a list: What information is needed to tell a sports story?

Next comes the role-play. Choose one climactic sports moment (for example, a game-winning home run) the students can enact, preferably one that everyone knows or can imagine. Half the group narrates the action while the other half acts out the scene in slow motion. Afterward, recast the students, and explain that this time, the story can be paused or rewound to add details. Encourage sensory details. For example: What does the crowd sound like? What scents are in the air? What is the batter thinking? Sports are a smelly, loud, tactile business, so have fun with it and get creative. At the end, explain to the students that details are part of **setting the scene.**

Discuss: Why is setting the scene so important to sports writing?

Explain: Sportswriters tell the people who weren't at the game what happened. They use details to put the reader in their seat. Sportswriters can't tell everything. Instead, they describe the most important moments of a game, especially when the game is either won or lost. This is **the dramatic moment.**

Have students complete the "Setting the Scene" handout, individually or in pairs (these exercises may also be adapted for a large-group format).

Then invite students to come up with their own examples for the "Elements of Dramatic Moments" handout. For example:

The Expiring Clock may be the last seconds of the quarter, or the bottom of the ninth, or . . .

The Underdog may be a very short basketball player, or a Jamaican bobsled team, or . . .

The Unexpected may be a sudden snowstorm, or a 100-point game, or . . .

Adversity may be a physical handicap, or a raucous crowd, or . . .

Finally, **the achievement** (or, the result) tells the reader what the dramatic moment accomplished. Most of the time, this will be: Who won the game?

Discuss: What results are there besides winning and losing? (Such as: setting records, learning teamwork, personal performance/confidence, entertainment, charity, physical health, raising community spirit, and so on.)

Finally, it's time to write. Let students write a sports story of their own choosing. (If they struggle to come up with one, they may retell a story brought up in the workshop.) Students should focus on setting the scene, telling the dramatic moment, and explaining the achievement—all using unique, interesting details.

We've done two variations of this workshop. For the first, we collected the students' finished sports stories and compiled them on the spot with volunteer help into a newspaper/booklet we titled the *All-Star Tribune*. During the assembling process, students drew illustrations for their stories and played extra rounds of the role-play game (a fan favorite). At the end of workshop, each student took home an *All-Star Tribune* containing the day's stories.

The second variation occurred when we had the chance to take the students to a live baseball game. Afterward, we adapted our workshop to create a pack of baseball cards, each featuring the students' game-inspired sports writing on the back.

Workshop leaders and students should feel free to invent their own creative outlets for student work. No matter your final product, students enjoy sharing their own sports stories and recognizing what goes into telling these stories most effectively.

Lastly, students who are not into sports can focus instead on games, which contain the same basic elements. Perhaps show a clip from the American Crossword Tournament to prove how intense gamers can get (or ask students what happens when they play video games with friends). Hide-and-seek, tag, Monopoly, spelling bees, and even solitaire can—with a little creativity—be just as dramatic and exciting. It's all in how you tell it.

SETTING THE SCENE

Sportswriters tell people what happened during the game. Details help readers recreate an important moment in their imagination.

Put a checkmark next to the line that best sets the scene for each sport below.

BASEBALL
- ❏ The pitcher ran out on the field to start the game.
- ❏ Tim trotted nervously to the mound, fired up to face the Yankees' lineup of heavy hitters.

GOLF
- ❏ Phil watched and hoped his putt would go in.
- ❏ Phil cried, "Go!" as his putt snaked down the green toward the hole.

BASKETBALL
- ❏ Kevin stepped to the free throw line. He tried to ignore the sound of 20,000 fans, louder than a jet engine.
- ❏ Kevin stepped to the free throw line. He made both shots.

SOCCER
- ❏ Brianna's heart pounded in her chest, and her legs felt like icicles.
- ❏ Brianna's uniform was blue. Her cleats were covered in mud.

Dramatic moments make sports and stories exciting. They are the most important moments of a game, especially when the game is either won or lost. Read these two descriptions of the end of a baseball game:

1. David Ortiz hit a home run, and the Red Sox won.

2. David Ortiz hit a home run with two outs in the bottom of the ninth inning to lift the Red Sox over the Yankees for the division title.

Which is more dramatic? Why?

ELEMENTS OF DRAMATIC MOMENTS

✓ **The Expiring Clock:** In the final seconds of a game, someone has to win and someone has to lose. Time is running out!

✓ **The Underdog:** A name for the player or team who is not expected to win because of a significant disadvantage (examples: size, training, experience...).

✓ **The Unexpected:** When something happens that almost never happens. Fans stand up and say, "Wow, did you see that?!"

✓ **Adversity:** Unique challenges a player or team has to overcome in order to win (examples: travel, weather, injury...).

✓ **The Achievement:** Every game has a result, and every sportswriter needs to say what it was. The most common results are: Who won? Who lost?

DISCUSSION

✓ What else can a player or team achieve besides winning or losing?

✓ Can a great sports story be told even in the face of defeat?

I WROTE A GUIDEBOOK AND ALL I GOT WAS THIS LOUSY T-SHIRT

TRAVEL WRITING

by SUSIE NADLER AND LAURIE SCHOLES

3 SESSIONS, 2 HOURS EACH
MATERIALS: *Tourist costume (optional)*
Travel guidebooks

Session 1

For this workshop we swallow our pride from the get-go, because we show up to the first session in costume. A tourist costume, to be specific— Bermuda shorts, Hawaiian shirt, dorky hat, fanny pack, and so on. In this case, the fanny pack is stuffed to bursting with travel guide-books. We get them from the library, since we need enough for the students to share in pairs or small groups.

To begin, we dump the guidebooks clumsily onto the desk at the front of the room and say, "We're planning a visit to [your town here], but these guidebooks are so dense and boring that every time we open them we instantly fall asleep. Since you kids live here, and you seem so kind and knowledgeable, do you think you can help us out?"

Then the students band together in pairs or groups of four. As a group, they prepare a written itinerary for us. We want to know: Where should we go? How do we get there? What will we find? We ask them to be as specific and detailed as possible, and to choose the most interesting destinations.

The results of their trip-planning exercise can be used to compile a list of necessary elements for the guidebook. Eventually this list becomes a kind of table of contents for the finished product. We ask them questions about the *purpose* of a guidebook, since *purpose* is so important in this kind of informative writing. What do you think people look for in a guidebook? Why do people use them? A little group brainstorming leads to a list of the things readers want from a guidebook: information about restaurants, museums, land-marks, and so on.

Instead of lecturing about guidebook style, we ask them to read bits from the books they used in the exercise. Do we want our guidebook to be funny and irreverent? Chatty? Serious and comprehensive? It's fun to treat this as a kind of "editorial board," and let all the kids weigh in. Usually they think the published guidebooks are dry as dust, so they're eager to figure out how to make theirs better. Define the different possibilities for style, then take a vote. Get specific: Should the guidebook be written in first or third person? Who is our audience? This is especially important; we encourage them to consider designing the book for kids their age, since they have an insider's perspective on what kids like to do.

Then we start talking about technique. How do these guidebooks make you *want* to go to the places they review? A member of each group reads the passage they chose out loud, and we ask them what makes the writing interesting and persuasive. Specific detail, sensory impressions, and authoritative language are three of the things we like to focus on. We remind them that as the writer, you're kind of like the tour guide waving that ridiculous red flag to make sure everyone on the tour follows you through Chinatown. But in this case, the red flag is your writing, and if somebody loses sight of the flag or gets tired of following it, you're in trouble. The reader has to trust you.

The handout helps to wrangle all these ideas together and review them.

To wrap up, the students are instructed to think of their favorite place in town, the one place where they *must* drag all unsuspecting out-of-town relatives. They close their eyes, and we lead them through a sensory experience of this place. What do they see? Hear? Smell? Taste? Feel? This is just a list-making exercise; they will use all of these details for a full-fledged description later on.

For homework, we let the students loose on our city, instructing them to visit the places they just visited in their minds. They are to take notes on their travels, including of course the essential facts of transportation, admission fees, hours of operation, and the like.

Session 2

To warm up, the students write an imaginary guidebook entry about a made-up place. They can make it up themselves or choose an existing fictional place, like Oz or Middle Earth or Fraggle Rock or Candyland. We remind them about the stylistic choices we made last time, and also about the important elements of guidebook writing. Students can read these out loud, for practice listening to and recognizing the writing style the class has chosen.

Now we ask the students to take out the notes from their travels. Another meeting of the "editorial board" provides a chance to divide their chosen locations into the existing table of contents from the last session. The students can see the book beginning to take shape as each of their locations is filed under a chapter on the board. Some choices defy categorization—that pet cemetery, for example, was a toughie—but a "Miscellaneous Fun and Learning" chapter should suffice.

The rest of this session is all about the writing. Students compile their list-making work from the first session with the notes from their homework travels. It might help to review the handout on guidebook writing, and to conference with the students individually as they work. The Internet is a great tool here, as we like to encourage the students to fact-check their information. (A phonebook will work just as well.) Students who finish early become the art department; they start working on illustrations, printing photographs, and developing sidebar material. (Our favorite sidebar from a recent class: "How to Survive in San Francisco on Burritos Alone.")

If there's time and ambition, we like to assign the students to visit a place where they've never been but always wanted to go, and this is the subject of their second contribution to the guidebook. The assignment is the same as before: go to this second place and take good notes.

Session 3

The structure of the third session pretty much follows the structure of the second. We like to pass out a handout with examples from each of the previous week's entries; we use these to show what makes guidebook writing great. Most of the quotes we choose contain persuasive detail, the kind of thing you wouldn't know unless you'd actually visited the place in question. One student's french fries were pilfered by a renegade seagull at the zoo; his warning served as both a funny aside and a helpful detail. We also like to emphasize the wit and approachability of their natural written voices.

At this point we call another meeting of the "editorial board" to organize their new entries into existing chapters. We assign the necessary production duties (copying, collating, and the like). Some ideas for fun "extras" the students can contribute: a page of author information (compiled through interviews with classmates); "top 10" sidebars; a cover page; a table of contents page. Once the students are finished writing and revising their second entries, they can get started on these extra elements. When everyone has finished a polished draft, we copy them all and bind them into real guidebooks.

The best thing about this workshop is that everyone takes home a fun and practical book. Their family and friends can use it, and every time it comes off the shelf, they'll feel proud.

BE A TOURIST IN YOUR OWN TOWN

HOW TO IMPART YOUR LOCAL WISDOM TO CLUELESS OUT-OF-TOWNERS

Bon voyage! By the end of this class, we'll have produced together a fabulously fun and informative book for you to share with visitors to our great city. Here are some tips to help you along the way:

GOALS OF GUIDEBOOK WRITING

1. **To INFORM** your readers about the place they intend to visit

2. **To EXCITE** your readers about the place they intend to visit

3. **To ASSIST** your readers in planning their travels, and in feeling comfortable once they arrive

ESSENTIALS OF GUIDEBOOK WRITING

1. **Get your facts straight.** You don't want your readers to end up at the museum when they're trying to get to the zoo. Check and double-check names, addresses, phone numbers, and hours of operation. Also give your readers helpful hints about the weather and other unexpected variables ("it's cold in them thar zoo!").

2. Facts, schmacts! Facts are great, but your entries should also **make your readers want to have the experience.** Make them feel like they *must* eat an amazing local burrito *now*. Describe the creaminess of the guacamole, the sharpness of the salsa, the messy carne asada juices that run down your chin. This is what makes guidebook writing fun. Focus on the unique experience of being in your town—the sounds, smells, textures, and sights.

3. Speaking of sounds, smells, and textures, don't forget to **use incredible detail.** Be specific about the experience of your chosen locale. Avoid vague adjectives like "super" and "cool" and "supercool."

4. **Remember your audience.** You should assume that your readers have never set foot in your town, and maybe they never will. Make the experience lively and real, even for those who will never have it.

5. Be a good reporter. When you're out on the town visiting your hot spots, take lots of notes. Don't just **write down the nuts-and-bolts facts—also note your impressions and feelings.** (Not to beat a dead horse, but how 'bout those sounds and smells?) If you just hate taking notes, bring a recorder, and record your thoughts on tape.

6. **Know your stuff and be confident.** It's very important that your writing have *authority*—in other words, your writing should be confident and approachable. Your readers need to trust you if they're going to follow you all over a strange city.

7. A guidebook is more than just words. **Use photos and drawings,** which can also help you tell your story. If you have a camera, great—take it with you. Otherwise, put your skills as an *artiste* to work.

COOKING FOR CRYPTIDS
THE DEFINITIVE CRYPTOZOOLOGICAL COOKBOOK
by SHANNON DIGREGORIO

1 SESSION, **90** MINUTES
MATERIALS: *Cookbooks*
Assorted cryptid-friendly snacks
Extra adult helpers (optional)

THIS WORKSHOP HAS ONE GOAL: TO DEFINE AND CREATE AND PUBLISH delicious recipes that would make any cryptid happy.

As the students enter the room they are encouraged to explore one of the many cookbooks that are set out on the workshop tables. (Cookbooks can range from general *Joy of Cooking*–style books, to books just about one item, such as cupcakes. If you have access to an old copy of *Larousse Gastronomique* definitely bring it along—it includes old-fashioned recipes for iguana and monkey!) Encourage each student to pick out his or her favorite cooking word from the cookbooks available, and be prepared to share it with the group. As workshop leaders we really want to stress the difference between recipes and creative writing. An emphasis should be made on the types of words used in recipes (measurements, quantities, and action words—baking, stirring, grating, and so on) and the importance of precise language and instructions.

As the students list the words, capture them each on a whiteboard or chalkboard and define them as you go—there will be many that the whole group might not be familiar with.

Next, ask the class to list as many cryptids as they can think of, and what their favorite food might be. For example, we try to make sure that Bigfoot, the Loch Ness Monster, and the Unicorn are all on the list, as they will play a big part later in the workshop. I personally think that Bigfoot really loves a nice trail mix of found items, that the Loch Ness Monster can't resist a good seaweed smoothie, and that Unicorns love to share a forest fruit salad—skewered on their horns, of course.

As a group, identify what Bigfoot might like in his favorite trail mix. Use questions like "What might Bigfoot find where he lives?" "What might grow there?" "What might tourists or trackers leave behind?"

As a group decide on:

☞ A recipe title

☞ A recipe short description

☞ What ingredients might be included

☞ What steps the recipe takes (first, measure ingredients, and so on)

Now the class divides up into small groups (three to five kids max), and groups are assigned (or they can choose) the cryptids they would like to focus on preparing a recipe for.

Now is the time to unveil all the exciting ingredients they will be working with as chefs and cookbook authors today. A short list includes:

☞ Raisins (yellow and purple)

☞ M&Ms

☞ Sunflower seeds

☞ Other dried fruit (pick what looks weird and cool!)

☞ 3–4 juice varieties that are green/yellow/blue

☞ Seaweed

☞ Herbs

☞ Pineapple

☞ Strawberries

☞ Other brightly colored fruit, if in season

The goal is to provide the students with an assortment of fun and possibly unknown ingredients to create with. With an older group, renaming each item as a weird and wonderful new ingredient can be both fun and gross—imagine your raisins as reindeer droppings, your mint as a magical herb, and your juice as the venom of a giant snake!

Now, with a specific cryptid in mind, each small group can review the cookbooks and decide on what recipe to create. Once the final recipe is decided upon, each group should follow the steps above to make the recipe and prepare a sample for each participant. While the team is making the recipe they should appoint one group member to either take a photo, or draw a picture of either the cooking process or their completed dish—this will be included in the master cookbook at the end.

Once each group has drafted and prepared their recipe they can present it to the larger group. Have students each write down a short blurb on what they think of each dish—this will be important as each will also get the chance to be a critic later on!

Collect the recipes and prepare them for the master cookbook that every student will take home. (You can copy and assemble these after class; or, if you have some extra adult volunteers, they can assemble them on the spot). If you need to kill time while the books are being assembled, the class can work on book review quotes for the back of the book, write their author bios, or help assemble a glossary of terms used in cryptid cooking.

With 5–10 minutes left to go, present students with their own copies of the completed cookbook (or hand them out the following day) and encourage them to add more recipes or illustrations.

RECIPE TEMPLATE

TITLE:

AUTHOR NAME(S):

PHOTO OR DRAWING OF RECIPE

SHORT DESCRIPTION OF RECIPE
For example, "This recipe for Bigfoot's Favorite Trail Mix is a foolproof favorite, whether you're a yeti or just out in the wilderness tracking one!"

Yield: _____ number of servings

INGREDIENTS
Item 1 & quantity _____
Item 2 & quantity _____
Item 3 & quantity _____
Item 4 & quantity _____
Item 5 & quantity _____
Item 6 & quantity _____
Item 7 & quantity _____
Item 8 & quantity _____

PREPARATION
Step 1: _____
Step 2: _____
Step 3: _____
Step 4: _____
Step 5: _____

SERVING INSTRUCTIONS

_____

_____

_____

_____

SCIENCE CLUB

ICE CREAM!

by ELAINE M. PALUCKI

1 SESSION, 90 MINUTES
MATERIALS: *See individual activities*
Three adult helpers (optional)

826 SCIENCE CLUB WORKSHOPS ARE designed to feature essential elements of science experimentation: curiosity, observation, measurement, data collection, and most of all FUN! In this lesson plan, we'll show you how to recreate them in your own classroom. The instructor checklists that follow the lesson plan will help you make sure you have everything you need.

Many students (and adults) mistake learning science as a job that involves memorizing a collection of facts, rather than as a creative search to discover the way elements in our world interact. To avoid this knee-jerk reaction, this workshop is designed as a mystery about how we can make ice cream from everyday ingredients. Science is a way of exploring and understanding our world, and what better way to do that than asking questions. With that in mind, this workshop begins with a good brainstorming session of what we know already and what questions we want to find the answers to.

As students begin the workshop, they are asked to jot down the answers to the questions on the "What Do You Know About Ice Cream?" handout. Then we go around the room, and the students share their favorite ice cream flavor. This is a good opportunity to talk about how science is collaborative and to inspire the students to work as a science team to figure out how ice cream can be made. The students should be encouraged to talk about what they like about their favorite ice cream. For example: *What ingredients might create that fabulous ice cream taste?*

Students will be quick to say broad things like "flavor" or that it's "creamy" or "sweet." Work with them to identify tangible ingredients. (Example: If you wanted to make your cereal sweet in the morning, what might you put in it? Sugar.) Students are often able to identify sugar, milk, ice, and vanilla flavoring as ingredients. As students correctly identify an ingredient I normally place it on a table for them to see. More often than not, they are unable to identify salt as the key ingredient, and you'll have to show it to them as one they didn't guess.

Ask them if they ever taste salt in their ice cream. Provide some clues to stimulate group discussion as to how it might be used: *Perhaps we just don't use very much salt in the recipe, so we don't taste it?* Don't explain its use here, though; let the students remain open to this ingredient having a broad range of functions. This keeps the mystery and curiosity and creativity flowing!

It's important to ask the group to think about each of these ingredients in terms of the states of matter they exist in (this is the third question on the worksheet the students completed at the beginning of the workshop). Students should know that ice cream is a solid and milk is a liquid. Ask them what happens when we put any one of the solid ingredients (salt, sugar, and ice) into a liquid like milk or water? Students will usually reply that the solid ingredients melt or dissolve into the liquid. Which is exactly the dissonance that you want. In fact, I normally reinforce here that milk is the creamy ingredient generating the taste, and the sugar seems dissolved into it, right?

So how is it, then, that we take the main ingredients, like milk, and somehow end up with ice cream, a solid?

Have the students brainstorm on how this transition might happen. The discussion can be started with the help of some silly suggestions: *Am I going to whip out a super big freezer, or run across the street to a deli and borrow the fridge? Perhaps I have superpowers? Or maybe I can stir really fast with a frozen spoon? Chop up the ice and put it in the milk?* Once several ideas for ways this change of state might happen have been suggested, pull out two Ziploc bags and tell the students: "Now we have everything we need to make ice cream!"

In order to keep a controlled environment, especially with a larger group of students, it helps to set up stations around the room for each of the ingredients. This spaces out the students in the group and allows students to individually measure their own ingredients. It's helpful to have three adult assistants, but you can also designate a student as the "leader" of each table if you don't have assistants available.

At each table, make sure there is a printout of the steps that the students will be performing there for easy reference (see "Get Your Ingredients!" handout for the steps). It is helpful to review the entire process as a group prior to beginning. While reviewing the procedure, point out the location of each station in the room and explain that the order in which the ingredients are added is important and the measurements of each ingredient are also critical to success.

Make sure they understand the tools they are using to measure. Encourage the students to ask questions and to write down any observations they have. Although we want them to measure and work as closely to the protocol as possible, that is unlikely to happen and is true of all science—so you want them to record **what they actually did.** For example: *Did they use a little too much milk, not quite enough sugar? Did anything change color? Did they shake for shorter or longer time periods than suggested? How much ice did they use?*

The slight differences in measurement and protocol between the students will give you a natural bridge to talk about the process of science—how even little changes can have big effects on the final results obtained. After they finish, students who used more milk can be asked to show their ice cream to the group. Did it take longer for it to become a solid? What other changes might they notice? Encourage students to talk about what differences they think were important to the process. I also allow students to try variations if they want to. For example, there are always students who firmly believe more flavor and more sugar will make their ice cream *more delicious.* Let them try—but the result is generally not more delicious, even to a 6-year-old!

Once the ice cream is made and is being eaten, ask the students to think about the questions on the "Observations" worksheet. This process works well as a group discussion. Ask if the plastic bags (with the milk, sugar, and flavor) had been placed directly in the freezer, would it turn into ice cream?

Revisit the subject of states of matter. The first change in going from milk to ice cream is from a **liquid** to a **solid.** Have the students identify which ingredient caused that to happen. Was it how they hypothesized in the initial discussion? If not, what happened that was different? The following paragraphs walk you through the science in the procedure.

The ice absorbs **energy** (represented by it melting), changing the phase of water from a solid to a liquid. Where does this energy come from? It comes from anything that is touching the ice: the ingredients, the air, and even your hands when you are shaking the bag of ice.

The "magic" ingredient for making the ice cream is the salt. When you add salt to the ice, it lowers the freezing point of the ice, actually making the ice "colder" than it was before. What this means is that the salt actually changes the temperature that ice will melt at! This decrease in temperature allows the milk to freeze while you are shaking the bag.

As students in winter climates might know, water will normally freeze when the temperature is below 32°F. If we make a 10% salt solution the water won't freeze until the temperature is below 20° F. If we add more salt, so that the solution is now 20% salt, the water won't freeze until the temperature is 2°F. By lowering the temperature at which ice is frozen, we are able to create an environment in which the milk mixture can freeze and turn into ice cream.

INSTRUCTOR CHECKLIST 1:

Physical Ingredients (listed per student):

Calculate the appropriate amount of each item you need for the number of students you have in your workshop/class. Then **at minimum** double it to account for spills, mismeasurement, students who want to try a variation on the protocol, and so on.

_____ 2 sizes of zipper style* Ziploc bags

_____ ½ cup milk

_____ 1 tbsp sugar

_____ ½ tsp vanilla extract**

_____ 4 tbsp kosher rock salt

_____ A minimum 2 cups of ice cubes

_____

*It is easy to tell with the zipper style bags that they are locked and truly closed, which prevents spilling.

**Other flavorings such as orange, almond, and chocolate syrup can be used, but vanilla works best.

INSTRUCTOR CHECKLIST 2:

Tools you need:

As with the ingredients list, make the list of what you need and then double or triple it depending on your class size and room orientation.

_____ Cup liquid measuring cup

_____ Tablespoon measures (for sugar)

_____ Teaspoon measures (for vanilla)

_____ Tablespoon measures (for salt)

_____ Cups or scoopers for scooping ice to cover the milk

_____ Printouts of directions for each station

_____ Lab notebook pages for each student

_____ Paper towels for each station

_____ A cooler large enough to hold the ice and keep milk cold while workshop is beginning

_____ Hand towels for students to wrap around their Ziploc bags in case of spilling. You might consider asking students to bring one from home to help reduce costs. The towel will not be damaged.

This protocol was put together after looking at a variety of Internet resources like the following. They may also be useful to you.

How to Make Ice Cream in a Bag in 5 Minutes:

www.ehow.com/how_4879437_ice-cream-bag-minutes.html

Homemade Ice Cream in a Bag:

http://crafts.kaboose.com/ice-cream-in-a-bag.html

WHAT DO YOU KNOW ABOUT ICE CREAM?

1. What is your favorite flavor of ice cream?

_____

_____

_____

2. What kinds of ingredients do you think you need to make ice cream?

_____

_____

_____

3. For every ingredient above, write whether you think this is a solid, liquid, or gas. What do we call water when it becomes a solid?

_____

_____

_____

4. How do you think we will turn these ingredients into ice cream? (Will we run with them? Stir them? Put them in the refrigerator?)

_____

_____

_____

GET YOUR INGREDIENTS!

STEP 1:

Get a small Ziploc bag from the table. Label it with your name.

With the help of the table leader, add **1/2 cup of milk.**

STEP 2:

Add a flavoring to your ice cream, such as **1/2 teaspoon of vanilla.**

Add **1 tablespoon of sugar.**

Seal your Ziploc bag, leaving as little air as possible on the inside. Show it to the table leader.

STEP 3:

Place your first bag with flavor, milk, and sugar into a gallon Ziploc bag.

Cover that bag of milk in **ice,** filling your gallon bag.

Add **4 tablespoons of salt** to the top of your ice.

Get all the extra air out of your bag. Show it to the table leader, then wrap your Ziploc bag in a towel.

NOW YOU ARE READY TO MAKE ICE CREAM!

Everyone should shake, roll, or move his or her bag for **8 minutes total.**

Do not look at what is going on in the bag; just make sure that the ice stays on top of the bag on the inside and that you keep moving it.

OBSERVATIONS

1. Did your ice cream look like ice cream you buy from the store? How was it similar or different?

_____

_____

_____

_____

2. Which ingredient do you think was most important in allowing you to make the milk turn into ice cream?

_____

_____

_____

_____

3. What do you think you would get if you shook the bag for only 2 minutes? 6 minutes? 15 minutes?

_____

_____

_____

_____

4. Do you think anything would change if you used less ice? More milk?

_____

_____

_____

_____

STICKY WORDS

by MAYA SHUGART AND RYAN SMITH

2 SESSIONS, 2 HOURS EACH
MATERIALS: *See each activity's instructions*

WHY SHOULD THE EARS HAVE ALL THE FUN WHEN IT COMES TO POETRY?
The eyes want in! How can we make poems that look as beautiful as they sound?

In this workshop students learn to write a cinquain, a five-line poetic form inspired by Japanese haiku. They use descriptive adjectives, moving verbs, and unique nouns to describe something that they see in a picture. They learn to speak in language that sounds slightly different from their everyday conversation, and they will begin to think of words as multisensory. They then write original poems and collage them into art for readers' eyes and ears to enjoy in harmony.

Session 1

MATERIALS: *Square construction paper cutouts*
Collection of 3–4 picture prompts
Thesaurus
Markers and pencils
Introduction name cards for students to work on
Collage materials: magazines, newspapers, pictures

Introduction: We start by having students describe themselves using nouns, adjectives, and verbs ("My name is <u>Ryan</u> and my favorite animal is the <u>squid</u> because it is <u>colossal</u> and it likes to <u>dance</u>"). It helps to have this sentence written on the board with the blanks provided. Pass around a textured object for students to hold while they introduce themselves.

Nouns, verbs, adjectives: Next, we read aloud an example cinquain, written in large letters on the board. Here are two to choose from:

SQUIRRELS

Flying
Gathering nuts
You are like monkeys there
Swinging from trees covered by leaves
Each fall.

TRASH TRUCK

Smelly
Like a sneaker
Stinking up my bedroom
You make me feel nauseous and slow
Go home.

We ask: Is this poem all verbs? Or all nouns? What other words make it up? What's your favorite word in it? Swinging? What does it look like to swing from trees? Can someone show us what it's like to feel nauseous and slow? Have one of the students demonstrate!

After going over the poem, scramble the words from this poem. Create three columns on the board (nouns, verbs, adjectives) and ask students to come up to the board to organize the words into each category.

Word bank: Next, we explain what a word bank is to students, and how they will use one later on when writing their cinquains. What makes up a sentence? Words do. What kinds of words? Nouns, adjectives, and verbs. Where do words come from? Our arms, legs, teeth, and mind. We are going to think of the best words we can—the "sticky" words that stick in our brains—and put them into a word bank on the board, which we'll use later on . . .

But first, our mind needs a picture! We show picture prompts of alligator skin, shiny rims, smokestacks, long hair, sticky buns, and muddy shoes. Then we say: Look at this picture and write down five different words to describe it. Go around and have each student give his or her stickiest, chewiest, messiest word. Then, have students place all of their words (as best they can) into a word bank. If there are words like "dog" ask the students, What kind of dog? If there are words like "walk" ask the students about synonyms, like shimmy or strut. For words like "happy" ask for synonyms like ecstatic or thrilled.

Mind pictures: Each student will choose TWO images from collage materials to write a poem about and collage. We say: Close your eyes and think of the word _____. What can you think of that's cold? What is that thing doing? Where is it going?

Syllables: We ask: What is a syllable? A syllable is the sound a vowel creates when we pronounce a word. We return to the cinquain on the board and have students count syllables (by clapping) as we read aloud:

Smelly (2)
Like a sneaker (4)
Stinking up my bedroom (6)
You make me feel nauseous and slow (8)
Go home. (2)

Writing time: Give students time to cut out pictures from magazines and start forming their cinquains. We ask: Where can we get these words? How about from the word bank that we created earlier?

Wrap up: Check in with students, answer any questions. Have one stellar student read aloud his or her cinquain once, then a second time while the class counts the syllables by clapping.

Session 2

MATERIALS: *Magazines, newspapers*
Scissors, paste, markers
Sample finished accordion book (optional)

Introduction: We like to start by asking a few students to share the cinquains they wrote in the last session. We talk about what makes them work well: good use of adjective, noun, verb, simile, and colorful language, used syllables correctly, and so forth.

Group exercise: At this point, you may have a few students who fell behind and aren't quite writing metric verse. So, besides reading more of them, it's helpful to talk through the cinquain and write one as a group. Why is it called a cinquain? (It has five lines.) What's the rhythm? (2, 4, 6, 8, 2.) We ask: How much can we say in just a few words? Then we invite the class to write a group cinquain using some images we've cut from a magazine.

The guidelines for this cinquain:

🖝 No articles (the, a, an)

🖝 Use simile (like a spider . . .)

🖝 Connect two images or things (for example, tightrope walker, spider)

🖝 Use a thesaurus: find a "sticky" word

Write the cinquain on the board as the class composes it.

Individual writing: We give the students time to work on their cinquains. Place a thesaurus at each table. Once they've finished, give them some time to collage.

 ## SUPERTEACHER BONUS ACTIVITY

Help the students turn their collages and cinquains into an accordion book!

MADDENING MAD LIBS

by DAN GERSHMAN

1 SESSION, 90 MINUTES
MATERIALS: *Book of Mad Libs*
Copies of the handouts

IN THE CHAOTIC WORLD OF POSTMODERN CREATIVE EXPRESSION, GRAMMAR is often considered one of the last outposts of formulaic order in written English. Maybe that's why it's dreaded and loathed. Luckily, children all over America have had access to fun instructional materials about the parts of speech since the 1950s: Mad Libs! This lesson capitalizes on the humor and chaos of Mad Libs to give young students an entry point into the more sober and orderly landscape of English grammar. Students leave with a booklet of their own original Mad Libs that they can enjoy at home.

At its heart, Mad Libs is a game of spontaneous word suggestion, so for a quick warm-up, it helps to get your students into the habit of picking words quickly without too much thought. Go around the room and have each student say a different word. You can ask them to choose their favorite word, or words in a given category, or (my personal favorite) progressively longer words.

Then it's time to bank on the momentum you've generated during the warm-up while doing some light grammar instruction. Present information about nouns (person, place, thing; singular, plural); adjectives; and verbs and verb tenses (simple present, simple past, and present progressive).

It sounds like a lot, but it really shouldn't take more than 10–15 minutes to cover all those concepts. Most students will already know how to use basic grammar—they'll just need to learn the names for everything. Give lots of examples, and have the students volunteer their own examples so they get practice identifying and selecting the parts of speech.

Great! Now the students have all the tools they need. Do a sample Mad Lib together as a class. Once they've done one as a group, they'll be ready for the next exercise.

Then you're ready for the real fun. Set up three writing stations, one for each of the three different worksheets. (If you've got a big class, or if the stations would be more chaotic than fun, the students can work at their own desks. Just give them 15 minutes or so with each worksheet, then pass out the next one.) At each station, direct the students to write a (very) short story in pencil on the white lines, then help them choose appropriate words to "blank out." When they've decided on some words to remove, they should label the missing word (noun, adjective, simple present verb, and so on) on the gray line beneath, then erase the word from the white line.

Give the students about 15 minutes at each station, then have them move on to the next one.

Once the students have been through all three stations, ask them to choose their best Mad Lib to put in the Mad Libs booklet, which you can photocopy later. Do a few Mad Libs together as a class to celebrate their hard work.

SUPERTEACHER BONUS ACTIVITY

If you have time, typing up the students' Mad Libs so they look like "real" Mad Libs will give them a big thrill.

When you get a chance, photocopy the Mad Libs and staple them into booklets. Then give each student a copy so they can (simple present) their friends with (adjective) Mad Libs!

A TRIP TO THE BEACH

Write your most excellent story on the white lines.

A DAY AT THE ZOO

Write your most excellent story on the white lines.

A BORING DAY AT HOME

Write your most excellent story on the white lines.

IF I WERE A KING OR QUEEN
CREATING YOUR OWN COUNTRY

by J. RYAN STRADAL AND ROBERT JURY

1 SESSION, 2 HOURS

ALL CHILDREN LIVE IN THEIR OWN world—albeit one restrained by the mores and demands of unfair, illogical adults—and the rules, wishes, and parameters of this world are often only expressed piecemeal, as in a desire to stay up until midnight, or a secret wish for a horse in the garage. This exercise lets students transcend all that.

When we explain to the students that they'll be creating their own country from scratch, many start working before we're even done explaining the guidelines. Fortunately, the setup is short and simple; we go over the aspects of what makes a country, we spend a couple hours creating our ideal nation, and then we share it, United Nations–style, with our fellow world leaders.

We've found that the students need little guidance beyond the introduction, although they do request an audience for their cartographical innovations (more on this shortly).

The first things we explain are a country's components, which the students then invent for themselves in whichever order they choose. They are:

Name of Country: The naming of one's country, though difficult, should be tackled first because it suggests boundaries that make the infinite scope of nation building seem less daunting. We've found that the students opt for simple, declarative names that suggest a theme (for example, Jungle World, Red and Blue Land) or hybrids with actual places (for example, Boston D.C. or Kittyville, California).

Who's in Charge: Now's a good time to engage your class in a brief lesson about different kinds of governments: monarchies, dictatorships, democracies, republics, empires, parliaments, and so on. What kind of government will they choose for their country? What will they call its leaders? Supreme Queen, Tribal Chief, King Awesome, Dude/Dudette in Charge, Duchess, Prime Minister, and El Presidente are all great choices. No students have ever chosen someone other than themselves to head their fictional country. Real-life authority figures rarely figure at all in these worlds, and when they do, they're usually demoted to a menial position. Try not to let it get to you.

Map of Country: After showing the students a quick example of a fictional map on a dry-erase board or chalkboard, this portion of the exercise is tackled with alarming alacrity and impressive imagination. Certain patterns will emerge: public repositories of money (usually in the form of rivers or lakes), buildings constructed from highly perishable comestibles, and sprawling personal estates (one student's eight-bed, six-bath mansion ultimately proved to be on the modest side and needed to be revised).

We go over the fictional map, and naturally, we see many variations on its themes. We blend the political, the topographical, and the edible, disregarding scale, mold, and zoning ordinances. The students often explore beyond these suggestions, inventing spectacular landmarks (a Tree of Life losing a war of attrition with a tornado) and unique urban centers (many students create cities populated exclusively by their favorite animal).

Flag of Country: Many students immediately gravitate toward creating their flag design, utilizing a palette that would cause accidents at the U.N.'s carport. We need few to no examples; the students often generate flags as if they were waiting their whole lives to do so.

Description of Country: This is the World Almanac entry. What is the population? What languages are spoken? What do people wear? Who is the most popular writer or musician? We explain that this is where the students can express their tastes and make their country truly ascribe to their own desired logic. We do not consider any pet-to-human ratio too outlandish.

Decree of Absolute Laws: We tell the students that for once they can make all the rules, and for many, this is as least as fun as drawing the map. Harsh tax codes are not unheard of, and parents, teachers, and siblings often experience a severe curtailment of civil liberties. However, many students also eliminate the insulting practice of charging money for food, so life for adults in these countries isn't a complete downer.

What's Next: Once we've guided the class through an explanation of each component, with examples, the next few hours are primarily composed of one-on-one consultation with students who are either stuck on a detail or have an exciting innovation to share.

In a project like this with few parameters, it can sometimes take the students a while to adjust to the idea that the aspects of this fictional country can be as far-flung as they wish them to be. We answer many questions pertaining to logic and boundary, such as: Can one trillion people fit on an island shaped like a teddy bear? (Of course.) If Matthew's map has a black hole, can Emily's have a white hole? (Why not?)

At the end of class, we ask the students who are so inclined to do a short presentation on their country for the edification of the other heads of state. This often emboldens some of the kings, queens, princesses, and lords who were initially hesitant to do so. Then we place the completed work in a royal binder for safekeeping and easy transport. They are now ready to make their new country a part of the world.

FIVE SUGGESTIONS FOR COUNTRY-BUILDERS

1. If you're having trouble with your map, ask yourself: What is your favorite food or beverage? Name anything you would like to have in close proximity or in great quantities, like a root beer lake, or an ice cream iceberg.

2. Are there any laws you currently consider to be unfair? Now is your chance to set the world straight. You can also decide how many school days you have a year, what is taught in school, and, naturally, if there even is school.

3. Consider dividing your country into different states or territories if you can't fit everything into just one nation. You can also banish or assign certain things to islands, like vegetables, snow, homework, pizza, or chores.

4. Take a look at the student sitting next to you. Does your country have relations to his or hers? Are they peaceful or problematic? Will Puppy Town and the Snowcone Island renew their peace talks this year? At last, it's your call.

5. Design a coat of arms, logo, or symbol to put upon your flag. Consider a representation of your favorite animal or pet. Nothing gets the point across at a border crossing better than a giant hamster.

HOW TO BE A DETECTIVE

by AMIE NENNINGER

1 SESSION, 2 HOURS
MATERIALS: *A strange costume (and a person to wear it)*
1 copy of the handout packet for each student

AS A FOUNDING MEMBER OF THE BLUEBIRD Detective Agency at age 8, I am well aware of the fascination kids have with mysteries. This lesson provides a fun way to introduce the necessary elements, or "usual suspects," of the mystery genre. The students practice both roles—mystery reader and writer—and learn to strike the balance of a fair but highly intriguing story.

Each junior detective receives the top-secret notebook handout, which provides materials for discussion and a number of activities for the kids to complete. The class begins with a general discussion about beloved mysteries and detectives. Trixie Belden, Harriet the Spy, Encyclopedia Brown, Nate the Great, and Nancy Drew always top the list. These characters all appear in engaging, clever stories, and the students are excited to hear that they are about to learn how to write an equally excellent mystery.

To warm up the detective side of the brain, the class incorporates a number of games that require an eagle eye for detail. This begins without the students' knowledge. As they enter the room, the instructor or an assistant greets them. This person is dressed oddly: skirt over pants, lots of layers, mismatched shoes, multiple watches, band-aid on the cheek, two pairs of glasses, a suspicious nametag (Jeremiah Fishmonger on a woman, FiFi Plendergrass on a man), and has unusual items tucked in pockets. This person may also make a lot of squeaks or sneezes, only walk backwards, or speak in an odd voice. After the class settles, that person disappears and removes all of the odd details. Then the kids take turns testing their powers of observation. What did they notice? Their notes are listed on the board.

Then the class takes turns reading aloud the story "Is the Principal Calling?" in the handout. The story ends abruptly, before the mystery is solved. We discuss what type of story we read. How can you tell that this is a mystery and not a romance novel or a science book? We also make predictions about the story and whom we think the prank caller might be. Finally, it is time to read the ending. We discuss it. Were the clues in the story good? Too hard? Too easy?

We take a break to play Investigator. One child (the Investigator) leaves the area, and a guilty suspect is selected to start a hand pattern (clap, clap, snap). The rest of the group begins the pattern and the Investigator returns. The guilty suspect changes the hand pattern every 30 seconds or so (shoulder tap, finger snap) and everyone else attempts to shift seamlessly to the new pattern. The Investigator has three chances to guess the guilty suspect. Then the guilty suspect becomes the Investigator, and the game continues.

After this, we turn to the "Usual Suspects in a Mystery" in the "Write Your Own!" page in the notebook. We discuss what the terms mean and give examples from the story "Is the Principal Calling?" Now that everyone is familiar with the important elements of a mystery, the kids generate possible settings, suspects, and motives in their notebooks.

For younger students, you may want to do a simpler activity. You could show the class a picture of a *The Cat in the Hat*–style mess (a broken fish bowl, a guilty-looking cat, a cunning bird) and ask the class to solve what they think happened from the clues in the picture. Who's the suspect? What was the motive?

For the last activity, you have two choices: you can either have each student write his or her own mystery, or you can write a mystery as a class, ending abruptly at a good point for a cliff-hanger, and have each student write his or her own solution. They are reminded to include the same characters, continue our story, and add one last fantastic clue that tips the scale to the guilty suspect. When everyone is finished, each child shares his or her own stunning revelation!

TOP SECRET

CASE #091804

THIS TOP-SECRET NOTEBOOK
BELONGS TO: _____, P.I.

CASE FILE #1:
IS THE PRINCIPAL CALLING?

Sam looked out the kitchen window at the new snow on the ground. He was thinking about going out to build a snow fort when the phone rang.

"May I speak with Sam Fredrickson?" the voice on the phone asked.

"This is Sam," answered Sam.

"Please hold for Principal Simmons."

Sam looked at the phone. Why was the principal calling? If Sam was in trouble, wouldn't the principal want to talk to his parents? Maybe Principal Simmons wanted to congratulate him, although Sam couldn't think of why.

Sam thought about all of the good and bad things he had done lately as he waited . . . and waited . . . and waited. Finally he realized the truth. Someone had played a trick on him, and it probably wasn't his principal.

Sam decided he probably knew the prank caller. But who could it be? Jenny was always goofing around. Maybe she called and pretended to be Principal Simmons. Sam dialed her number. It was busy.

"I'm going to get to the bottom of this!" he said, as he bundled up and headed out into the crunchy white snow.

Sam was walking over to Jenny's house, when he spotted someone building a snowman. It was his friend Emma.

"Hey Sam, I'm glad you walked by. I wanted to know if you could play this afternoon. I was going to call you, but my mom just grounded me from using the phone."

Sam explained that he would be back to play later, and headed over to Jenny's house.

It had been snowing all morning, and when Sam reached Jenny's house, a blanket of snow covered the lawn and the sidewalk. He walked up to the front door, making footsteps in the spotless snow. Sam rang the doorbell.

"Hi Sam," Jenny said as she opened the door.

"Hey Jenny, the oddest thing happened this morning. Principal Simmons called me. But I don't think it was really her. Did you call me this morning?"

"No Sam," Jenny explained. "It sounds like someone played a trick on you, but it wasn't me! I walked over to the library this morning to work on my report, and I just got home. I wonder who tricked you?"

"I think I have a pretty good idea who called," said Sam.

Did the principal really call Sam? What do you think? Discuss it with your class, then turn the page to find out. No peeking!

PART 2

THE THRILLING CONCLUSION!

"I know who called," said Sam. "And I also know that you weren't at the library this morning."

Jenny smiled. "All right, maybe it wasn't Principal Simmons, but how did you know it was me?"

"Well, I was the first person to walk in the snow on your porch. No one's come in or out of your house yet today. You were definitely at home."

Jenny giggled, "I can't trick you!" Sam and Jenny headed outside to help Emma build her snow fort.

PART 3

WRITE YOUR OWN!

THE USUAL SUSPECTS IN A MYSTERY:
Crime: The bad/sad/exciting mysterious thing that happens

The crime in my mystery is: _____

Detective: The smart and curious character who solves the crime

The detective in my mystery is: _____

Setting: An interesting environment where the story takes place

The setting in my mystery is: _____

Suspects with motives: Characters with good reasons and opportunities to commit a crime

The suspects in my mystery are: _____

SUSPECT #1

Name: _____

Motives: _____

SUSPECT #2

Name: _____

Motives: _____

SUSPECT #3

Name: _____

Motives: _____

YOUR MYSTERY WILL ALSO NEED:

CLUES: Evidence, pieces of the puzzle.

RED HERRINGS: Fake or distracting clues. Can you find any red herrings in "Is the Principal Calling?"

SOLUTION: Solving the mystery, putting the pieces together.

HARRY POTTER SPIDER-MAN VS. THE EVIL ZOMBIE NINJAS

by ERIC CANOSA

1 SESSION, **90** MINUTES

MATERIALS: *Pictures of superheroes*
Art supplies like magazines to cut up, glue, paint (optional)

THIS LESSON PLAN HAS AN AWFUL LOT TO DO WITH A TRADE I ONCE witnessed: 20 purple Skittles for a third-edition Marvel card featuring Wolverine. Clearly, my subjects were not diplomats working to solve Important Crises (which is not to say that Skittles and Marvel cards don't exchange hands behind closed doors at the U.N.). These were third graders interacting with an emerging sense of value, distribution, and trade. Fun fact: On average there are fewer than 10 purple Skittles in a package, and I've *never* seen more than 12.

The point I'm trying to make is that students between 6 and 8 years old are, psychologically, really into rules. This is the age when students begin to develop a keen sense of right and wrong. As a result, they start to think about the world in terms of "good guys" and "bad guys." The development of a moral compass incites students to greater identification with a number of role models, or personal heroes. This lesson is designed to capitalize on students' interest in heroes and channel it into a productive creative writing experience.

The first part of the lesson is intended to increase the students' motivation and interest in the activity at hand. This shouldn't be too difficult a task! Superheroes are intrinsically pretty motivating, after all. Sit the students down in any formation that affords a view of the blackboard/whiteboard/projection screen. I suggest either the classic semicircle or groups of four. If you feel adventurous you may try a lightning-bolt or spider-web pattern. (Harry Potter Spider-Man, get it?)

You're going to make a presentation on your favorite heroes and villains. I recommend putting images of your beloved characters up on the board and giving a pseudo-anatomy lesson. Something along the lines of, "These are Superman's eyes. No big deal, but he CAN SHOOT LASERS out of them."

You'll want to give your students copies of the handout to provide structure to your presentation and get them writing. Do this for not more than four characters. If you have time, make up problems or obstacles for the heroes and villains to face and ask the students what they think the characters would do in those situations.

Next, have the students come up with their own original ideas for a hero or villain and ask them to record their ideas on a fresh handout. This might take a while, but don't give more than 20 minutes for the activity. Seriously. Time it and don't go over the limit.

Remember how, for the presentation, the students went from looking at the images you displayed to writing an analysis on the handout? Great news! Now they're going to go from the notes on their handout to creating an image! Get as creative as you can with how they construct these images. Magazine collages are always fun! Computer technology provides lots of options! Finger paint? Go for it! Just plain drawing? Also good!

When the students have their *awesome* original heroes or villains fleshed out with both words and a picture of some manner, you can take them to the extended writing portion of the lesson. Using whatever selection method you feel comfortable with (I've always preferred tarot cards) separate the students into pairs. Ask them to introduce their characters to each other, then have them write a paragraph about what happens when they meet! I recommend asking for a solid paragraph of four to five sentences, but the length and complexity of the writing assignment should be based on the skills of the students you're working with. Again, 20 minutes is about the maximum I would allow for this task.

That's it! You're done! Now go fight crime.

CHARACTER FACT FILE

CHARACTER'S NAME: _____

This character is a: (check all that apply)

❑ Hero ❑ Villain ❑ Animal ❑ Ghost ❑ Regular person

Write a sentence about this character's costume:

_____

_____

_____

_____

Write a sentence about this character's powers and abilities:

_____

_____

_____

_____

Write a sentence about this character's personality:

_____

_____

_____

_____

Do you think this character is cool?

❑ Yes ❑ No

Do you want this character to be the next president of the United States?

❑ Yes ❑ No

How many heavy bricks could this character lift?

❑ One ❑ Two ❑ Ten ❑ Twenty ❑ More: _____

How many marshmallows could this character eat IN A ROW?

❑ One ❑ Two ❑ Ten ❑ Twenty ❑ More: _____

OUT THERE: DRAWING AND WRITING NEW WORLDS

AN INTERDISCIPLINARY ART AND WRITING LESSON

by MEGHAN McCOOK

2 SESSIONS, **90** MINUTES EACH
MATERIALS: *See each activity's instructions*

CALLING ALL KIDS! ARE YOU A DAYDREAMER? DO YOU THINK ABOUT alternate universes and far-off places that only exist in your mind? Well, get it out of your mind and onto paper! Check out some art and then create your own 2-D piece of artwork using lots of texture, shape, and color. You're not done portraying your universe yet, though! Explain it to us in a written description or "sketch" of the universe only YOU could imagine!

This workshop was originally designed to first take place in a contemporary art gallery for the art-making session, and then at 826CHI for the second session where the writing craziness would ensue. We've adapted it for classroom use here. Whether students are more comfortable with art or reading/writing, it gives them the chance to excel, but also work on what they may be less inclined toward. Combining art and writing will get your students' creative juices flowing and build confidence!

Start with Art...

Session 1

> **MATERIALS:** *Artwork for inspiration, colored markers, crayons, magazines, blank white paper, colored construction paper, pencils with erasers, string, aluminum foil, cardboard, scissors, watercolor pencils, water, brushes, paper towels, salt and resist crayons, any material that can be used for texture, clipboards and lined paper for taking notes, Sobo or Elmer's Glue, and so on*

In this session students hear a brief explanation of the chosen artist and his or her work by the teacher. They take their own notes, then come back together as a group and discuss what they saw in the art. Following a brief demonstration and given provided materials, students create their own 2-D piece of artwork depicting their own "universe."

There's nothing that can fully compare to a students experiencing artwork by standing in front of, around, or in it, wherever it may be . . . like a gallery, museum, artist studio, sculpture garden, or even his or her own home. The sensory and emotional things that happen to a viewer when experiencing the original piece of art, in person, are quite different from the experience of seeing it as a small image in a book. If you can manage a field trip to experience art firsthand with your students, I highly encourage it. If not, bring the art to your students. You can use a painting from your home, a poster, or an image from a book or the Internet. If you're feeling ambitious, you could even create a faux gallery in your room with reproductions. If you're feeling really ambitious, invite a working artist to visit your class with his or her artwork.

A big part of this lesson is giving the students a chance to experience new and *contemporary* artwork, not the historical, well-known art that we're all used to seeing. Students are rarely exposed to and educated about contemporary art, and it gives them an opportunity to approach new art without the same backstory and inhibitions. Picasso, Matisse, Leonardo da Vinci, and many others have their place in art education, but why not also give your students a fresh new experience that may be more relevant to their lives? Choosing the artwork that will inspire the students is tons of fun and can be a chance to expose yourself to new art as well.

Present the chosen artwork to the class. Give them a little background about the artist and the subject. Encourage them to take notes. Then, ask them what they think of it. What do they see?

Next, they'll create some artwork of their own. You can start by doing your own teacher demonstration. Have your own example partially started or a few examples in multiple stages of completion. It can be a painting, a drawing, or, best of all, a collage . . . who doesn't love collage?! Depending on what artwork you provided for inspiration, encourage the students to use related art elements, concepts, and techniques. Give them the option to work in an abstract, surreal, or realistic way. Tell the students that they will be writing about this place that they are creating next time, so that whatever they can't represent visually, they can use words to describe next session! Circulate among the students, offering help and asking questions. Make sure you provide at least 30 minutes for art making only, and of course plenty of time for cleanup.

. . . End with Writing

Session 2

MATERIALS: *Dry-erase board or chalkboard, pencils, erasers, lined notebook paper, original student artwork from last week, images of or actual artwork from last week that was used for inspiration, dictionaries, thesauruses, examples of description paragraphs from books or other sources*

After the students create their own artwork inspired by a contemporary artist and his or her work, they will switch gears and write about their very own invented place. Instead of creating a "character sketch," the students will use the same ideas and technique to write about a place instead . . . a "place sketch." This place is the space, environment, or universe that they created in their artwork. This is their opportunity to describe this place and what happens there. How can they describe this place in a creative and interesting way? Does everyone walk backwards here? Do animals talk? Do candy canes grow from trees? Is there a sky, and if so, is it always orange with polka dots? Do cars fly?

Having very inventive, creative, and inspiring writing samples is very important to communicate to the students the task at hand! Have the students read a couple of teacher-provided examples of descriptive paragraphs from novels or short stories. Even better, the teacher can use his or her own written example describing his or her own artwork sample from last time. This is a great opportunity for the students to take turns reading out loud. Encourage the students to think about their senses if they get stuck on ideas. If they were to imagine themselves in this place, what would they see, hear, smell, feel or touch, and maybe even taste? Remind the students that this is their very own place of their own making. Maybe it's a place they've always wished existed, or a place they dreamed about before. Use the chalkboard or dry-erase board to write down ideas or questions for them to refer to while writing. Or if you feel like your students might need more structure or prompts to help them get their ideas flowing, create a simple worksheet with questions like: If you were standing in this place right now, what would you see? Or, How is this place different from the world you live in now? What is unique about it?

Each student must write at least a short paragraph of five to seven sentences, but most will write several paragraphs, depending on how much time you give them. Remember, this is a "sketch," so there is no beginning and no end, but many descriptive sentences and words. But if a student wants to write a story about his or her place, all the better! Circulate, helping students. Provide at least 30 minutes of writing time.

Combine Art and Writing

Finally, near the end of the second session, leave enough time for each student to share his or her work. Hold up their art for the others to see while they read their stories out loud. Students are usually wiggling in their chairs with laughter and excitement to share their own invented place! Students who may have been a bit timid before to read out loud in front of the class are often confident as they beam over at their artwork they are describing. Success!

SUPERTEACHER BONUS ACTIVITY

I highly recommend publishing a workshop booklet with an image of each student's artwork and writing. It's a great way for them to see their finished work all together, and they are always proud!

WHINING EFFECTIVELY; OR, HOW TO PERSUADE YOUR PARENTS

by TAYLOR JACOBSON AND ABIGAIL JACOBS

3 SESSIONS, 2 HOURS EACH
MATERIALS: *4 adults for a last-session panel*

THIS WORKSHOP TEACHES STUDENTS to write proposals so convincing no parent can resist them. We have tested them on real parents, so we know. We've seen students exhibit iron-clad persuasive reasoning as they've tried to change their bedtime, raise their allowance, or increase their candy quota. It's quite impressive.

Session 1

We begin with a brainstorm on what we think "persuasive" means. This usually gets a lot of very interesting answers. We talk about what makes writing persuasive; why someone would want his or her writing to be persuasive; when and where persuasive writing is used; and what it means to persuade someone. The kids get pretty riled up when they start to understand they might really be able to talk their parents into ANYTHING if they craft the right argument.

We emphasize the difference between persuasive writing and opinion writing. This is sometimes hard for them to grasp but we try to work through it by defining emotion versus reason. We give examples: "Raw eggs are disgusting" is an opinion. "Raw eggs are a proven health risk" is persuasive. "Fourteen-year-olds should be able to drive" is an opinion. "In many countries, 14-year-olds are permitted to drive, and do so safely" is persuasive. "The school day starts too early" is an opinion. "Studies have shown that teenagers' comprehension improves after 10 AM" is persuasive. And so on.

We begin by going over the Five Commandments of Persuasive Writing, which we write on the board. They are:

1. Know your audience

   Are you trying to persuade your parents? Your teachers? Your friends? Society at large? Tailor your writing to your audience. Don't use slang with your teachers; don't use stiff, formal language with your friends.

2. Choose your position, and prepare for the opposition

   If you truly know your audience, you probably already know their opinion on your topic, and can counter it. "Though some parents may think kids are likely to lose an iPhone, research shows that's an extremely infrequent occurrence."

3. Back up the argument with research

   We tend to get asked "Can we make the research up?" here, so a brief discussion of what research is may be necessary.

4. Don't state your opinion unless you can back it up with good arguments

   We remind them: don't confuse facts with what *you* see as the truth.

5. Restate your point and summarize your supporting points

   A little repetition helps drive your argument home.

Next, we read an example of good persuasive writing and an example of not-so-persuasive writing aloud (handouts). We let the students tell us which one is good and which one is bad and why.

If time permits, we spend some time brainstorming topics and methods of research (statistics, interviews and quotes, examples). Topics usually involve persuading parents to buy something (Wii, cable TV, cell phone, puppy); or allow something (walk home from school alone, have a sleepover, forgo homework one day a week).

The assignment for the first class is to bring your topic, a brief definition of your audience including their opinion on the topic (if you already know), three strong points in your favor, and three possible counterarguments.

Session 2

In the second session we roll up our sleeves and work. We read what the students have written so far, then fix what needs fixing. If you have time to meet one-on-one with each student, great. If not, peer editing can be really helpful.

Usually, what the essays need at this point is more research to back up their arguments. We look for answers on the Internet. We also look for some good experts for them to interview and help them draft questions. Their assignment is to have the essay all finished for the last class.

Session 3

In the last session, we put our papers to the test. We bring in a panel of "parents and parent-like experts" to whom the students must present their work. The panel for our last workshop included a teacher, a journalist, a writer, and a self-described parent-persuading expert.

Each student stands up and presents his or her persuasive paper. The panel then comments on the style, writing, delivery, and overall persuasiveness, keeping in mind the parts and steps of a persuasive essay that we have discussed throughout the workshop. Feedback usually sounds something like, "At first I thought, 'Is this kid crazy? There is no benefit to video game playing that could persuade his parents to buy him an Xbox.' But you completely persuaded me with your statistic that linked video game playing with higher standardized test scores. If I were your parents, I would buy you one today." Music to our ears. Success!

A Not-So-Persuasive Essay

Dessert should always be served before any meats, fruits, and especially vegetables because dessert is definitely the best part of any meal. I mean, who can argue with the yumminess of cookies, cake, and ice cream as compared to spinach or meatloaf? I can't, and I'm sure you can't either. Let me tell you why I think that dessert should always be served first at every meal and you will certainly have to agree with me when I'm done.

First of all, we have the issue of how delicious dessert really is. As far as I can tell, everyone feels this way, so I shouldn't even have to convince you. Anyone who likes vegetables better than dessert is nuts—and I don't mean the kind of nuts you'll find in some chocolate brownies. I have asked most of my friends and they agree with me on this point: dessert tastes better than any other part of a meal. So, why shouldn't we get to enjoy dessert first and the other stuff later? Well, we shouldn't, which is what I'm trying to tell you here.

Aside from how good dessert tastes, we need to talk about how *bad* other kinds of foods taste in comparison. Nutrition, schmootrition, spinach just plain doesn't taste good and everyone knows it. Besides, if I'm really supposed to eat something as *unappetizing* as spinach, shouldn't I be allowed to eat an *appetizer* of double fudge ice cream first? Every restaurant menu I've ever seen serves appetizers, so there's no reason we shouldn't do the same thing at home.

My last point is probably the most important one, so listen up. By putting dessert at the end of a meal, you risk running out of time before you have to go to bed. That's right: all that time you spend eating eggplant, asparagus, and—if you're really unlucky—liver and onions, you could be eating dessert. But instead, due to the unreasonable rules placing dessert at the end of a meal, you sometimes have to wolf it down at an unreasonable pace due to time considerations. I don't know about you, but my bedtime is 9:00 PM *sharp,* so after spending an hour and a half pushing lima beans around my plate (that makes it look like you've eaten more than you have) I never have enough time to properly enjoy my dessert. That is not only unfair to me, it is also kind of dumb.

In summary, dessert should be eaten first because of the following:

1. It's the best.

2. Other food is very often the worst.

3. It's the only way to enjoy dessert at the leisurely pace in which it should be enjoyed.

Thank you for your time and consideration. I expect our next meal together to reflect the changes I have outlined above.

A Good Persuasive Essay

Children should be allowed to eat dessert before salad, main course, and vegetables at dinnertime because it improves their overall happiness, it assists in digestive functions, and it allows parents to spend less time washing dishes. Many parents think that healthy foods such as salad or vegetables are more important to a child's well-being, but recent studies have proven that consumption of dessert first is beneficial in more ways than one.

First, contradictory to the belief that a healthy balance of proteins and carbohydrates aids digestion, it is the sticky sugar found in most desserts that coats the belly and allows for improved absorption of nutrients. In his best-selling book *Digestive Functions*, the well-known digestive scientist Dr. Stomach Acid says, "Basically, the stomach is happy when it eats dessert and therefore more able to digest other, less satisfying foods such as salad and vegetables." Dr. Acid strongly supports the primary position of dessert in the meal and suggests that brownies, ice cream, and cake are the most beneficial desserts to serve on a regular basis.

Furthermore, eating dessert first improves children's overall level of happiness, making them more pleasant to be around, nicer, and more responsive to their parents. Children who eat dessert first have been known to clean their rooms more often and assist their parents with household chores. Sally Smothers, a fourth-grade student at San Francisco Elementary School, notes, "If my parents served dessert first, I would be so excited that I would wash the dishes after every meal and help my brother with his homework. In fact, I might even volunteer to walk the dog and clean my room once a week."

Finally, when salad, main course, and vegetables are served before dessert they often leave a messy residue on the plate, forcing parents to use new, clean plates when they serve dessert and therefore increasing the number of plates they must wash. But when dessert is served as the first course of the meal, there is no residue left on plates because dessert is so delicious. Therefore, the plates can be reused immediately for the other courses of the meal. Only one plate used means fewer dishes to wash. A recent study conducted by the Institute for Parental Relaxation (IPR) found that 9 out of 10 parents prefer doing "almost anything else" to washing dishes. Further, in his essay "Dessert Is Tasty: Researching Dessert and Its Benefits for Parents," Dr. Green Beans agrees and says that "serving dessert first would result in reduction of plate usage by no less than 50%. This is a clear indicator that serving dessert at the beginning of the meal would benefit parents as much as it would please their children."

In conclusion, the benefits of serving dessert before the main course clearly outweigh the drawbacks. With this one small change to the order of food consumption, parents could help make their children happier and healthier, all the while improving their own lives.

FOR THE BIRDS!

by SCARLETT STOPPA

1 SESSION, 2 HOURS
MATERIALS: *Bird magazines (birds already cut out of magazines, if possible), decorative paper, construction paper, poster board, cloth, scissors, glue, large dry-erase board and markers, pens, pencils, lined paper.*

EVER FED THE PIGEONS? OR WADDLED LIKE A PENGUIN? DO YOUR BIRDS OF a feather flock together, EVEN when you use conditioner? Wish you could fly like an eagle? To the sea? Well, Turkey, you're no lonesome dove! This lesson lets budding ornithologists imagine new avian species as they practice the fundamentals of storytelling.

The (Bird) Brainstorm

As students arrive, have them sit on the floor in front of the dry-erase board and guide them through generating ideas for the stories they will write later in the lesson. Headings include CHARACTERS (types of birds, who birds hang with, predators, prey, and so on), SETTING (bird habitats, places where no bird would dare to flap, and so on), and PLOT (situations birds get themselves into and out of, something that has never happened to a bird, and so forth). No answer is wrong. There are no limits to the imagination!

The Nests

After the brainstorm, assign each student to the safety of a nest. At one nest, the students combine bird parts (from the bird magazines, decorative paper, construction paper, and cloth raw materials) to create a giant bird on poster board that will make the classroom its new habitat. Next to each bird part have the students describe the purpose of that bird part.

At another nest, students craft their own bird (or birds) from provided bird parts (same raw materials as for the giant bird). They get to take these birds home!

Hatching Plots

After the nest activities, students sit down to write their stories. They should have lots of great ideas from the brainstorms and the bird collages they have crafted (for even more inspiration, invite the students to bring in stuffed animal birds or bird costumes from home, or bring in some of your own). Their bird should be the protagonist, and they are welcome to work the other students' birds into their stories. To get them started, give them the "Story Outline" handout so that they can generate some loose ideas for the flow of their story. Once they have finished this, go over the story checklist on the handout, then give the students lined paper for writing their stories.

Avian Dramas

Students are invited to read their stories while the other students act them out using props and costumes on hand. Expect mad chaos and many laughs!

Extra Time?

If there is extra time, lead the students in writing a group story based on the giant class bird they created. Each student adds a sentence or two—with some guidance from the teacher so that plot, character, description, dialogue, and so forth are included in the story.

STORY OUTLINE

BEGINNING (Introduce characters, describe the setting, dig into the conflict or challenges, start in the midst of the excitement!):

_____

_____

_____

_____

MIDDLE (How will the conflict climax? What will happen?):

_____

_____

_____

_____

END (Tie up loose ends; answer the questions the reader had at the beginning and middle of the story.):

_____

_____

_____

_____

STORY CHECKLIST*

❏ Beginning   ❏ Conflict or challenge

❏ Middle   ❏ Conflict or challenge resolved

❏ End   ❏ Action!

❏ Hero/Heroine   ❏ Dialogue

❏ Villain/Nemesis   ❏ Setting described

❏ Characters described

_____

*Not every story will have all of these pieces, but most do!

THERE'S POETRY IN AN ATOM

WRITING CREATIVELY ABOUT SCIENCE

by NICOLE MOORE AND RYAN MOORE

3 SESSIONS, 6 HOURS
MATERIALS: *Laptop, LCD projector (optional), flip chart (optional), access to videos on YouTube, worksheet, poem, short story, comic*

THIS CLASS SEEKS TO MAKE THE SCIENCES LESS ESOTERIC FOR THOSE WHO like to write, and to make writing more manageable for those who love science. Too often students are told that they will be naturally better at one type of thinking than the other, but this class sets out to show that everyone is capable of bridging that divide in their brains, and has the power to think creatively about something naturally logical.

Session 1

We begin the class by showing a video of Daniel Radcliffe (better known as the actor who played Harry Potter in the movie series) singing the periodic table on a British television show. His enthusiasm is contagious, and inevitably some of the students start giggling or bopping their heads along to the rhythm. Afterward, we ask: Why would a young, handsome, famous actor choose to declare his apparent love for the periodic table on a television show? The students have all kinds of answers, ranging from the notion that since he's famous, he can do whatever he wants, all the way to thinking that he's trying to be ironic. We ask about the song itself: Is it catchy? You bet. Why would someone want to create a song out of memorizing the periodic table? Because it sticks in your head, and if you need to know that sort of thing, a song will last longer than just the words by themselves. After this first discussion, the students begin to see that creative people can love logical things, including orderly, dependable science.

After that, we ask for students' own opinions about the two major aspects of this workshop: writing and science. As students talk, we write their responses down on a flip chart or chalkboard, using a Venn diagram. First we talk about the challenges of both: on one side of the chart stands "writing," and on the other is "science." As the students list their personal challenges with one or the other, we write down what they have to say either under the writing section, the science section, or in the middle, showing that this challenge applies to both. This serves a couple of purposes: first, it helps unite students who face similar challenges in both subjects, and it also creates evidence of the similar feelings that both subjects incite in students. Many students are surprised to see that the challenges they face in science are the same challenges that other students face in writing, and vice versa. We repeat this exercise with the positive feelings associated with both, and students can see again how success can look similar for both subjects.

Now that the students understand the obstacles and rewards of both subjects, we ask the students to brainstorm a list of scientific topics that are particularly interesting to them. These will range from ROYGBIV (the acronym that represents the order of colors in the rainbow) to parasites to pterodactyls. Err on the side of having too many ideas rather than too few, and encourage students to mine topics they might have covered recently in their science classes. As the ideas are flying, write them down on the whiteboard or blackboard. Once the students have thrown a goodly amount of ideas into the air, pair students up and ask them to choose one of the topics on the board. The student pairs are given about 5–10 minutes to quickly free-write on their chosen topic. This free-write can take on just about any form: poem, song lyric, comic, or vignette. The idea is to start getting those minds cranking out creative views of scientific ideas. At the end of the free-write, invite students to share their work out loud with the group.

The students should now start to feel more confident about this whole enterprise, and this is a good time to share with them some more examples of creativity inspired by science. YouTube is overflowing with excellent examples: in our workshop, we used music by They Might Be Giants, from the *Here Comes Science* album; a video of Tom Lehrer singing about pollution; and clips from the children's TV shows *Beakman's World* and *Bill Nye the Science Guy.* As you show the clips, ask students to jot down notes about anything that stands out to them: it might be a term, an effect used, a personal reaction, or a question that they still have. After showing each clip, ask students to react to the material. What was the concept being introduced? How was it addressed? Who do you think they were trying to teach? Why did they choose to present that particular concept in a certain way? Students are more media savvy than you might realize; they will quickly see that complicated concepts need the time and visual component that video clips provide, whereas concepts that just need a little memorization make really catchy songs.

We finish the first day with time to free-write. Students may choose a topic from their group brainstorm, or they may choose to write about something that was brought up in the songs or videos they just experienced. They can choose any genre they feel comfortable with—the point is to get words on the page, and to encourage viewing their topic in nonliteral ways. Students are again invited to share what they've written, and other students can offer constructive feedback to each other.

Session 2

Building upon the confidence to grapple with logical ideas in fanciful ways, we jump right in and ask the students to consider creating figurative descriptions of particular scientific topics. (A quick review of certain terms, such as alliteration, simile, metaphor, and hyperbole is helpful.) Ask students to create an alliterative description of atoms; a simile representing the movement of ions; a metaphor illustrating how a snake jaw works; and a hyperbole explaining what parasites feed upon. Feel free to make up different examples, of course, or let students pick! After each prompt, invite students to share their responses. You will be surprised how quickly they are able to draft beautiful phrases, even about ugly parasites!

Now that everyone has practiced using particular types of figurative language, we discuss with the group the types of messages that are best conveyed by different types of writing. Students offer the types of themes that they feel are best delivered in songs, comics, short stories, and poems. We pass around examples of a poem and a short story, both based on scientific ideas, and ask the students to share why they think the respective authors chose that medium for their message. Everyone starts to see the benefits and limitations of each type of writing, and we combine this with the discussion from the first session about why artists might have chosen a song or a short video clip to explain their particular scientific topic. The periodic table makes an excellent song, but it might not make the best short story. In contrast, explaining how cloning works would fit well into a comic book or a short story, but it might feel rushed in a poem or a song.

We finish the second session the same way we finish the first, with a nice chunk of time for the students to settle upon a topic that interests them and free-write. They can continue writing about the topic from the first session, or they can choose something new. We use a worksheet (see handout) that encourages the students to follow the same procedure in their writing as is used in developing scientific experiments. They first decide what they will investigate, and after they have observed their item of interest, they develop a hypothesis about its behavior. They are guided to develop some kind of test for this theory, and then report on these findings in the form of creative writing.

The focus of today's writing is to increase the use of figurative language. Really encourage the students to stretch as they make their scientific topic relatable through their writing. Perhaps they should personify the fossil of a triceratops, or maybe they need to add some sensory details to their poem about how baby birds learn to fly. At the end of the free-write, students read aloud what they have so far, and their peers offer constructive feedback. Students are asked to continue working on this particular piece, and have a second draft of it in time for the third and final session.

Session 3

This session is dedicated to the students writing and editing as many pieces as there is time for. After every editing session, students may share their progress and solicit additional feedback on the piece they are currently working on. At the end of the session, students are invited to share their favorite pieces, and all bask in the glory of having written creatively about science.

LINKS:

Here are some of the links we used during the workshop.

Daniel Radcliffe and the periodic table:
www.youtube.com/watch?v=rSAaiYKF0cs

Tom Lehrer on pollution:
www.youtube.com/watch?v=JPrAuF2f_oI&feature=related

Beakman's World on gas density:
www.youtube.com/watch?v=w7G4o2alLww&feature=related

Bill Nye on the Earth's crust:
www.youtube.com/watch?v=oTFX8Gn9K-c

Bill Nye on volcanoes:
www.youtube.com/watch?v=tfXGbzgGJ74&feature=related

They Might Be Giants (TMBG) in "Science Is Real"
www.youtube.com/watch?v=ty33v7UYYbw

TMBG on the sun:
www.youtube.com/watch?v=me06I9GDM_k&feature=related

TMBG on the rainbow:
www.youtube.com/watch?v=Gf33ueRXMzQ&feature=related

TOPIC: _____

	OBSERVATIONS ABOUT YOUR TOPIC
SEE	
SMELL	
TOUCH	
HEAR	
TASTE	

HYPOTHESIS ABOUT YOUR TOPIC, BASED ON OBSERVATIONS LISTED ABOVE

How will you prove this hypothesis?

_____

_____

_____

Write your notes from your experiment below:

_____

_____

_____

How does your experiment affect your hypothesis?

_____

_____

_____

Which type of writing would best convey your message? WHY?

_____

_____

_____

Write a draft of your "report" below:

_____

_____

_____

GUERRILLA POETRY

by BECKY EIDELMAN

1 SESSION, 90 MINUTES
MATERIALS: *Images of superheroes*
Blank paper
Books of poetry (Shel Silverstein or other children's poets)
Chalk (lots of it!)
A few extra adults to supervise and help

THE GOAL OF THIS CLASS IS TO SHOW students how poetry can jump out at you *anywhere*—and when you know this, you start to see it in places you never expected to find it.

After the students are seated, the instructor mentions that we have some company today, and that students will see them if they look down at the table. In front of each student is a picture of a superhero. We explain: each one of these superheroes was chosen because of his or her ability to jump out from nowhere—Spider-Man swings down from his string, the incredible Hulk jumps out from behind a building—and scare the pants off everyone walking along the sidewalk. The students have five minutes to come up with what their superhero would say if he/she/it jumped out from behind a dumpster/telephone booth/bank and saw something bad going on. (We can also make the sound effects that would obviously happen if our superhero were really riled up.) After we do this exercise, the instructor calmly explains that as scary as that was, we know something that can be just as scary: finding a poem somewhere you didn't expect it to be, and having it talk to you like a superhero would.

We're going to write poetry that talks as loudly as your superhero does. Since superheroes disapprove of vandalism, we'll be using notepaper and chalk.

Then we launch into the "flash poetry" assignment. Tell students to look around the classroom and find a spot (which can be any surface but the ceiling or the floor) where they want to hide a poem later. They have to be sneaky about deciding where their spot is, because no one else can know about it until the end of the lesson. Give them a few minutes to pick out the hiding spot. If you have a small class, you can let them get up and look around, but if this would create chaos, just have them choose a spot from their desks.

Next, they'll write flash poems—poems on the spot—to hide. The poems can be suited to the hiding place the student chose (for example, ode to a chair, old-gum-stuck-on-table blues, poem about a cold, dark cabinet—you can write these ideas on the board) or something they already had in mind. Alternately, they can choose poems they like from a book of poetry and copy them down. Give them 15 minutes or so to complete this assignment.

Then we go around the room and share our poems, or a few lines that we like from a poem, standing up and reading with a loud voice (this can also be done at the end of the lesson instead). Students can share the flash poem, a poem they found in the poetry books, or both. After they've shared, we'll collect the flash poetry poems and tell them that the super-secret project will continue later.

Then the instructor explains the next part of the lesson: we'll be going outside to the schoolyard and writing, in chalk, some lines from the poems we've just shared. To minimize chaos, it helps to designate a set area for them to write in. A few extra adults will also come in handy here. Students can chalk drawings next to their poems and write their poems in funny ways—anything to make it look like street art.

While students are chalking, have a grown-up helper take a few students at a time back into the class to hide the flash poems they wrote earlier. We'll come inside after all the students have hidden their flash poetry poems.

The lesson ends with a hunt to find all the poems. If there are any undiscovered poems at the end of the session, the poets can reveal where they hid their poems.

FRANKENFILMS

by LINDSEY ROBINSON AND JON ZACK

1 SESSION, 2 HOURS
MATERIALS: *DVD player or computer
Movie clips Sample screenplay*

IN THIS CLASS STUDENTS LEARN THE BASIC ELEMENTS OF SCREENWRITING BY rewriting and reimaging scenes from popular movies. Students will work as script doctors, the writers a studio calls upon to polish and rewrite an existing script.

Every movie starts with a screenplay; it's the foundation and blueprint upon which a movie is built. Every movie also features three basic elements: a protagonist, a goal, and obstacles. There is a main character (protagonist) who wants something badly (goal) and is met with obstacles when he or she tries to reach this goal.

Step 1: Everyone has a favorite movie. In fact, it is often difficult to choose just one. We remember the plot, characters, and dialogue from movies we love. Ask the students to name their favorite movies. Then list the protagonist, his or her goal, and the obstacles standing in the way of the protagonist from these favorites.

Step 2: Show a scene from a popular movie, such as *Elf, Night at the Museum,* or *The Karate Kid*. Ask the students to identify the protagonist, goal, and obstacles in each film. For example, in *Elf* the protagonist is Buddy the Elf. *Hint:* if the movie is named after a character in the film, that person is usually the protagonist! Elf wants to find his father, which is his goal for the movie. However, Elf's father lives in a land that is foreign to Elf: NYC.

Step 3: Ask the students to give the main character from the film a different goal and set of obstacles. For example, Elf could now search for his mother instead. It helps to consider changing location, such as moving Elf from NYC to LA. Perhaps Elf's mother is a famous actress. What types of people would Elf then encounter on his journey? What different locations throughout LA could serve as a backdrop for the action? Brainstorm a list of locations with students.

Step 4: Put pen to paper or fingers to the keyboard and write the new scene! It is useful to pass out a page from a screenplay, to show the proper format.

Step 5: Bring the scene to life. The writer will cast students to play the characters in each scene and perform it for the class.

Step 6: Repeat the exercise with another movie.

Watch in amazement as your script doctors write scenes that are funnier and more creative than the original. Your students are on their way to writing scenes for the big screen!

THE RULES OF MAGIC

by JULIUS DIAZ PANORIŃGAN

1 SESSION, 2 HOURS

ONE OF THE LURES OF FANTASY IS possibility: a reader can stumble upon a magic ring or receive an unasked-for letter of acceptance to an unheard-of wizarding school. While exploring these possibilities as a young writer, it can be difficult to see and process that these worlds still have rules. (Once, I was working with a student at 826LA to come up with his superhero alter-ego: he came up with All-Powers-No-Weaknesses Man.) The thing is, it's these rules that make fantasy both accessible and satisfying. We cheer in part because (minor spoiler alert) Harry masters the Deathly Hallows and defeats Voldemort, but it's just as important that Harry stayed true to himself and trusted his gut.

This lesson has two major phases. First, the class spends some time going over the rules of magic, doing a bit of brainstorming and prewriting along the way. After that, the students basically have time and space to write short fantasy stories where—you guessed it—someone tries to break or abuse the rules.

The plan is flexible, depending on which rules you want to go over, how much time your students need for prewriting versus the actual writing of the story, and so forth. I usually plan on about 40 minutes for writing the actual story,

and that includes time for some students to share at the end.

Part One: The Rules

For each rule, we have

> A period of discussion and instruction

> Time for each student to write

> A check-in period where students share

Pick some fantasy the students are familiar with, and be loose and flexible with that definition. Harry Potter is an easy story to discuss (and indeed, several students who've taken this workshop have done a lot of explication for me), but don't discount something like *Pokémon* (the TV series, or even the video games). Have examples for them, and let them participate. Give them a writing prompt, and then let them share. The last part is particularly important here; sharing keeps excitement up and spurs greater heights of creativity for the next round.

I list the rules that follow, along with examples I've used, and the little writing prompt I give them for each section. Each rule should get at least 20 minutes, more if you're focusing on just two or three rules, which is entirely your choice.

(Please note: depending on the ages of the students you teach this to, the sophistication of the rules and relationships they come up with can vary. Rules 1 and 2 are pretty easy to work with, even for students under 10; Bonus Rule 1a can be pretty difficult, period, and this rule is the easiest to skip.)

Rule 1: Fantasy Is Reality (Except Awesome)

The idea here is that things in fantasy worlds mirror things in the real world. Clearly, elements of fantasy works have inspiration from reality. Some examples of the rule:

☞ Ents are like old trees, but they're also like old people!

☞ Lothlórien is Middle-earth's most amazing treehouse!

☞ Put-Outers are like lighters, except they turn everything on and off, not just themselves!

☞ A Pikachu is a little less direct, but it's explainable as a cross between a mouse (the adorable part) and an electric eel (the shocking part).

☞ Don't forget to let the students share some.

Ask the students to come up with things they like in the real world, then have them convert them into things that are magical and awesome. I ask for at least two to three things (creatures, objects, whatever) in the real world, and two to three settings to go along with that. Magical pets are pretty common (for example, a dog familiar or protector), as are magic doors and cities in some pretty out-there places: clouds, swamp bottoms, and so on.

Rule 2: Everything Is Connected

Here's where we start to get serious, where we start to lay down the foundation for the magic

rules that will inform the students' stories. Some examples of the rule:

☞ Harry's and Voldemort's wands share the same phoenix-feather core.

☞ Sauron pours most of his power into the One Ring.

☞ Godric Gryffindor has a magical sword and magical hat.

Here, the students' task is to come up with a few new magical things that connect to their original set of magical things. Perhaps a dog familiar has a magical collar, or the bog people from the bottom of the swamp need to have swamp water or swamp grass to survive.

Rule 3: Magic Moves (and so *Really* Funny Things Happen)

This one's a corollary to Rule 2, and it's highly likely that discussion on this rule has already started. When exploring Rule 2, students are setting out the connections—the way their magical world is supposed to work. Rule 3 has them go into the ramifications of those connections. Some examples of the rule:

☞ Because Harry's and Voldemort's wands are brothers, they don't properly work against each other.

☞ The One Ring wants to find Sauron, so it exerts control over the people who wear it. (Super advanced! If a ringbearer can control the One Ring, that ringbearer basically turns into the new Sauron!)

☞ True Gryffindors can draw Gryffindor's sword from the Sorting Hat.

So, what happens when our magic dog loses its magic collar? Or when a regular person drinks water from the magic bog? Have the students determine what happens when their magical connections are disrupted.

Bonus Rule 1a: Real-World Rules Are Fantasy Rules

This most difficult rule runs in parallel to the first three. Essentially, here we get into theme. Tolkien was big on the power of friendship and loyalty; Rowling cast it differently and wrote about love as the most powerful magic. Sam is able to bear the One Ring exactly because he did it for Frodo, and it's Voldemort's underestimation of love that sets up his downfall.

These are a couple of the better-known examples, with lots of other magical rules woven into the mix. There are simpler ones out there:

☞ Don't lie. This underpins Pinocchio, and there are magical consequences for when he breaks the rule.

☞ Names are personal and private and sometimes sacred. Think of Rumpelstiltskin, or Ursula K. Le Guin's "The Rule of Names," where the knowledge of someone's true name gives the protagonist power over that person.

But, as mentioned earlier, this rule is the toughest. To simplify this rule, you can ask the students for rules from the real world—you can't go out past curfew, you can't drive without a license, you can't shout "Fire!" in a theater—and have them come up with magical consequences.

Part Two: The Stories

At this point, students have at least imagined magical people and objects and settings, along with connections between them. They probably also have some idea of what happens when the usual connections are broken, and they may have explored the tie-in of real-world rules and themes. They're ready to go; have them write a story where the usual magic of their world breaks down, and see where things go from there! Happy endings are definitely not required.

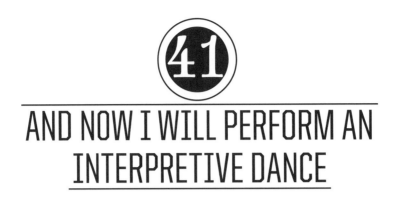

AND NOW I WILL PERFORM AN INTERPRETIVE DANCE

KINETIC WRITING

by ANGELA HERNANDEZ

1 SESSION, 1 HOUR

MATERIALS: *Island props (these are optional, but a coconut, seashells, beachwear, sunglasses, and sunscreen are recommended)*

THIS LESSON GETS EVERYONE UP AND moving, so it's great for students who have trouble staying in their seats. It's a good way to explore different forms of storytelling, and can be adapted for other subjects as well. I've also used it in my U.S. History class to review material. Letting the students get out of their seats and act out the lesson really helps them connect.

This class might also work well for the second language learner. For many second language learners, gesturing often helps facilitate the communication process and boosts confidence when speaking their nonnative language.

Here's how it works:

Pass out the handout. The prompt invites students to create a desert island story. Give the students 10 minutes or so to write. Because this is such a physical lesson, it's great to bring in physical props to inspire creativity. Let the students touch a hairy coconut, smell sunscreen, or listen to a shell. Sunglasses or a beach hat might help get them into character, and the props can lead to some inventive improv.

Next, have the students come to the front of the class one at a time, and act out their story, using only movement, facial expressions, and the island props—no words. (You could also have students trade papers, if they're squeamish about acting out their own story). Then have the class guess what the story was about. Let's see, there was armpit scratching, funny faces, and running in circles . . . Was it about a monkey dance troupe? An allergic reaction? Hyperactive toddlers?

Finally, have the student read the story out loud so the class can see if they guessed correctly. Ah, so it *was* about a monkey dance troupe after all! Fine work!

SHIPWRECKED!

Last week, I was out sailing, when all of a sudden there was a storm! My boat was shipwrecked on an island! I wandered around, and you wouldn't believe what I saw . . .

Tell us what you saw here. What did you smell, hear, feel? How did you react? Were you scared? Excited? What did you do? Then what happened?

_____

_____

_____

_____

_____

_____

_____

_____

_____

_____

_____

_____

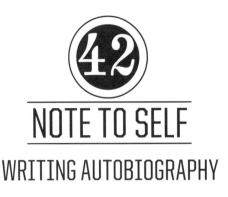

NOTE TO SELF

WRITING AUTOBIOGRAPHY

by TANIA KETENJIAN

6 SESSIONS, 1–2 HOURS EACH

THIS WORKSHOP WAS INSPIRED BY THE FACT THAT KIDS BETWEEN THE AGES OF 8 and 14 are very much in the midst of trying to understand themselves and where they fit in. Being a journalist, I often speak with people about who they are and how they see the world, and I knew hearing it from younger people would have a resonance for people of any age. What is your story? What do you think about? How did you grow up? Where are you from? What have you done that you are proud of? What scares you? Who are you? This workshop invites the students to take a closer look at themselves and share it with the world around them.

Each session begins with a simple assignment, a sort of introduction about what we are going to be writing about that day. This introduction gets the students' juices flowing and opens up a discussion. Since writing about yourself can be very personal, I want the kids to feel comfortable in the classroom and with each other. So there is a lot of sharing, about family, about school, about friends and fears and hopes. It's a very personal class and there tends to be a lot of bonding and support. There's also silliness and humor—these are kids after all—but the main thing is to get the students in a mindset where they can and will be open on the page.

Session 1: What Is Autobiography?

The very first day of class begins with a description of what autobiography is. It's actually a complicated question: What is writing about myself all about? How do I remain truthful? Can't my feelings change from day to day? What do I choose to write about? What if I am going to hurt someone's feelings? Can I write about other people or am I breaking someone's trust? Will my parents see this? Do I have to show them? We talk about all these issues and more.

Then we start writing. The first assignment is titled "MY STORY." What is your name, where do you live, where is your family from, where do you go to school, what languages do you speak, what are some of your favorite things (color, animals)? We want to get a general overview of the lives of the students so that later in the class we can delve deeper in other topics.

Session 2: What Do You Love?

The second assignment invites students to speak and write about what they love. Sometimes this is about a family member, a classmate, a good friend, a type of food, a place, a past experience. One student wrote about his love for fried chicken, another wrote about her love for her best friend, and another wrote about how much he loves his mom. The key thing here is to get the students writing and thinking about both the "what" and the "why." They like fried chicken, but why do they like it? Is it because it's juicy? Did they eat it when they were with someone they love? Do they like the smell it makes in the house? Does it remind them of something? These follow-up questions are just as important as the initial assignment.

Session 3: What Scares You?

The third assignment goes a bit deeper. We ask the students to write about what they find difficult or what they are scared of. For some, the writing just flows. Others find they need us to go over the assignment and talk things through with them so that when they land on something they like, or feel comfortable with, they can expand upon it. I go around the room and check in with the students as they write. When they've finished, we share. One girl wrote about a scary experience she once had at camp, another wrote about her brothers and how they are sometimes mean, another girl wrote about her friends at school and a particular one she has difficulty with.

Session 4: How Does the World See You?

In the fourth assignment, we ask the students to think about how the world sees them, not just how they see the world. What is the effect that they are having? How do they think they are perceived? This can be metaphorical or it can be actual. It can be through a story or it can be through a poem. Near the end of class, the students share their writing and the other kids in the class get a chance to ask questions. This way, the student gets to see where gaps can be filled. The student also gets some positive feedback and support, which encourages openness and sharing.

Session 5: Dream and Imagine

I give students the option either to write about a dream they had the night before (because dreams can be so vivid and, in their cryptic way, can tell so much about a person) or to write about how they see themselves in the next five years. These are a bit challenging because they are a little vague and they take imagination and creativity and a certain willingness to let go of what is "real" and explore possibilities. This assignment garnered some amazing results.

Session 6: Publish and Celebrate

In the final class, we look over all the writing from the past five lessons, decide on a few we really loved, and make any revisions necessary, knowing they are going to go into a book. Then we copy and assemble them into a class autobiography anthology, and everyone gets a copy. We share our favorite bits, eat cookies, and celebrate a job well done.

Now there's a book, the students have grown, and hopefully they have a better understanding of themselves so that they can make responsible choices that are right for them in the world.

43

SMELL THIS STORY, TASTE THIS POEM

by GABRIELA PEREIRA

5 SESSIONS, 90 MINUTES EACH
MATERIALS: *See sidebar and each session's instructions.*

AT 826, EVERYTHING WE DO IS HANDS-ON. THIS WORKSHOP GOES A STEP FURTHER: it's eyes-on, noses-on, ears-on and tastebuds-on as well. We'll be honest: it requires a fair amount of prep gathering all the materials, but the end result is totally worth it.

Session 1: SOUND

MATERIALS: *CD player and the songs you prepared ahead of time*

Part I—Soundtracks

Play a selection of soundtracks (1 minute of each) and have the students guess what movie the music is from. This is to help students warm up their ears. (You'll want to choose themes that are easy to recognize but also set a mood. Suggestions: *Harry Potter, Jaws, Indiana Jones, The Simpsons Movie, 2001: A Space Odyssey*.)

Part II—Music Paints a Picture (Handout Page 1)

Play segments (1–2 minutes) from the mix you made ahead of time. Assign each segment a number to help the students keep track of them.

After listening to 1–2 minutes of each piece, discuss the mood established by the piece. What specific sounds inspired a given image? What story is this piece of music telling?

Part III—Music Tells a Story (Handout Page 2)

Ask students to choose one of the pieces they listened to before and write a story that goes with that music. Go around the room and let kids listen to the music again if they wish. (It helps to break students into groups according to which piece they selected, then you can move from table to table and play the selected piece for each group.)

Session 2: SIGHT

MATERIALS: *A copy of Oscar Wilde's poem "Symphony in Yellow"; face pictures; paint chips in a variety of colors*

Part I—True Colors (Handout Page 3)

Have one or two students read "Symphony in Yellow" aloud, then discuss the poem and the symbolism of the color yellow. Some questions to help kick-start the discussion:

☛ What picture is the poet painting with his words?

☛ How many places do we see the color yellow in this poem?

☛ What does yellow mean to you and why?

☛ What is the symbolism of the color yellow in this poem?

☛ What do other colors make you think of?

☛ Anything else that strikes you as pertains to the poem or the color yellow.

Hand out paint chips at random. Ask students to write a poem or story that evokes the mood of that color. The only "rule" is that the title should be: "Symphony in _____."

Part II—Creating a Character (Handout Page 4)

Tell students to take a face picture and examine it in detail. They can give the face a name, a job, a backstory, even a family if they want. Now ask students to write a story about this character.

Session 3: TOUCH

MATERIALS: *A copy of Wallace Stevens's "Thirteen Ways of Looking at a Blackbird"; lunch bags with "monsters" inside (crayon, coin, eraser, and so on each hidden in a paper bag)*

Part I—Warming up

Play Zip! Zap! Zop! to get warmed up and to shake the sillies out.

Gather students in a circle. Start the game by pointing at one student in the circle and saying "Zip." That student must point to another player and say "Zap." This player must, in turn, point to another person in the circle and say "Zop." And that last person must immediately point to someone else and say "Zip." Continue in this way until someone says the wrong word or hesitates for too long.

Hint: It helps to do one or two rounds slowly until students get the hang of the game. Then speed it up to make it more challenging.

Part II—Ways of Looking (Handout Page 5)

Discuss "Thirteen Ways of Looking at a Blackbird." One way to start the discussion is by asking the kids which stanza they like best and why. Let each student share his or her favorite. Also, be prepared to answer questions about vocabulary ("bawds of euphony") and to share your own favorite stanza as well.

After the discussion, have each student write one stanza for the workshop's very own "Ways of Looking" poem. Start by choosing the object that will be the subject of the poem. A good way to do this is to ask the kids for suggestions and make a list on the board. Then, have students vote for their favorite, and the topic with most votes wins.

"X Ways of Looking at a _____"

[Replace X with the number of students in the class.]

Compile all the stanzas into one collaborative poem written by the whole class.

Part III—Monster in My Lunch Bag (Handout Page 5 Continued)

Hand out the lunch bags containing everyday objects (pencil, paper clip, eraser, coin, and the like) and ask students to study the object using only their hands and sense of touch. They are not allowed to look inside the paper bag. Now students must describe the object in as much detail as possible. They cannot say what the object is or make assumptions about the object; they must focus on describing how the object feels.

Afterwards, students will read their piece aloud and the class will try to guess what the object was. Notice how the sense of touch allows everyday objects to become extraordinary, much in the same way as the blackbird becomes so much more than a blackbird in the poem.

Session 4: TASTE

MATERIALS: *A copy of Jack Prelutsky's poem "Bleezer's Ice Cream"; Billy Collins's poem "Introduction to Poetry"; and Eve Merriam's poem "How to Eat a Poem"*

Part I—Bleezer's Ice Cream

Read the Jack Prelutsky poem "Bleezer's Ice Cream" and review topics like consonance, alliteration, assonance, and rhyme. Make up some wacky ice cream flavors using these figures of speech.

Part II—Feast of Words

Discuss "How to Eat a Poem" and "Introduction to Poetry" (which are both poems that talk about how to interact with and take in poetry).

Some things to consider:

☞ Why do we read poems?

☞ Why do we write poems?

☞ What is a metaphor?

☞ How does the metaphor of reading-as-eating work in the Merriam poem?

☞ What are some of the metaphors in the Billy Collins poem?

☞ What effect does the metaphor have on the reader? On the tone of the poem?

Part III—Writing a Delicious Feast (Handout Page 6)

Write a short piece where eating is a central image. The title is: "How to Eat a _____."
The only trick is that the subject of the piece cannot be food. It can be anything else, but not food.

Session 5: SMELL

Part I—My Life as a Dog (Handout Page 7)

Imagine you're a dog (or other animal that experiences the world through scent). Write a piece from this point of view, describing the world the way a dog would see it: through its nose. *Note*: You can make up words for scents, but you shouldn't have to explain them. The scents should all be self-explanatory.

Part II—Collecting Words

Have students collect the handouts from the entire workshop (total of seven) and assemble them into booklets. If students finish Part I with enough time before the reading, they can decorate their booklet covers.

Part III—Sharing Words: A Reading

Have students select one or two pieces they wrote, ones that they liked best from the workshop, and ask them to share these poems or stories aloud. A fun way to end the reading is to read the "Ways of Looking" poem that the class wrote together in Session 3 (Touch). You can either read the whole thing or have each student read the stanza he or she wrote.

YOU WILL NEED . . .

1. Poems

We used the following ones. The Collins, Prelutsky, and Stevens poems are available online at www.poets.org, and the others are available in various anthologies and poetry collections.

Collins, Billy. "Introduction to Poetry." *The Apple That Astonished Paris*. University of Arkansas Press, 1988.

Merriam, Eve. "How to Eat a Poem." In Stephen Dunning (Ed.), *Reflections on a Gift of Watermelon Pickle*. New York: Morrow, 1966.

Prelutsky, Jack. "Bleezer's Ice Cream." *The New Kid on the Block*. New York: Greenwillow, 1984.

Stevens, Wallace. "Thirteen Ways of Looking at a Blackbird." *In Richard Ellmann and Robert O'Clair (Eds.), The Norton Anthology of Modern Poetry (2nd ed.).* New York: Norton, 1988.

Wilde, Oscar. "Symphony in Yellow." In Richard Ellmann and Robert O'Clair (Eds.), *The Norton Anthology of Modern Poetry* (2nd ed.). New York: Norton, 1988.

2. Songs

Create an MP3 playlist or a mix CD featuring the following pieces:

- A small selection of movie theme songs
- Copland, Aaron. "Fanfare for the Common Man"
- Saint-Saëns, Camille. "Aquarium" from *Carnival of the Animals*
- Holst, Gustav. "Mars"
- Ponchielli, Amilcare. "La Giaconda: Dance of the Hours"
- Saint-Saëns, Camille. "The Swan" from *Carnival of the Animals*
- Mussorgsky, Modest. "Night on Bald Mountain"

. . . or substitute the songs you like best.

3. Sights

Put together an image file with various pictures of faces. One great resource is a book called *Faces* by François and Jean Robert (Chronicle Books, 2000). Alternately, you could just cut out some face pictures from a magazine.

Go to a local paint store and collect a variety of paint chips in different colors. Make sure you have at least one for each student in the class.

4. Things to Touch

Assemble props for the "Monster in my Lunch Bag" exercise. Take random objects (bottle cap, small stone, ball of yarn, and so on) and place them each in a paper bag. Assemble enough bags so that each student has one.

SESSION 1: SOUND

Name: _____

MUSIC PAINTS A PICTURE

Use these boxes to write words or draw pictures that describe each piece of music.

SESSION 1: SOUND

MUSIC TELLS A STORY

Name: _____

Musical segment number: _____

    Story title: _____

_____

_____

_____

_____

_____

_____

_____

_____

_____

_____

_____

_____

_____

_____

SESSION 1: SOUND

MUSIC TELLS A STORY

SESSION 2: SIGHT

Name: _____

TRUE COLORS

What color is your paint chip? _____

Paste your paint chip here:

_____

_____

_____

_____

_____

_____

_____

_____

What mood is this color? Happy? Sad? Angry? Silly? Where do you find this color in the world? List animals, foods, and objects that are this color.

_____

_____

Write a poem or short story using your paint chip color to set the mood.

_____

_____

SYMPHONY IN

_____

_____

_____

SESSION 2: SIGHT

Name: _____

CREATING A CHARACTER

Character's Name: _____

Age: _____   Girl/Boy: _____   Species: _____

What does your character look like? _____

_____

_____

Who's in your character's family? _____

_____

_____

Who's your character's best friend? Why? _____

_____

_____

Who's your character's worst enemy? Why? _____

_____

_____

Does your character have a secret? What is it? _____

_____

_____

What does your character want most in the world? What's standing in his/her way?

_____

_____

_____

_____

SESSION 3: TOUCH

Name: _____

WAYS OF LOOKING

Write one stanza for a poem with the title below. When we put everybody's stanzas together, we will have one collaborative poem.

WAYS OF LOOKING AT A

_____

_____

_____

_____

_____

_____

MONSTER IN MY LUNCH BAG
Without looking inside the bag, describe what the monster feels like.

_____

_____

_____

_____

_____

_____

_____

After you've described the monster, turn the page over and draw a picture of it on the back.

SESSION 4: TASTE

WRITING A DELICIOUS FEAST

Name: _____

Write a poem with the following title:

HOW TO EAT A _____

_____

_____

_____

_____

_____

_____

_____

◄──◆──►

Use the boxes below to jot down ideas for your poem.

Alliteration words:	Words that rhyme with: _____
Assonance words:	Words that rhyme with: _____
Consonance words:	Words that rhyme with: _____

SESSION 5: SMELL

Name: _____

MY LIFE AS A DOG

What kind of animal are you? _____

Tell us your story:

MY LIFE AS A _____

_____

_____

_____

_____

_____

_____

_____

_____

_____

_____

_____

_____

_____

_____

_____

GRAMMARAMA

HOMONYM STAND-OFF

by MARGARET MASON

3 SESSIONS, 1 HOUR EACH
MATERIALS: *See individual activities*

THE WORD "GRAMMAR" MAY NEVER inspire your kids to pull out noisemakers and party hats, but grammar doesn't have to be boring. This lesson turns grammar into an extreme sport. It's the Homonym Stand-Off!

Homonyms are the curse of professional writers and editors. They confound even intelligent, well-educated adults. They won't confound your students, however—your students are about to become homonym fiends.

These words will pop up again and again throughout students' lives, but it can be difficult to remember the discrepancies. The student handout provides mnemonic devices for each word set, introducing students to the idea of using mnemonic devices for any memorization exercise.

This is a very flexible lesson plan that spans about three class periods. It includes one day of in-class instruction, a quiz day, and a game day. You can leave a few days of study time between each lesson. Each activity involves the included homonym word list.

Session 1: Instruction

You'll need:

☞ An overhead projector and transparencies of the student handout, *or* . . .

☞ A blackboard where you can write words out as you discuss them

☞ Handouts for students to study at home, or you can have them take notes

Start by explaining what a homonym is and why it's important to learn the distinctions between words that sound alike but have different meanings. Tell the class that they'll be learning the differences between words, and will be quizzed in preparation for the Homonym Stand-Off. Briefly explain what mnemonic devices are, and how they can help students remember things more easily.

Review each set of words from the word list of your choice, and go over any questions kids may have about the definitions and memory hints. Set a date for the quiz, and distribute the handouts if you've decided to use them.

Session 2: Quiz

Be sure to grade and return the quiz before the Homonym Stand-Off so students know what they've missed.

Session 3: Homonym Stand-Off

This is where things get fun. The Homonym Stand-Off is a cross between charades, Pictionary, and a spelling bee. One student pulls a homonym clue out of a bag, and attempts to act it out or draw it on the board. His or her teammates must guess the word, and then you choose a team member to spell the word.

Of course, to win, everyone involved must know what the words mean and how to spell them correctly.

You'll need:

☞ A one-minute timer or clock with a second hand

☞ A chalkboard or whiteboard

☞ A bag of Hershey's Kisses or hard candy.

☞ A bag of individual clues you've written out in advance. Not all the words will work for this game, so just write out these:

> adaptor
>
> capital
>
> capitol
>
> compliment
>
> Earth
>
> earth
>
> hippie
>
> hippy
>
> loathe
>
> naval

> navel
>
> pail
>
> poor
>
> pour
>
> stationary
>
> stationery
>
> wrapped

How to Play:

☞ **Make teams.** Divide the students into two teams and let them choose their team names. Write each team name on the board.

☞ **Establish incentive.** Tell the teams that the winning team gets to choose whether to make the other team perform "I'm a Little Teapot," complete with actions, or get one Hershey's Kiss each for themselves.

☞ **Explain the rules.** You choose a student from the first team to select a clue. He or she has one minute to act out the clue or draw it on the board while teammates guess. Once someone has guessed the word, choose another student from the same team to spell it.

Each team has the potential to earn three points per turn. They get one point each for:

· Guessing the word

· Acting out the right word

· Spelling the word correctly

(Note: Before you ask a student to spell, let the team know whether their actor was acting out the correct version of the word by giving or withholding the point.)

☞ **Let the game begin.** Teams take turns guessing and spelling words until you run out of time. Winner takes all!

HOMONYM STAND-OFF STUDY SHEET

accept—to receive willingly, to approve, to endure. "I accept your conditions."

except—with the exception of. "I'll go any day except Sunday."

Memory hint: Except crosses out what you don't want. Accept means you'll take two.

adapter—a person who adapts things, books into screenplays, and so on.

adaptor—a device that makes incompatible parts compatible. "That plug won't fit in the outlet, you need an adaptor."

Memory hint: The O in adaptor stands for outlet. Adapter ends in -er because most words for people who do things end the same way: baker, skater, butcher, player.

capital—a town or city that is the official seat of government; material wealth; an upper-case letter.

capitol—a building in which a state legislature meets.

Memory hint: A capitol is the kind of fancy building that makes you say, "Oh!"

complement—to make whole, to go well with something. "That painting complements your couch."

compliment—when someone says something nice, offers praise.

Memory hint: Compliments make people say, "I am the best."

Earth—the planet on which we live.

earth—dirt.

Memory hint: The planet Earth is much bigger than a handful of earth, so the first letter is bigger too.

ensure—to make certain. "She ensured his safety."

insure—to make certain, "She insured his safety," but also to provide insurance for, "She insured the house."

Memory hint: If you use insure, you'll always be right. "I am always right."

hippie—a liberal nonconformist.

hippy—used to describe a person with ample hips.

Memory hint: A hippy person's hips and legs make the shape of a Y. Stereotypical hippies are slim, like the letter I.

It's—the short way of saying "it is."

Its—the possessive form of "it."

Memory hint: "*Its*" *is so possessive of the letter S that it won't even let a little apostrophe sneak in between.* "*It's*" *used to be two words, so the apostrophe butting in isn't such a big deal.*

loath—reluctant. "He was loath to pass up the cake."

loathe—to despise. "She loathed her enemy."

Memory hint: The E on the end of loathe is for evil, which most of us dislike.

naval—having to do with a navy.

navel—belly button.

Memory hint: Al is in the navy; his uniform is naval.

pail—a bucket.

pale—light in color.

Memory hint: A guy who wears his swimsuit for the first time that summer is a pale male.

poor—lacking money.

pore—to study carefully. "She pored over her books."

pour—to make liquid flow from a container.

Memory hint: The U in pour is shaped like a bucket that collects liquid. Poor has two O's like little holes in your pockets. To pore over your books is a bore.

rapt—engrossed, absorbed.

wrapped—enveloped or covered.

Memory hint: Rapt is a short word, because the person who coined it had a short attention span. Wrapped has more letters because it has to cover something up.

stationary—in a fixed position.

stationery—office supplies, specifically writing paper.

Memory hint: In stationery, the E is for envelope. Stationary is for anything else.

your—the possessive form of the word "you." "Your bag, your clock."

you're—the short way to write "you are."

Memory hint: The apostrophe in "you're" is just saving a seat for the missing A from "you are." (He'll be back any minute.) "Your" is for everything else.

HOMONYM QUIZ

WORD LIST

accept

except

adapter

adaptor

capital

capitol

complement

compliment

Earth

earth

ensure

insure

hippie

hippy

it's

its

loath

loathe

naval

navel

pail

pale

poor

pore

pour

rapt

wrapped

stationary

stationery

your

you're

DEFINITIONS

1. _____ Reluctant.

2. _____ The planet on which we live.

3. _____ A person who adapts things.

4. _____ A person with ample hips.

5. _____ Lacking money.

6. _____ Having to do with a navy.

7. _____ Office supplies, specifically writing paper.

8. _____ To make whole, to go well with something.

9. _____ To receive willingly, to approve, to endure.

10. _____ Dirt.

11. _____ Light in color.

12. _____ A building in which a state legislature meets.

13. _____ Something that makes incompatible parts compatible.

14. _____ To make liquid flow from a container.

15. _____ When someone offers praise.

16. _____ The possessive form of "it."

17. _____ With the exception of.

18. _____ Engrossed, absorbed.

19. _____ To despise.

20. _____ A bucket.

21. _____ To make certain, and to provide insurance for.

22. _____ Enveloped or covered.

23. _____ An upper-case letter.

24. _____ To remain in a fixed position.

25. _____ Belly button.

26. _____ To make certain.

27. _____ The possessive form of the word "you."

28. _____ An extremely liberal nonconformist.

29. _____ The short way of saying "it is."

30. _____ To study carefully.

31. _____ The short way to write "you are."

ANSWER KEY

1. loath
2. Earth
3. adapter
4. hippy
5. poor
6. naval
7. stationery
8. complement
9. accept
10. earth
11. pale
12. capitol
13. adaptor
14. pour
15. compliment
16. Its
17. except
18. rapt
19. loathe
20. pail
21. insure
22. wrapped
23. capital
24. stationary
25. navel
26. ensure
27. your
28. hippie
29. It's
30. pore
31. you're

HOW TO BE THE NEXT PRESIDENT OF THE UNITED STATES!

OR, HOW TO WRITE A REALLY, REALLY, REALLY GOOD LETTER

by JENNY HOWARD

1 SESSION, 90 MINUTES

WE FIRST LED THIS WORKSHOP TO HELP STUDENTS WRITE LETTERS FOR the 826 book *Thanks and Have Fun Running the Country: Kids' Letters to President Obama*. The workshop has two main goals: to get students thinking about politics through writing a letter to anyone from their local congressional representative or candidate to the president or first lady, and to ensure that the lost art of letter writing makes it to the next generation.

To start, I love a good icebreaker. Ask the students to share something related to the topic at hand, like who's their favorite public figure, and why.

Next we talk politics. The discussion will all depend on the age range that you're working with, but the big takeaway from the conversation should be that even though our students might not be of age to vote, they can still be heard. Oddly enough in this age of e-mail, the legislative process is probably one of the few places left that still puts emphasis on the (hand) written word. Depending on the office where you're looking to send the letter, they may have employees whose whole job is responding to constituents!

Our group was writing about the upcoming governor's election in our state, so we focused a lot on how states work, our state specifically. But you can discuss anything you want, from presidential elections to congressional bills. Again, the big takeaway is to make sure that students can somehow connect their personal experiences to the larger picture (whether that's the United States or their hometown) so they can feel excited about writing, and know that what they're doing has a purpose. One student wrote about his mother's struggling small business and how he thinks it's great that our governor cares about small businesses.

We asked our students what facts they know about our state, what it means to be a citizen of the state, and what they know about politics. We asked them what the job of the governor is and if anyone knew any specific duties the governor has. Having a biographical discussion about the person students are writing to is a great idea—our students loved hearing that Governor Rick Snyder went to the University of Michigan, and really enjoyed writing to Michelle Obama about Bo and her fabulous J. Crew wardrobe. Also, throwing in a silly fact *always* goes over well (as long as it's true!).

Onward, to letter writing: I had a sample letter on hand to read out loud to students that we also handed out for future reference (see handout). We also had a template handout on each table that split the letter into pieces (see handout). Splitting up the letter works really well—it moves students along if necessary, but it also gives other students the opportunity to work ahead of they are grasping the concept better.

The format of the letter worked well, too—students were comfortable writing their first paragraphs about themselves, and it helped them to be more confident when it came to addressing the politicians they were writing to (it's cool to think that the president cares about your dog and your favorite teacher in school). Reading portions of their letters aloud was key, also, for giving students ideas and examples (and it's always a good way to spotlight good work and boost confidence).

It's just as important to make sure students are writing the body of the letter as it is to make sure they've properly addressed, dated, greeted, and signed off on their letters, too—the more realistic, the better. I had one parent tell me that this letter-writing workshop helped her son see why writing was important because he felt that writing a letter was doing something real.

We wrapped up by letting students share their letters aloud. If there's time, you can also have everyone share something new they've learned about politics, their state, or their politician. We made a little pageant out of it, too—we had a "spotlight" and microphone set up, and we invited parents to come toward the end of class to listen to their students.

After making copies for us to keep and to give to parents and students to take home, we mailed the handwritten letters to our politicians and eagerly awaited their replies.

SAMPLE LETTER

Neil Tambe
5555 Wolverine Drive
Ann Arbor, MI 48104

July 5, 2010

Mr. Rick Snyder
P.O. Box 7371
Ann Arbor, MI 48107

Dear Mr. Snyder:

My name is Neil Tambe. I am 23 years old, and I currently live in Ann Arbor. I have lived in the State of Michigan since I was 6 years old, so I care a lot about our state and the upcoming election. I know that you are running for governor of Michigan. I wanted to write you a letter to tell you about my opinion for keeping young people in the state. I hope you consider this letter when making decisions during the campaign and in the future.

I saw on your Web site that you support keeping young people who just graduated from college living in the state. I agree with you that this is very important. After all, young people are great people to start companies, fill new jobs, and help keep our neighborhoods fun and active. I know this issue is tricky, so thank you for spending time thinking about it.

Please keep working on this issue. I think it would be a good idea for you, if you win the election, to recruit a group of young people from all across the state to talk with you about what it's like to be a young person in Michigan and help you make decisions about this issue.

Thank you for your time and service. Good luck in the election!

Best Regards,

Neil Tambe
Ann Arbor Resident
University of Michigan-Ann Arbor, Class of 2009

SAMPLE LETTER TEMPLATE

[Your Name]
[Your Address]
[Date]

1. Greeting!

2. Information about YOU.

How old are you? Where do you live? Where do you go to school? What do you like to do?

3. Your views.

What do you like about your world? What do you think should change? What is important to you?

4. What you know about the person you're writing to.

Why do you like this person? Is there a specific issue that you like or don't like? Talk about it here.

5. Signing Off!

Sincerely, Thank you very much, Best wishes, and so on,

[Your Name]
[Your Town, Your State]

CHARACTER ASSASSINATION!

by ERIC CANOSA

TWO SESSIONS, 90 MINUTES EACH
MATERIALS: *Graph paper and lined paper*

CHARACTERS ARE THE HEART AND SOUL OF A STORY. EVEN THE MOST incredible, thematically rich, imagery-filled story will fall flat on its face without engaging characters. In this lesson, students learn to flesh out their characters with all the details that make them feel real. Then they kill them off (sort of), using a brief obituary to really figure out what's important in the character's life. Students will learn everything from what is in their characters' trash, to how they eat breakfast, to the layout of their home.

Session 1

Before class, you'll need to find or write a paragraph that establishes a setting and describes an event through a character's first-person point of view without revealing many details about that character. It's best if the scene involves other people, or could credibly involve other people. For example, your paragraph might describe a baseball player sliding into home from third base, or a recently exonerated defendant walking out of the courthouse following the trial. Just make sure the paragraph doesn't describe the character, only his or her their actions and perceptions. Distribute the paragraph as a handout so the students can read along, or write or project it on the board.

As class starts, ask them to read the paragraph and have a quiet conversation with their neighbor about who the point-of-view character might be. They can jot down some notes if it helps them think!

After the students have had a few minutes to contemplate and discuss, lead a short discussion about who the point-of-view character might be. Then, brainstorm other characters who might be present at the scene and talk briefly about how their EXPERIENCE of the scene would be different. Next, have students choose one of the other characters from the brainstorm and then write a paragraph describing the scene from that character's point of view. If there's time, students can share their paragraphs with the group, and their peers can guess details about the point-of-view character.

This next part is one of my favorite writing activities to do with students: OBITUARY WRITING! Here, we're doing brief one-sentence obituaries, but ambitious or older students might want to write longer ones. Start by writing a few one-sentence obituaries on the board. Some samples:

Since Gene Marx lived on the squash court, it came as no surprise to his loved ones when he died on it, as well.

Neighbors never complained about Martha Maxwell's unkempt yard; they knew she was too busy with her charity work to devote much time to such trivial things.

Guy Lewis could do many things: lift a car, pave a parking lot, wrestle an alligator.

What makes these one-sentence obituaries powerful is their scope (they encompass a person's ENTIRE life, not just a particular snippet), and the fact that they are written from a compassionate viewpoint. That's a good thing, because authors should want their readers to sympathize with the protagonists in their story. Finally, the one-sentence obituaries are great because they essentially function as very concise character summaries—and they are rich grounds for all manner of delightful inferences. Give your students a little time to think about the character they'll want to create, then have them write the character's one-sentence obituary. If time permits, have the students share these aloud.

Now that your students have a general idea of where they want to go with their characters, they should start fleshing out the details. Basically, they'll make a character sheet containing Name, Age, Date of Birth, Eye Color, Hair Color, Size, Other Characteristics, Virtues, Flaws, Garbage.

Here's an example from a sci-fi story I'm writing:

Name: Michel Perez

Age: 31

Date of Birth: 4/23/3015

Eye Color: Brown

Hair Color: Brown

Size: Smallish for a man

Other Characteristics: Wears glasses; smoker

Virtues: Intelligent problem solver

Flaws: Arrogant and cowardly

Garbage: Crumpled up memos, junk food wrappers, tissues, cigarette packages

To wrap up Session 1, the students should write a paragraph from their new character's point of view. My suggestion: have them write about the character's morning rituals. If there's time, the students should share their paragraphs with the group. For homework between Session 1 and Session 2, the students should eat breakfast as their character would, EVERY DAY.

Session 2

Session 1 consists of a number of structured activities; Session 2 involves a lot more creative writing time. You'll need to find enough graph paper to distribute to all your students, and a bunch of lined paper.

Distribute graph paper to the students as they arrive and ask them to draw a rough blueprint of their character's home. Yes, I know some characters may live in a cardboard box or the middle of a forest—the students should map out the alley or the glade, respectively. Afterwards, students can share what their character's home is like with the class.

Next, ask the students to write a scene that takes place in their character's lovely home. The catch: the scene has to start with the phrase, "Nobody has ever loved me as much as I've loved them." The phrase could be dialogue, or it could be coming from a TV or radio, or it could be something a character is thinking. You'll want to model how this works with an example—the scene doesn't have to be long, certainly less than a page. Presumably, the scenes your students write will be at least somewhat emotional in nature, which is appropriate, because now you're going to ask them to give each other therapy!

One student will assume the ego of his or her character, while the other will be a therapist. The character should talk about . . .

☞ What his or her goals and dreams are.

☞ If he or she will achieve them, and how.

☞ If not, why not? What character traits keep him or her from going after the dream? Why do situational obstacles become insurmountable?

After 10 minutes or so, the students should switch so that the therapist becomes a character and vice versa.

Finally, the students should be separated into small groups of two or three, and work together to write a scene where their characters meet and interact with each other. My suggestion is the classic "trapped in an elevator" scene, but students can be as creative as they want.

That's it! Make copies of what the students wrote so they can take their group production home, and encourage them to write lots of new scenes with the characters they've come to know and love!

SONNETS WITH SUPERPOWERS

by SARAH GREEN

2 SESSIONS, 1 HOUR EACH

POEMS AREN'T STATIC WORDS ON A PAGE. Good ones can see in the dark, travel invisibly, breathe underwater, or fly faster than light. In this workshop, we look at the basics of the sonnet form, and learn how to craft creative new sonnets that can do anything.

Session 1: Rhyme and Meter Overview

Opener: Names and Stresses

To get a feel for stresses in words, we locate the stresses in the word we know best: our own name. Go around the room, and have students say their name and locate the stress: ReBECCa, JamAL. Let students briefly practice getting those stresses right, without officially teaching meter yet, just playing with the music of the names.

Go around one more time and this time count syllables as a group. Rebecca: 3. Jamal: 2. List these on the board or chart paper.

Breakfast Foods

I taught this lesson in the morning; lunch or dinner food might be more appropriate depending on your lesson's time of day. Ask: "What's your favorite breakfast food?" Make a list on the board so students can see the words. Then, going one by one, as with the names, listen for where the stresses are. Example: PANcakes. Scrambled EGGS. Scan these using traditional scansion marks. Again, no need to make a big deal about these marks—just work them in. Make sure all students can hear the difference in emphasis.

Sonnet Preview

Write out one line of a sonnet, for example, "Thou art more lovely and more temperate." Going slowly, see if students can help you "scan" this line—they tell you where the emphasis marks go. Wherever it gets tricky, stop and read out loud, accenting correctly yourself. No need to teach iambs, or use the word "pentameter" (though feel free to for older students); it's just great to let students count syllables.

Rhyme: One-Syllable Words

Switching gears now, take a break and have fun with rhyme. Use one-syllable words, even words as easy as "cat." Make as long a list as students have the attention span for with a particular vowel (that "a in cat") before moving on to maybe one or two more vowel rhymes ("go/snow/no"; "ice/dice/nice"). This should be a fun part of the day for everyone. Feel free to graduate to two syllables if that makes sense.

Session 2: Reading and Writing Sonnets, Questions and Wishes

Distribute the handout.

Introduce the word "sonnet," which means "little song" in Italian. Start with Browning's sonnet, which rhymes. Students should still have rhyme on the brain. Read (or have a volunteer read) this sonnet aloud. See if students can figure out why some people might call this a song. Write down the words that rhyme. Notice that Browning starts with a question and then answers that question. Why is the person writing this poem? What do students think the story is behind it? How does she feel? Why? Point out that many, but not all, sonnets are written about love.

Next, move on to Shakespeare. Read or have a student read this poem aloud. Again pay attention to rhyme. Make a (student-led) list of the words that rhyme. Explain vocabulary that may be foreign. Again: What does this person want? How does he feel? What story do students imagine? Notice there is also a question in this sonnet. When students are ready, see if they can count the syllables in a few lines of this poem. Go back to Browning and count the syllables in her poem. Aha! Ten syllables per line, plus rhyme. These are features of a traditional sonnet.

You can add these features to the board under "Sonnet: Little Song." I tend not to get into iambic pentameter using those specific words, but again, feel free. Finally: How many lines does this poem have? Fourteen. Explain that traditional sonnets always have 14 lines and that's one of the biggest clues that a poet is using the sonnet form.

An Original Sonnet

Have the students write their own 14-line poem. If they are overwhelmed by this length, see if they can write 7 lines to start. The topic is completely up to them; it doesn't have to be about love. It might be useful to give them an assignment, such as "Write about a question or a wish. Any question or any wish." Older students should be invited to incorporate as many other sonnet aspects into their draft as they can—I have had students successfully include rhyme, 10 syllables, and even (intuitively) iambic pentameter. Aiming for 10-syllable lines is a good sneaky way to arrive at iambic pentameter with fifth graders (or grown-ups) much of the time.

Let students write for however long makes sense for the time you have.

Make sure to leave room to share poems!

Optional Valentine's Day activity: Students can take their sonnet's last two lines and illustrate them on construction paper, doilies, or whatever other material you have available for craft making. These do not have to be valentine heart shapes (I've seen some sonnet lines written on robot pictures), but they can be.

FROM *SONNETS FROM THE PORTUGUESE* (XLIII)

How do I love thee? Let me count the ways.
I love thee to the depth and breadth and height
My soul can reach, when feeling out of sight
For the ends of Being and ideal Grace.
I love thee to the level of everyday's
Most quiet need, by sun and candle-light.
I love thee freely, as men strive for Right.
I love thee purely, as they turn from Praise.
I love thee with the passion put to use
In my old griefs, and with my childhood's faith.
I love thee with a love I seemed to lose
With my lost saints—I love thee with the breath,
Smiles, tears, of all my life!—and, if God choose,
I shall but love thee better after death.

—Elizabeth Barrett Browning

SHALL I COMPARE THEE TO A SUMMER'S DAY? (SONNET 18)

Shall I compare thee to a summer's day?
Thou art more lovely and more temperate:
Rough winds do shake the darling buds of May,
And summer's lease hath all too short a date;
Sometimes too hot the eye of heaven shines,
And often is his gold complexion dimmed;
And every fair from fair sometime declines,
By chance of nature's changing course untrimmed;
But thy eternal summer shall not fade,
Nor lose possession of that fair thou ow'st;
Nor shall death brag thou wand'rest in his shade,
When in eternal lines to Time thou grow'st:
      So long as men can breathe, or eyes can see,
      So long lives this, and this gives life to thee.

—William Shakespeare

BEST IMAGINARY VACATION EVER!

by MICAH PILKINGTON

1 SESSION, 2 HOURS

THIS WORKSHOP HAS A SIMPLE BUT urgent goal: to combat the threat of dull summer vacations.

Once everyone is seated, we go around the room and talk about some fun places for imaginary vacations: the woods, the lake, Grandma's house. We point out that while fun, every single place we named had gravity. We know we can do better. Before jumping into a fantasy vacation plan, we list on the board the vacation activities that we do *not* recommend:

Getting bitten by angry spiders

Eating tuna and Jell-O sundaes

Being chased by a mob of any sort

Bee taming

Bear taming

Sock darning

Mosquito ranching

Downhill skiing without snow

Going to piano repair camp

Hair mowing

We ask the class to add to our list of bad vacation ideas; cleaning your room, math, and yard work are often mentioned.

The instructor then gives the class a brief example of an ultimate dream vacation. In one class, the instructor used her cat's itinerary, which involved snorkeling, lots of accordion music, and a whole roast turkey for dinner every night. Other ideas have included a two-week stay in a candy store and a trip to the waterslide factory.

Now it's time for students to gather their own vacation ideas, so we go to the handout and get started on specifics. Where will they go? Who will they bring? How will they spend their days? This section goes quickly; the instructor merely pushes for details and discourages conventional ideas about the laws of time and space. This is a good time to emphasize fiction and fantasy and to encourage the students to be as creative as they can. We agree that every vacation must end with a party, so we throw in some ideas for that, too.

The final step is to use all the ideas we've worked on to write a story about a typical day in the best vacation ever. If they're stuck, we encourage students to look at their notes for inspiration. The class ends with students sharing their awesome plans. Ice cream and flying figured largely into one vacation story; in another, Madonna appeared and gave everyone dance lessons. If there's time at the end of class, kids decorate their handouts with vacation pictures.

Write Your Dream Vacation Itinerary!

Where I will go:

_____

_____

_____

_____

What I will bring (supplies, clothes, toys, dodge balls, and so on. Be as detailed as possible. Is it a red dodge ball, or is it a red glitter light-up dodge ball with a jet pack?):

_____

_____

_____

_____

Who I will bring (family members? pets? friends? Why would they be good travel companions?):

_____

_____

_____

What I will do for a job (ice cream taster? professional hoverbiker? Tell us all about it!):

_____

_____

_____

What I will do for fun:

_____

_____

_____

_____

Transportation to and from my vacation spot (surely nothing so boring as a car—get creative):

_____

_____

_____

_____

Things I will not have to do, not even once, because you can't make me:

_____

_____

_____

_____

What my end-of-vacation blowout party will be like:

_____

_____

_____

_____

_____

WHAT'S THE SCOOP? HOW TO GET THE REAL STORY

by MARK DE LA VIÑA

1 SESSION, 90 MINUTES PLUS HOMEWORK

HOW MANY PEOPLE CAN SAY THEY ARE PAID TO BE CURIOUS? HOW MANY GET to pose the kinds of questions that everyone wishes they could ask?

Journalists not only get to explore and write about compelling subjects, but they can break stories that have a positive impact if they ask the right questions in an interview.

What all good stories, both big and small, have in common is a newsworthy subject that is timely and important. What also helps make the article newsworthy is if it's local or if it involves a critical conflict, such as a dispute between students and teachers. Sometimes, it's a simple, powerful story about how a student won a major award by working long hours outside of class.

You don't have to cling to a lamppost in a hurricane or join the White House press corps to get a good story. But you have to know how to conduct an interview. In this lesson, students learn how to do just that.

Step 1: Ask the students to find a possible story, preferably about a subject that interests them. It should also be newsworthy. It doesn't have to be the kind of article that will turn an election or clear someone of wrongdoing, but the information should be of value to anyone reading about this subject.

Step 2: Students find the right person to approach for an interview. A good source is someone who can give you firsthand information, rather than rumor or hearsay.

Step 3: Go over the "Good Interview Tips" handout to prep the students for conducting their interviews. If you want to practice, it can be really fun to bring in someone—posing as an expert on a given topic—to practice on. This is even more fun if, say, the given topic is a little ridiculous (like Hannah Montana trivia) and the expert is in full costume.

Step 4: Turn the students loose to write their stories.

SUPERTEACHER BONUS ACTIVITY

Once the students have turned in their stories, compile them all into a class newspaper!

GOOD INTERVIEW TIPS

❖ **Research.** Research your subject *before* your interview. Subjects are more comfortable with an informed reporter.

❖ **Be respectful.** The person you talk to is doing you a favor by granting the interview. Introduce yourself by telling him or her who you are; what class, publication, or outlet you are writing for; and what your story is about. Thank the person interview is over.

❖ **Listen.** Pay attention to what the person says, and to *how* he or she says it. Did he or she answer the question you asked, or did the person answer the question he or she wished you had asked?

❖ **Observe.** If you're talking to an art teacher, does he or she have paintings on the wall? If you're writing a story about sneakers, is the person you are interviewing wearing a certain kind of shoe? Ask about these things—they could provide an important detail in the story you write. Be inquisitive *and* observant.

❖ **Ask.** If you are in doubt about something, or there is some element of the subject you do not understand, don't be afraid to ask. You can't write a story well if you don't fully grasp the subject.

❖ **Check spelling and facts.** Make sure all names are spelled correctly. When a person spells his or her name aloud, read back the spelling to make sure it is correct. Check your facts. Don't print rumors or hearsay.

❖ **Be strong.** Don't shy away from hard questions. Don't let the person you are interviewing control the interview by giving information that doesn't answer the questions. Your job is not just to gather information, but to gather the right information.

QUESTIONS TO ASK:

1. Get the person's complete name. And ask how to spell his or her *entire* name. Is there a middle initial? Or a nickname? Example: Francisco D. "Paco" Williams. Spell out the person's name aloud to make sure it is correct.

2. What is the subject's age? If he or she is a student, what grade is he or she in?

3. Who is involved? Is your interview subject the best person to talk to, or is there perhaps someone else who knows more or is closer to the subject?

4. What is the time element? Sample questions: How long has 826 Valencia been around? When did the Writers' Room start? How long has Ms. Johnson been teaching at Everett Middle School? When does the football season start and end?

5. Is this an event you're covering? If so, where is it taking place? In what classroom? In the gym? At some club? Again, be specific. If necessary, include the address.

6. How did this happen? Examples: How did the Animal Room come together? How did the Kid Power club get started? How did the story of the nonexistent school swimming pool first circulate? How did a rapper begin his career?

7. Why is this person doing what he or she is doing? Examples: Why is the coach using a defense-oriented system? Why does an actor keep making comedies? Why do more students at the school prefer Nike Air Force to Converse All-Stars?

8. Ask the person to specify. If your subject says he or she has been a singer "forever," find out when he or she started. If a person wins a scholarship, find out the dollar amount of the award, the full name of the scholarship, and how many people competed for it. Get as complete a picture as possible.

9. What is your subject looking forward to? Does he or she have any goals or long-range plans? Examples: Now that George Lucas has filmed six *Star Wars* movies, what will he work on next?

10. At the end of the interview, ask if there is anything your subject wants to add. Are there any questions he or she thinks you missed asking?

11. Is there any additional information you can include to help readers? A teacher they should contact? A phone number readers can call if they have any questions? The URL of a Web site they can visit?

12. Be sure to tell the person you're interviewing that you might contact him or her again if another question comes up—you or your editor later might think of something that was overlooked. These are called follow-up questions.

⑤⓪

THE ILLUSTRATED BOOK REPORT

by REBECCA STERN AND BRAD WOLFE

3 SESSIONS, 1 HOUR EACH

SAY GOODBYE TO BORING FILL-IN-THE-BLANK AND TELL-ME-WHAT-HAPPENED-NEXT book report worksheets. Having each child create a comic strip showing what happened in the reading is a creative and fun way to evaluate where students are in terms of their understanding of a particular book. We like to have our students make these comics in addition to our lively book discussions, thought-provoking written responses, and boring old quizzes, as all of these components together form a holistic assessment of the children's reading comprehension.

Session 1

We begin the comic project by reading the first chapter of a book we've been reading together (this can really be done with any text). Then, as a class, we list the main events from the chapter on the board. There's usually some debate as to what events are considered "important" or "main," but we've found that these conversations are helpful as they instigate interesting discussions. Once we're all satisfied with the list, we tell the kids that their task is to convert the list on the board into a comic strip. The only rule is that they have to stay true to the story, meaning they can't add in their own characters, plot twists, and so on.

"What is a comic strip?" a student may ask. To that, we tell them that a comic strip consists of pictures with some words and captions to help the reader understand what's happening. To help the students fully understand their task, we draw some boxes on the board and then tell them that we're going to make a comic strip of our list. We draw the first event in the first box—for example, if the first event is Odysseus's ship heading off towards Ithaca, we would draw a boat, with a person waving at the shore. Out of Odysseus's mouth we draw a speech bubble and write, "Toward Ithaca!" It's important to explain speech bubbles (dialogue) and captions (brief sentences explaining the action) to the students—often kids want to write tons and tons in their comics and we have to teach them to write only what is essential. Also, we try to stress to the kids that effort is important, but drawing perfect pictures is not! After drawing the first box on the board, we have the kids sketch out the rest of the events listed.

We provide the comic paper (see handout), though we tell the students that they can make their own paper if they prefer. Technology can be incorporated into this project by having the students create their comics on computers, using software like Comic Life (this also works for kids who have a difficult time drawing or who have dysgraphia).

Session 2

We tell the kids that they are going to do a comic for each chapter of the book (this can be the book you've been reading together as a class, or a book students have read on their own). At the end, they will put all of their comics together to make a comic book (or graphic novel). For the comic books to work, it's important to tell the kids to keep their papers in the same direction—if their first comic is laid out horizontally across the page, then all of their subsequent comics should go horizontally, as well. Then we set them loose to work.

Session 3

Once they have put their comic books or graphic novels together, we share them so that they can see all of their peers' works of art. Even though they're based on the same story, each one turns out completely unique.

RESPONDING TO LITERATURE:
COMIC BOOK ASSIGNMENT

Directions: You are to draw a comic strip for each chapter in _____.
The comic should show the main events from the chapter—you do not need to include
every detail. (*Hint:* Make a list of the main events first, and then begin your comic.) You
should include chapter numbers, captions (speech and thought bubbles work as well), and
labels. Please put time and effort into this project. You may use the cartoon boxes provided,
or make your own.

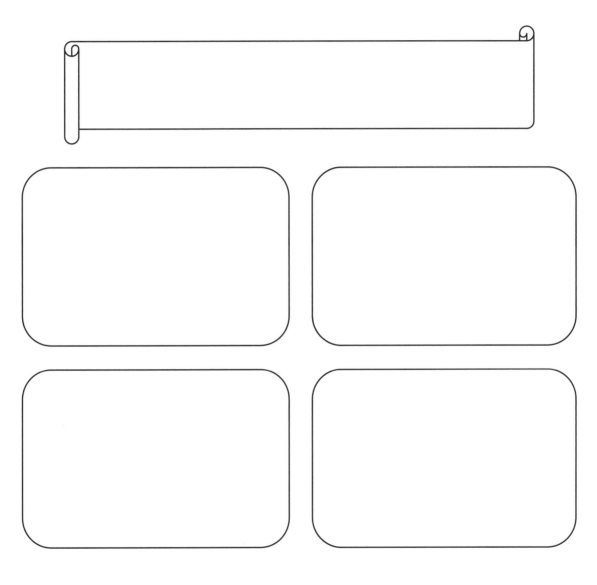

APPENDIX

Evaluation Rubric

	Structure		Style	Grammar & Usage
	Nonfiction	**Fiction**		
Great	• Clearly expresses a main idea • Points are well supported • Shows evidence of strong research • Points flow logically from paragraph to paragraph • Has a strong conclusion	• Setting, characters, and plot are vibrant, rounded, and connected • Story has strong imaginative fictional elements • Action flows logically or naturally • Dialogue is strong • Ending is effective and fitting	• Includes lots of descriptive detail • Writing reflects a unique voice • Word choice is inventive and appropriate	• Uses advanced punctuation, like semicolons and dashes • Harder words are spelled and used correctly • Sentences are complete and don't run on
Good	• Expresses a main idea, but occasionally wanders off • Points are sometimes supported • Shows evidence of some research • Uses paragraphs, though transitions may be rough • Has a definite conclusion, but may end on a weak note	• Setting, characters, and plot are fairly well rounded but underdeveloped or disconnected at points • Story has some imaginative fictional elements • Dialogue is present and fairly strong • Ending is present but may feel somewhat sudden or disjointed	• Includes some descriptive detail • Words are well chosen	• Uses correct punctuation and capitalization most of the time • Most words are spelled and used correctly • Sentences are complete and don't run on most of the time
Basic	• Doesn't express a main idea • Statements lack development or support • Shows no evidence of research • No paragraphs • Conclusion is weak or missing	• Story features characters, setting, and a plot, but they may not be developed or connected • Story lacks imaginative elements • Little or no dialogue • Ending is missing or very abrupt	• Includes little descriptive detail • Word choice is basic	• Many words are spelled or used incorrectly • Lacks punctuation or capitalization • Sentences may be fragmented • Writing is hard to read

Self-Assessment Checklist

☐ I showed that I know a lot about my topic.

☐ I expressed what I think and feel.

☐ My paper has a main idea.

☐ My ideas are supported.

☐ My paper has paragraphs that flow from one idea to the next.

☐ My paper has a beginning, middle, and end.

☐ I spelled words correctly. When I didn't know how to spell a word, I looked it up.

☐ I used punctuation correctly.

☐ My sentences are complete.

☐ I capitalized words correctly.

☐ I included descriptive details.

☐ I used colorful, energetic, meaningful words instead of bland words like "nice."

☐ I had fun writing it!

Common Core Curriculum Standards

To help ensure that you're satisfying necessary standards, we've prepared charts to show you which of the Common Core Curriculum Standards each lesson plan meets. The standards were created as part of the Common Core State Standards Initiative, which aims to align diverse state standards and curricula. Forty-eight states are members of the initiative, and most states have adopted the standards.

Some grades have been combined here for convenience, occasionally with slight modifications. You can read the full text of the standards and learn more about them at www.corestandards.org.

FIRST–SECOND GRADE	TEXT TYPES AND PURPOSES		
	Write opinion pieces in which they introduce the topic or name the book they are writing about, state an opinion, supply a reason for the opinion, and provide some sense of closure.	Write informative/ explanatory texts in which they name a topic, supply some facts about the topic, and provide some sense of closure.	Write narratives in which they recount two or more appropriately sequenced events, include some details regarding what happened, use temporal words to signal event order, and provide some sense of closure.
TRAGIC LOVE TALES (BY SIX-YEAR-OLDS)		◆	◆
WRITING FOR PETS		◆	◆
FORT PARTY!		◆	◆
MAKE-BELIEVE SCIENCE		◆	◆
OH, YOU SHOULDN'T HAVE, REALLY			◆
SPACE EXPLORATION FOR BEGINNERS		◆	◆
WHY DID THE CHICKEN CROSS THE LESSON PLAN?			
PJ PARTY			◆
ANY WHICH WAY			◆
BRAINS! OR, WRITING WITH ZOMBIES			◆
COOKING FOR CRYPTIDS		◆	
SCIENCE CLUB	◆	◆	
IF I WERE A KING OR QUEEN	◆	◆	
HARRY POTTER SPIDER-MAN VS. THE EVIL ZOMBIE NINJAS			◆
FOR THE BIRDS!			◆
AND NOW I WILL PERFORM AN INTERPRETIVE DANCE			◆
BEST IMAGINARY VACATION EVER!			◆

	With guidance and support from adults, focus on a topic, respond to questions and suggestions from peers, and add details to strengthen writing as needed.	With guidance and support from adults and peers, focus on a topic and strengthen writing as needed by revising and editing.	With guidance and support from adults, use a variety of digital tools to produce and publish writing, including in collaboration with peers.
Tragic Love Tales (by Six-Year-Olds)	❖	❖	
Writing for Pets	❖	❖	
Fort Party!	❖	❖	
Make-Believe Science	❖	❖	
Oh, You Shouldn't Have, Really	❖	❖	
Space Exploration for Beginners	❖	❖	
Why Did the Chicken Cross the Lesson Plan?	❖	❖	
PJ Party	❖	❖	
Any Which Way	❖	❖	
BRAINS! Or, Writing with Zombies	❖	❖	
Cooking for Cryptids	❖	❖	
Science Club	❖	❖	
If I Were a King or Queen	❖	❖	
Harry Potter Spider-Man vs. the Evil Zombie Ninjas	❖	❖	
For the Birds!	❖	❖	
And Now I Will Perform an Interpretive Dance	❖	❖	
Best Imaginary Vacation Ever!	❖	❖	

	Participate in shared research and writing projects (e.g., read a number of books on a single topic to produce a report; record science observations).	With guidance and support from adults, recall information from experiences or gather information from provided sources to answer a question.
Tragic Love Tales (by Six-Year-Olds)		❖
Writing for Pets		❖
Fort Party!		❖
Make-Believe Science	❖	❖
Oh, You Shouldn't Have, Really	❖	❖
Space Exploration for Beginners	❖	❖
Why Did the Chicken Cross the Lesson Plan?		❖
PJ Party	❖	❖
Any Which Way	❖	❖
BRAINS! Or, Writing with Zombies	❖	❖
Cooking for Cryptids	❖	❖
Science Club	❖	❖
If I Were a King or Queen	❖	❖
Harry Potter Spider-Man vs. the Evil Zombie Ninjas		❖
For the Birds!	❖	❖
And Now I Will Perform an Interpretive Dance		❖
Best Imaginary Vacation Ever!		❖

	Write opinion pieces on topics or texts, supporting a point of view with reasons and information. Introduce a topic or text clearly, state an opinion, and create an organizational structure in which related ideas are grouped to support the writer's purpose. Provide reasons that are supported by facts and details. Link opinion and reasons using words and phrases (e.g., for instance, in order to, in addition). Provide a concluding statement or section related to the opinion presented.	Write informative/explanatory texts to examine a topic and convey ideas and information clearly. Introduce a topic clearly and group related information in paragraphs and sections; include formatting (e.g., headings), illustrations, and multimedia when useful to aiding comprehension. Develop the topic with facts, definitions, concrete details, quotations, or other information and examples related to the topic. Link ideas within categories of information using words and phrases (e.g., another, for example, also, because). Provide a concluding statement or section related to the information or explanation presented.	Write narratives to develop real or imagined experiences or events using effective technique, descriptive details, and clear event sequences. Orient the reader by establishing a situation and introducing a narrator and/or characters; organize an event sequence that unfolds naturally. Use dialogue and description to develop experiences and events or show the responses of characters to situations. Use a variety of transitional words and phrases to manage the sequence of events. Use concrete words and phrases and sensory details to convey experiences and events precisely. Provide a conclusion that follows from the narrated experiences or events.
TRAGIC LOVE TALES (BY SIX-YEAR-OLDS)		◆	◆
WRITING FOR PETS		◆	◆
FORT PARTY!		◆	◆
MAKE-BELIEVE SCIENCE		◆	◆
OH, YOU SHOULDN'T HAVE, REALLY			◆
SPACE EXPLORATION FOR BEGINNERS		◆	◆
RECYCLED ELVES			◆
HOW TO WRITE A HOW-TO		◆	◆
TALKING TRASH!		◆	◆
WHY DID THE CHICKEN CROSS THE LESSON PLAN?			
SPY SCHOOL		◆	◆
PJ PARTY			◆
ANY WHICH WAY			◆
LIFE-SIZE BOARD GAME!			◆
BRAINS! OR, WRITING WITH ZOMBIES			◆
HOW TO WRITE A COMIC			◆
THE MEANING OF LIFE	◆	◆	◆
HOW TO SURVIVE ANYTHING		◆	◆
VINDICATED VILLAINS			◆
ONO-MATO-WHAT NOW?			◆

	With guidance and support from adults, produce writing in which the development and organization are appropriate to task, purpose, and audience.	With guidance and support from peers and adults, develop and strengthen writing as needed by planning, revising, and editing.	With some guidance and support from adults, use technology, including the Internet, to produce and publish writing as well as to interact and collaborate with others; demonstrate sufficient command of keyboarding skills to type a minimum of one page in a single sitting.
TRAGIC LOVE TALES (BY SIX-YEAR-OLDS)	❖	❖	
WRITING FOR PETS	❖	❖	
FORT PARTY!	❖	❖	
MAKE-BELIEVE SCIENCE	❖	❖	
OH, YOU SHOULDN'T HAVE, REALLY	❖	❖	
SPACE EXPLORATION FOR BEGINNERS	❖	❖	
RECYCLED ELVES	❖	❖	
HOW TO WRITE A HOW-TO	❖	❖	
TALKING TRASH!	❖	❖	❖
WHY DID THE CHICKEN CROSS THE LESSON PLAN?	❖	❖	
SPY SCHOOL	❖	❖	
PJ PARTY	❖	❖	
ANY WHICH WAY	❖	❖	
LIFE-SIZE BOARD GAME!	❖	❖	
BRAINS! OR, WRITING WITH ZOMBIES	❖	❖	
HOW TO WRITE A COMIC	❖	❖	
THE MEANING OF LIFE	❖	❖	
HOW TO SURVIVE ANYTHING	❖	❖	
VINDICATED VILLAINS	❖	❖	
ONO-MATO-WHAT NOW?	❖	❖	

THIRD-FOURTH GRADE	RESEARCH TO BUILD AND PRESENT KNOWLEDGE			RANGE OF WRITING
	Conduct short research projects that build knowledge through investigation of different aspects of a topic.	Recall relevant information from experiences or gather relevant information from print and digital sources; take notes and categorize information, and provide a list of sources.	(Begins in grade 4) Draw evidence from literary or informational texts to support analysis, reflection, and research. Apply grade 4 reading standards to literature (e.g., "Describe in depth a character, setting, or event in a story or drama, drawing on specific details in the text [e.g., a character's thoughts, words, or actions]."). Apply grade 4 reading standards to informational texts (e.g., "Explain how an author uses reasons and evidence to support particular points in a text").	Write routinely over extended time frames (time for research, reflection, and revision) and shorter time frames (a single sitting or a day or two) for a range of discipline-specific tasks, purposes, and audiences.
TRAGIC LOVE TALES (BY SIX-YEAR-OLDS)		◆		◆
WRITING FOR PETS		◆		◆
FORT PARTY!		◆		◆
MAKE-BELIEVE SCIENCE	◆	◆	◆	◆
OH, YOU SHOULDN'T HAVE, REALLY		◆	◆	◆
SPACE EXPLORATION FOR BEGINNERS	◆	◆	◆	◆
RECYCLED ELVES	◆	◆		◆
HOW TO WRITE A HOW-TO		◆	◆	◆
TALKING TRASH!	◆	◆	◆	◆
WHY DID THE CHICKEN CROSS THE LESSON PLAN?	◆			◆
SPY SCHOOL	◆	◆	◆	◆
PJ PARTY	◆	◆	◆	◆
ANY WHICH WAY	◆	◆	◆	◆
LIFE-SIZE BOARD GAME!		◆	◆	◆
BRAINS! OR, WRITING WITH ZOMBIES	◆	◆	◆	◆
HOW TO WRITE A COMIC	◆	◆	◆	◆
THE MEANING OF LIFE	◆	◆	◆	◆
HOW TO SURVIVE ANYTHING	◆	◆	◆	◆
VINDICATED VILLAINS		◆	◆	◆
ONO-MATO-WHAT NOW?	◆	◆	◆	◆

TEXT TYPES AND PURPOSES

	Write opinion pieces on topics or texts, supporting a point of view with reasons and information. Introduce a topic or text clearly, state an opinion, and create an organizational structure in which related ideas are grouped to support the writer's purpose. Provide reasons that are supported by facts and details. Link opinion and reasons using words and phrases (e.g., for instance, in order to, in addition). Provide a concluding statement or section related to the opinion presented.	Write informative/explanatory texts to examine a topic and convey ideas and information clearly. Introduce a topic clearly and group related information in paragraphs and sections; include formatting (e.g., headings), illustrations, and multimedia when useful to aiding comprehension. Develop the topic with facts, definitions, concrete details, quotations, or other information and examples related to the topic. Link ideas within categories of information using words and phrases (e.g., another, for example, also, because). Provide a concluding statement or section related to the information or explanation presented.	Write narratives to develop real or imagined experiences or events using effective technique, descriptive details, and clear event sequences. Orient the reader by establishing a situation and introducing a narrator and/or characters; organize an event sequence that unfolds naturally. Use dialogue and description to develop experiences and events or show the responses of characters to situations. Use a variety of transitional words and phrases to manage the sequence of events. Use concrete words and phrases and sensory details to convey experiences and events precisely. Provide a conclusion that follows from the narrated experiences or events.
ALL-STAR SPORTS STORIES		◆	◆
COOKING FOR CRYPTIDS		◆	◆
SCIENCE CLUB	◆	◆	◆
STICKY WORDS			
MADDENING MAD LIBS			
IF I WERE A KING OR QUEEN	◆	◆	◆
HOW TO BE A DETECTIVE		◆	◆
HARRY POTTER SPIDER-MAN VS. THE EVIL ZOMBIE NINJAS		◆	◆
FOR THE BIRDS!		◆	◆
THERE'S POETRY IN AN ATOM	◆	◆	◆
GUERILLA POETRY			
FRANKENFILMS			◆
AND NOW I WILL PERFORM AN INTERPRETIVE DANCE		◆	◆
NOTE TO SELF	◆	◆	◆
SMELL THIS STORY, TASTE THIS POEM		◆	◆
HOW TO BE THE NEXT PRESIDENT OF THE UNITED STATES!	◆	◆	◆
CHARACTER ASSASSINATION!			◆
SONNETS WITH SUPERPOWERS			
BEST IMAGINARY VACATION EVER!		◆	◆
THE ILLUSTRATED BOOK REPORT			◆

THIRD-FOURTH GRADE	PRODUCTION AND DISTRIBUTION OF WRITING		
	With guidance and support from adults, produce writing in which the development and organization are appropriate to task, purpose, and audience. (Grade-specific expectations for writing types are defined in preceding standards for 1–3.)	With guidance and support from peers and adults, develop and strengthen writing as needed by planning, revising, and editing.	With some guidance and support from adults, use technology, including the Internet, to produce and publish writing as well as to interact and collaborate with others; demonstrate sufficient command of keyboarding skills to type a minimum of one page in a single sitting.
ALL-STAR SPORTS STORIES	❖	❖	
COOKING FOR CRYPTIDS	❖	❖	
SCIENCE CLUB	❖	❖	
STICKY WORDS		❖	❖
MADDENING MAD LIBS	❖	❖	
IF I WERE A KING OR QUEEN	❖	❖	
HOW TO BE A DETECTIVE	❖	❖	
HARRY POTTER SPIDER-MAN VS. THE EVIL ZOMBIE NINJAS	❖	❖	
FOR THE BIRDS!	❖	❖	❖
THERE'S POETRY IN AN ATOM	❖	❖	❖
GUERRILLA POETRY	❖	❖	
FRANKENFILMS	❖	❖	
AND NOW I WILL PERFORM AN INTERPRETIVE DANCE	❖	❖	
NOTE TO SELF	❖	❖	
SMELL THIS STORY, TASTE THIS POEM	❖	❖	
HOW TO BE THE NEXT PRESIDENT OF THE UNITED STATES!	❖	❖	
CHARACTER ASSASSINATION!	❖	❖	
SONNETS WITH SUPERPOWERS	❖	❖	
BEST IMAGINARY VACATION EVER!	❖	❖	
THE ILLUSTRATED BOOK REPORT	❖	❖	❖

THIRD-FOURTH GRADE	RESEARCH TO BUILD AND PRESENT KNOWLEDGE			RANGE OF WRITING
	Conduct short research projects that build knowledge through investigation of different aspects of a topic.	Recall relevant information from experiences or gather relevant information from print and digital sources; take notes and categorize information, and provide a list of sources.	(Begins in grade 4) Draw evidence from literary or informational texts to support analysis, reflection, and research. Apply grade 4 reading standards to literature (e.g., "Describe in depth a character, setting, or event in a story or drama, drawing on specific details in the text [e.g., a character's thoughts, words, or actions]"). Apply grade 4 reading standards to informational texts (e.g., "Explain how an author uses reasons and evidence to support particular points in a text").	Write routinely over extended time frames (time for research, reflection, and revision) and shorter time frames (a single sitting or a day or two) for a range of discipline-specific tasks, purposes, and audiences.
ALL-STAR SPORTS STORIES	◈	◈	◈	◈
COOKING FOR CRYPTIDS	◈	◈	◈	◈
SCIENCE CLUB	◈	◈	◈	◈
STICKY WORDS	◈			◈
MADDENING MAD LIBS		◈		◈
IF I WERE A KING OR QUEEN	◈	◈	◈	◈
HOW TO BE A DETECTIVE	◈	◈	◈	◈
HARRY POTTER SPIDER-MAN VS. THE EVIL ZOMBIE NINJAS			◈	◈
FOR THE BIRDS!	◈	◈	◈	◈
THERE'S POETRY IN AN ATOM	◈	◈	◈	◈
GUERRILLA POETRY		◈		◈
FRANKENFILMS	◈	◈	◈	◈
AND NOW I WILL PERFORM AN INTERPRETIVE DANCE			◈	◈
NOTE TO SELF	◈	◈	◈	◈
SMELL THIS STORY, TASTE THIS POEM	◈	◈	◈	◈
HOW TO BE THE NEXT PRESIDENT OF THE UNITED STATES!	◈	◈	◈	◈
CHARACTER ASSASSINATION!		◈	◈	◈
SONNETS WITH SUPERPOWERS		◈		◈
BEST IMAGINARY VACATION EVER!			◈	◈
THE ILLUSTRATED BOOK REPORT	◈	◈	◈	◈

FIFTH GRADE	TEXT TYPES AND PURPOSES		
	Write opinion pieces on topics or texts, supporting a point of view with reasons and information. Introduce a topic or text clearly, state an opinion, and create an organizational structure in which ideas are logically grouped to support the writer's purpose. Provide logically ordered reasons that are supported by facts and details. Link opinion and reasons using words, phrases, and clauses (e.g., consequently, specifically). Provide a concluding statement or section related to the opinion presented.	Write informative/explanatory texts to examine a topic and convey ideas and information clearly. Introduce a topic clearly, provide a general observation and focus, and group related information logically; include formatting (e.g., headings), illustrations, and multimedia when useful to aiding comprehension. Develop the topic with facts, definitions, concrete details, quotations, or other information and examples related to the topic. Link ideas within and across categories of information using words, phrases, and clauses (e.g., in contrast, especially). Use precise language and domain-specific vocabulary to inform about or explain the topic. Provide a concluding statement or section related to the information or explanation presented.	Write narratives to develop real or imagined experiences or events using effective technique, descriptive details, and clear event sequences. Orient the reader by establishing a situation and introducing a narrator and/or characters; organize an event sequence that unfolds naturally. Use narrative techniques, such as dialogue, description, and pacing, to develop experiences and events or show the responses of characters to situations. Use a variety of transitional words, phrases, and clauses to manage the sequence of events. Use concrete words and phrases and sensory details to convey experiences and events precisely. Provide a conclusion that follows from the narrated experiences or events.
FORT PARTY!		✦	✦
MAKE-BELIEVE SCIENCE		✦	✦
MAGIC REALISM			✦
RECYCLED ELVES			✦
CREATING A GUIDE TO MODERN GIRLHOOD	✦	✦	✦
HOW TO WRITE A HOW-TO		✦	✦
TALKING TRASH!		✦	✦
SPY SCHOOL		✦	✦
LITERARY MASH-UPS			✦
BRAIN SPELUNKING			✦
PJ PARTY			✦
ANY WHICH WAY			✦
LIFE-SIZE BOARD GAME!			✦
BRAINS! OR, WRITING WITH ZOMBIES			✦
HOW TO WRITE A COMIC			✦
THE MEANING OF LIFE	✦	✦	✦
HOW TO SURVIVE ANYTHING		✦	✦
VINDICATED VILLAINS			✦
ONO-MATO-WHAT NOW?			✦
ALL-STAR SPORTS STORIES			✦
I WROTE A GUIDEBOOK	✦	✦	✦
STICKY WORDS			
MADDENING MAD LIBS			

	Produce clear and coherent writing in which the development and organization are appropriate to task, purpose, and audience. (Grade-specific expectations for writing types are defined in preceding standards for 1–3.)	With guidance and support from peers and adults, develop and strengthen writing as needed by planning, revising, editing, rewriting, or trying a new approach.	With some guidance and support from adults, use technology, including the Internet, to produce and publish writing as well as to interact and collaborate with others; demonstrate sufficient command of keyboarding skills to type a minimum of two pages in a single sitting.
FORT PARTY!	❖	❖	
MAKE-BELIEVE SCIENCE	❖	❖	
MAGIC REALISM	❖	❖	
RECYCLED ELVES	❖	❖	
CREATING A GUIDE TO MODERN GIRLHOOD	❖	❖	
HOW TO WRITE A HOW-TO	❖	❖	
TALKING TRASH!	❖	❖	❖
SPY SCHOOL	❖	❖	
LITERARY MASH-UPS	❖	❖	
BRAIN SPELUNKING	❖	❖	
PJ PARTY	❖	❖	
ANY WHICH WAY	❖	❖	
LIFE-SIZE BOARD GAME!	❖	❖	
BRAINS! OR, WRITING WITH ZOMBIES	❖	❖	
HOW TO WRITE A COMIC	❖	❖	
THE MEANING OF LIFE	❖	❖	
HOW TO SURVIVE ANYTHING	❖	❖	
VINDICATED VILLAINS	❖	❖	
ONO-MATO-WHAT NOW?	❖	❖	
ALL-STAR SPORTS STORIES	❖	❖	
I WROTE A GUIDEBOOK	❖	❖	❖
STICKY WORDS	❖	❖	
MADDENING MAD LIBS	❖	❖	

FIFTH GRADE	RESEARCH TO BUILD AND PRESENT KNOWLEDGE			RANGE OF WRITING
	Conduct short research projects that build knowledge through investigation of different aspects of a topic.	Recall relevant information from experiences or gather relevant information from print and digital sources; summarize or paraphrase information in notes and finished work, and provide a list of sources.	Draw evidence from literary or informational texts to support analysis, reflection, and research. Apply grade 5 reading standards to literature (e.g., "Compare and contrast two or more characters, settings, or events in a story or a drama, drawing on specific details in the text [e.g., how characters interact]"). Apply grade 5 reading standards to informational texts (e.g., "Explain how an author uses reasons and evidence to support particular points in a text, identifying which reasons and evidence support which point[s]").	Write routinely over extended time frames (time for research, reflection, and revision) and shorter time frames (a single sitting or a day or two) for a range of discipline-specific tasks, purposes, and audiences.
FORT PARTY!		❖		❖
MAKE-BELIEVE SCIENCE	❖	❖	❖	❖
MAGIC REALISM		❖	❖	❖
RECYCLED ELVES		❖	❖	❖
CREATING A GUIDE TO MODERN GIRLHOOD	❖	❖	❖	❖
HOW TO WRITE A HOW-TO		❖	❖	❖
TALKING TRASH!	❖	❖	❖	❖
SPY SCHOOL	❖	❖	❖	❖
LITERARY MASH-UPS		❖	❖	❖
BRAIN SPELUNKING		❖	❖	❖
PJ PARTY	❖	❖	❖	❖
ANY WHICH WAY	❖	❖	❖	❖
LIFE-SIZE BOARD GAME!		❖	❖	❖
BRAINS! OR, WRITING WITH ZOMBIES	❖	❖	❖	❖
HOW TO WRITE A COMIC	❖	❖	❖	❖
THE MEANING OF LIFE	❖	❖	❖	❖
HOW TO SURVIVE ANYTHING	❖	❖	❖	❖
VINDICATED VILLAINS		❖	❖	❖
ONO-MATO-WHAT NOW?	❖	❖	❖	❖
ALL-STAR SPORTS STORIES	❖	❖	❖	❖
I WROTE A GUIDEBOOK	❖	❖	❖	❖
STICKY WORDS		❖		❖
MADDENING MAD LIBS		❖		❖

	Write opinion pieces on topics or texts, supporting a point of view with reasons and information. Introduce a topic or text clearly, state an opinion, and create an organizational structure in which ideas are logically grouped to support the writer's purpose. Provide logically ordered reasons that are supported by facts and details. Link opinion and reasons using words, phrases, and clauses (e.g., consequently, specifically). Provide a concluding statement or section related to the opinion presented.	Write informative/explanatory texts to examine a topic and convey ideas and information clearly. Introduce a topic clearly, provide a general observation and focus, and group related information logically; include formatting (e.g., headings), illustrations, and multimedia when useful to aiding comprehension. Develop the topic with facts, definitions, concrete details, quotations, or other information and examples related to the topic. Link ideas within and across categories of information using words, phrases, and clauses (e.g., in contrast, especially). Use precise language and domain-specific vocabulary to inform about or explain the topic. Provide a concluding statement or section related to the information or explanation presented.	Write narratives to develop real or imagined experiences or events using effective technique, descriptive details, and clear event sequences. Orient the reader by establishing a situation and introducing a narrator and/or characters; organize an event sequence that unfolds naturally. Use narrative techniques, such as dialogue, description, and pacing, to develop experiences and events or show the responses of characters to situations. Use a variety of transitional words, phrases, and clauses to manage the sequence of events. Use concrete words and phrases and sensory details to convey experiences and events precisely. Provide a conclusion that follows from the narrated experiences or events.
IF I WERE A KING OR QUEEN	❖	❖	❖
HOW TO BE A DETECTIVE		❖	❖
HARRY POTTER SPIDER-MAN VS. THE EVIL ZOMBIE NINJAS		❖	❖
OUT THERE	❖	❖	❖
WHINING EFFECTIVELY	❖	❖	❖
THERE'S POETRY IN AN ATOM	❖	❖	❖
GUERRILLA POETRY			
FRANKENFILMS			❖
THE RULES OF MAGIC			❖
AND NOW I WILL PERFORM AN INTERPRETIVE DANCE		❖	❖
NOTE TO SELF	❖	❖	❖
SMELL THIS STORY, TASTE THIS POEM		❖	❖
GRAMMARAMA			
HOW TO BE THE NEXT PRESIDENT OF THE UNITED STATES!	❖	❖	❖
CHARACTER ASSASSINATION!			❖
SONNETS WITH SUPERPOWERS			
BEST IMAGINARY VACATION EVER!		❖	❖
WHAT'S THE SCOOP?	❖	❖	❖
THE ILLUSTRATED BOOK REPORT			❖

	Produce clear and coherent writing in which the development and organization are appropriate to task, purpose, and audience. (Grade-specific expectations for writing types are defined in preceding standards for 1–3.)	With guidance and support from peers and adults, develop and strengthen writing as needed by planning, revising, editing, rewriting, or trying a new approach.	With some guidance and support from adults, use technology, including the Internet, to produce and publish writing as well as to interact and collaborate with others; demonstrate sufficient command of keyboarding skills to type a minimum of two pages in a single sitting.
IF I WERE A KING OR QUEEN	❖	❖	
HOW TO BE A DETECTIVE	❖	❖	
HARRY POTTER SPIDER-MAN VS. THE EVIL ZOMBIE NINJAS	❖	❖	❖
OUT THERE	❖	❖	
WHINING EFFECTIVELY	❖	❖	❖
THERE'S POETRY IN AN ATOM	❖	❖	❖
GUERRILLA POETRY	❖	❖	
FRANKENFILMS	❖	❖	
THE RULES OF MAGIC	❖	❖	
AND NOW I WILL PERFORM AN INTERPRETIVE DANCE	❖	❖	
NOTE TO SELF	❖	❖	
SMELL THIS STORY, TASTE THIS POEM	❖	❖	
GRAMMARAMA	❖	❖	
HOW TO BE THE NEXT PRESIDENT OF THE UNITED STATES!	❖	❖	
CHARACTER ASSASSINATION!	❖	❖	
SONNETS WITH SUPERPOWERS	❖	❖	
BEST IMAGINARY VACATION EVER!	❖	❖	
WHAT'S THE SCOOP?	❖	❖	
THE ILLUSTRATED BOOK REPORT	❖	❖	❖

FIFTH GRADE	RESEARCH TO BUILD AND PRESENT KNOWLEDGE			RANGE OF WRITING
	Conduct short research projects that build knowledge through investigation of different aspects of a topic.	Recall relevant information from experiences or gather relevant information from print and digital sources; summarize or paraphrase information in notes and finished work, and provide a list of sources.	Draw evidence from literary or informational texts to support analysis, reflection, and research. Apply grade 5 reading standards to literature (e.g., "Compare and contrast two or more characters, settings, or events in a story or a drama, drawing on specific details in the text [e.g., how characters interact]"). Apply grade 5 reading standards to informational texts (e.g., "Explain how an author uses reasons and evidence to support particular points in a text, identifying which reasons and evidence support which point[s]").	Write routinely over extended time frames (time for research, reflection, and revision) and shorter time frames (a single sitting or a day or two) for a range of discipline-specific tasks, purposes, and audiences.
IF I WERE A KING OR QUEEN	✦	✦	✦	✦
HOW TO BE A DETECTIVE	✦	✦	✦	✦
HARRY POTTER SPIDER-MAN VS. THE EVIL ZOMBIE NINJAS			✦	✦
OUT THERE	✦	✦	✦	✦
WHINING EFFECTIVELY	✦	✦	✦	✦
THERE'S POETRY IN AN ATOM	✦	✦	✦	✦
GUERRILLA POETRY		✦		✦
FRANKENFILMS	✦	✦	✦	✦
THE RULES OF MAGIC		✦	✦	✦
AND NOW I WILL PERFORM AN INTERPRETIVE DANCE			✦	✦
NOTE TO SELF	✦	✦	✦	✦
SMELL THIS STORY, TASTE THIS POEM	✦	✦	✦	✦
GRAMMARAMA		✦		✦
HOW TO BE THE NEXT PRESIDENT OF THE UNITED STATES!	✦	✦	✦	✦
CHARACTER ASSASSINATION!		✦	✦	✦
SONNETS WITH SUPERPOWERS		✦		✦
BEST IMAGINARY VACATION EVER!			✦	✦
WHAT'S THE SCOOP?	✦	✦	✦	✦
THE ILLUSTRATED BOOK REPORT	✦	✦	✦	✦

	Write arguments to support claims with clear reasons and relevant evidence. Introduce claim(s) and organize the reasons and evidence clearly. Support claim(s) with clear reasons and relevant evidence, using credible sources and demonstrating an understanding of the topic or text. Use words, phrases, and clauses to clarify the relationships among claim(s) and reasons. Establish and maintain a formal style. Provide a concluding statement or section that follows from the argument presented.	Write informative/explanatory texts to examine a topic and convey ideas, concepts, and information through the selection, organization, and analysis of relevant content. Introduce a topic; organize ideas, concepts, and information, using strategies such as definition, classification, comparison/contrast, and cause/effect; include formatting (e.g., headings), graphics (e.g., charts, tables), and multimedia when useful to aiding comprehension. Develop the topic with relevant facts, definitions, concrete details, quotations, or other information and examples. Use appropriate transitions to clarify the relationships among ideas and concepts. Use precise language and domain-specific vocabulary to inform about or explain the topic. Establish and maintain a formal style. Provide a concluding statement or section that follows from the information or explanation presented.	Write narratives to develop real or imagined experiences or events using effective technique, relevant descriptive details, and well-structured event sequences. Engage and orient the reader by establishing a context and introducing a narrator and/or characters; organize an event sequence that unfolds naturally and logically. Use narrative techniques, such as dialogue, pacing, and description, to develop experiences, events, and/or characters. Use a variety of transition words, phrases, and clauses to convey sequence and signal shifts from one time frame or setting to another. Use precise words and phrases, relevant descriptive details, and sensory language to convey experiences and events. Provide a conclusion that follows from the narrated experiences or events.
MAGIC REALISM			❖
RECYCLED ELVES			❖
CREATING A GUIDE TO MODERN GIRLHOOD	❖	❖	❖
HOW TO WRITE A HOW-TO		❖	❖
TALKING TRASH!		❖	❖
SPY SCHOOL		❖	❖
LITERARY MASH-UPS			❖
BRAIN SPELUNKING			❖
ANY WHICH WAY			❖
LIFE-SIZE BOARD GAME!			❖
HOW TO WRITE A COMIC			❖
THE MEANING OF LIFE	❖	❖	❖
HOW TO SURVIVE ANYTHING		❖	❖
ALL-STAR SPORTS STORIES			❖
I WROTE A GUIDEBOOK	❖	❖	❖
MADDENING MAD LIBS			
IF I WERE A KING OR QUEEN	❖	❖	❖

	Produce clear and coherent writing in which the development, organization, and style are appropriate to task, purpose, and audience. (Grade-specific expectations for writing types are defined in preceding standards for 1–3.)	With some guidance and support from peers and adults, develop and strengthen writing as needed by planning, revising, editing, rewriting, or trying a new approach.	Use technology, including the Internet, to produce and publish writing as well as to interact and collaborate with others; demonstrate sufficient command of keyboarding skills to type a minimum of three pages in a single sitting.
MAGIC REALISM	❖	❖	
RECYCLED ELVES	❖	❖	
CREATING A GUIDE TO MODERN GIRLHOOD	❖	❖	
HOW TO WRITE A HOW-TO	❖	❖	
TALKING TRASH!	❖	❖	❖
SPY SCHOOL	❖	❖	
LITERARY MASH-UPS	❖	❖	
BRAIN SPELUNKING	❖	❖	
ANY WHICH WAY	❖	❖	
LIFE-SIZE BOARD GAME!	❖	❖	
HOW TO WRITE A COMIC	❖	❖	
THE MEANING OF LIFE	❖	❖	
HOW TO SURVIVE ANYTHING	❖	❖	
ALL-STAR SPORTS STORIES	❖	❖	
I WROTE A GUIDEBOOK	❖	❖	❖
MADDENING MAD LIBS	❖	❖	
IF I WERE A KING OR QUEEN	❖	❖	

SIXTH GRADE	RESEARCH TO BUILD AND PRESENT KNOWLEDGE			RANGE OF WRITING
	Conduct short research projects to answer a question, drawing on several sources and refocusing the inquiry when appropriate.	Gather relevant information from multiple print and digital sources; assess the credibility of each source; and quote or paraphrase the data and conclusions of others while avoiding plagiarism and providing basic bibliographic information for sources.	Draw evidence from literary or informational texts to support analysis, reflection, and research. Apply grade 6 reading standards to literature (e.g., "Compare and contrast texts in different forms or genres [e.g., stories and poems; historical novels and fantasy stories] in terms of their approaches to similar themes and topics"). Apply grade 6 reading standards to literary nonfiction (e.g., "Trace and evaluate the argument and specific claims in a text, distinguishing claims that are supported by reasons and evidence from claims that are not").	Write routinely over extended time frames (time for research, reflection, and revision) and shorter time frames (a single sitting or a day or two) for a range of discipline-specific tasks, purposes, and audiences.
MAGIC REALISM		❖	❖	❖
RECYCLED ELVES		❖	❖	❖
CREATING A GUIDE TO MODERN GIRLHOOD	❖	❖	❖	❖
HOW TO WRITE A HOW-TO		❖	❖	❖
TALKING TRASH!	❖	❖	❖	❖
SPY SCHOOL	❖	❖	❖	❖
LITERARY MASH-UPS		❖	❖	❖
BRAIN SPELUNKING		❖	❖	❖
ANY WHICH WAY	❖	❖	❖	❖
LIFE-SIZE BOARD GAME!		❖	❖	❖
HOW TO WRITE A COMIC	❖	❖	❖	❖
THE MEANING OF LIFE	❖	❖	❖	❖
HOW TO SURVIVE ANYTHING	❖	❖	❖	❖
ALL-STAR SPORTS STORIES	❖	❖	❖	❖
I WROTE A GUIDEBOOK	❖	❖	❖	❖
MADDENING MAD LIBS		❖		❖
IF I WERE A KING OR QUEEN	❖	❖	❖	❖

	Write arguments to support claims with clear reasons and relevant evidence. Introduce claim(s) and organize the reasons and evidence clearly. Support claim(s) with clear reasons and relevant evidence, using credible sources and demonstrating an understanding of the topic or text. Use words, phrases, and clauses to clarify the relationships among claim(s) and reasons. Establish and maintain a formal style. Provide a concluding statement or section that follows from the argument presented.	Write informative/explanatory texts to examine a topic and convey ideas, concepts, and information through the selection, organization, and analysis of relevant content. Introduce a topic; organize ideas, concepts, and information, using strategies such as definition, classification, comparison/contrast, and cause/effect; include formatting (e.g., headings), graphics (e.g., charts, tables), and multimedia when useful to aiding comprehension. Develop the topic with relevant facts, definitions, concrete details, quotations, or other information and examples. Use appropriate transitions to clarify the relationships among ideas and concepts. Use precise language and domain-specific vocabulary to inform about or explain the topic. Establish and maintain a formal style. Provide a concluding statement or section that follows from the information or explanation presented.	Write narratives to develop real or imagined experiences or events using effective technique, relevant descriptive details, and well-structured event sequences. Engage and orient the reader by establishing a context and introducing a narrator and/or characters; organize an event sequence that unfolds naturally and logically. Use narrative techniques, such as dialogue, pacing, and description, to develop experiences, events, and/or characters. Use a variety of transition words, phrases, and clauses to convey sequence and signal shifts from one time frame or setting to another. Use precise words and phrases, relevant descriptive details, and sensory language to convey experiences and events. Provide a conclusion that follows from the narrated experiences or events.
HOW TO BE A DETECTIVE		❖	❖
HARRY POTTER SPIDER-MAN VS. THE EVIL ZOMBIE NINJAS		❖	❖
OUT THERE	❖	❖	❖
WHINING EFFECTIVELY	❖	❖	❖
THERE'S POETRY IN AN ATOM	❖	❖	❖
GUERRILLA POETRY			
FRANKENFILMS			❖
THE RULES OF MAGIC			❖
AND NOW I WILL PERFORM AN INTERPRETIVE DANCE		❖	❖
NOTE TO SELF	❖	❖	❖
SMELL THIS STORY, TASTE THIS POEM		❖	❖
GRAMMARAMA			
HOW TO BE THE NEXT PRESIDENT OF THE UNITED STATES!	❖	❖	❖
CHARACTER ASSASSINATION!			❖
SONNETS WITH SUPERPOWERS			
WHAT'S THE SCOOP?	❖	❖	❖
THE ILLUSTRATED BOOK REPORT			❖

	Produce clear and coherent writing in which the development, organization, and style are appropriate to task, purpose, and audience. (Grade-specific expectations for writing types are defined in preceding standards for 1–3.)	With some guidance and support from peers and adults, develop and strengthen writing as needed by planning, revising, editing, rewriting, or trying a new approach.	Use technology, including the Internet, to produce and publish writing as well as to interact and collaborate with others; demonstrate sufficient command of keyboarding skills to type a minimum of three pages in a single sitting.
HOW TO BE A DETECTIVE	❖	❖	
HARRY POTTER SPIDER-MAN VS. THE EVIL ZOMBIE NINJAS	❖	❖	❖
OUT THERE	❖	❖	
WHINING EFFECTIVELY	❖	❖	❖
THERE'S POETRY IN AN ATOM	❖	❖	❖
GUERRILLA POETRY	❖	❖	
FRANKENFILMS	❖	❖	
THE RULES OF MAGIC	❖	❖	
AND NOW I WILL PERFORM AN INTERPRETIVE DANCE	❖	❖	
NOTE TO SELF	❖	❖	
SMELL THIS STORY, TASTE THIS POEM	❖	❖	
GRAMMARAMA	❖	❖	
HOW TO BE THE NEXT PRESIDENT OF THE UNITED STATES!	❖	❖	
CHARACTER ASSASSINATION!	❖	❖	
SONNETS WITH SUPERPOWERS	❖	❖	
WHAT'S THE SCOOP?	❖		
THE ILLUSTRATED BOOK REPORT	❖	❖	❖

	Conduct short research projects to answer a question, drawing on several sources and refocusing the inquiry when appropriate.	Gather relevant information from multiple print and digital sources; assess the credibility of each source; and quote or paraphrase the data and conclusions of others while avoiding plagiarism and providing basic bibliographic information for sources.	Draw evidence from literary or informational texts to support analysis, reflection, and research. Apply grade 6 reading standards to literature (e.g., "Compare and contrast texts in different forms or genres [e.g., stories and poems; historical novels and fantasy stories] in terms of their approaches to similar themes and topics"). Apply grade 6 reading standards to literary nonfiction (e.g., "Trace and evaluate the argument and specific claims in a text, distinguishing claims that are supported by reasons and evidence from claims that are not").	Write routinely over extended time frames (time for research, reflection, and revision) and shorter time frames (a single sitting or a day or two) for a range of discipline-specific tasks, purposes, and audiences.
RESEARCH TO BUILD AND PRESENT KNOWLEDGE 				**RANGE OF WRITING**
HOW TO BE A DETECTIVE	✦	✦	✦	✦
HARRY POTTER SPIDER-MAN VS. THE EVIL ZOMBIE NINJAS			✦	✦
OUT THERE	✦	✦	✦	✦
WHINING EFFECTIVELY	✦	✦	✦	✦
THERE'S POETRY IN AN ATOM	✦	✦	✦	✦
GUERRILLA POETRY		✦		✦
FRANKENFILMS	✦	✦	✦	✦
THE RULES OF MAGIC		✦	✦	✦
AND NOW I WILL PERFORM AN INTERPRETIVE DANCE			✦	✦
NOTE TO SELF	✦	✦	✦	✦
SMELL THIS STORY, TASTE THIS POEM	✦	✦	✦	✦
GRAMMARAMA		✦		✦
HOW TO BE THE NEXT PRESIDENT OF THE UNITED STATES!	✦	✦	✦	✦
CHARACTER ASSASSINATION!		✦	✦	✦
SONNETS WITH SUPERPOWERS		✦		✦
WHAT'S THE SCOOP?	✦	✦	✦	✦
THE ILLUSTRATED BOOK REPORT	✦	✦	✦	✦

	Write arguments to support claims with clear reasons and relevant evidence. Introduce claim(s), acknowledge alternate or opposing claims, and organize the reasons and evidence logically. Support claim(s) with logical reasoning and relevant evidence, using accurate, credible sources and demonstrating an understanding of the topic or text. Use words, phrases, and clauses to create cohesion and clarify the relationships among claim(s), reasons, and evidence. Establish and maintain a formal style. Provide a concluding statement or section that follows from and supports the argument presented.	Write informative/explanatory texts to examine a topic and convey ideas, concepts, and information through the selection, organization, and analysis of relevant content. Introduce a topic clearly, previewing what is to follow; organize ideas, concepts, and information, using strategies such as definition, classification, comparison/contrast, and cause/effect; include formatting (e.g., headings), graphics (e.g., charts, tables), and multimedia when useful to aiding comprehension. Develop the topic with relevant facts, definitions, concrete details, quotations, or other information and examples. Use appropriate transitions to create cohesion and clarify the relationships among ideas and concepts. Use precise language and domain-specific vocabulary to inform about or explain the topic. Establish and maintain a formal style. Provide a concluding statement or section that follows from and supports the information or explanation presented.	Write narratives to develop real or imagined experiences or events using effective technique, relevant descriptive details, and well-structured event sequences. Engage and orient the reader by establishing a context and point of view and introducing a narrator and/or characters; organize an event sequence that unfolds naturally and logically. Use narrative techniques, such as dialogue, pacing, and description, to develop experiences, events, and/or characters. Use a variety of transition words, phrases, and clauses to convey sequence and signal shifts from one time frame or setting to another. Use precise words and phrases, relevant descriptive details, and sensory language to capture the action and convey experiences and events. Provide a conclusion that follows from and reflects on the narrated experiences or events.
MAGIC REALISM			❖
RECYCLED ELVES			❖
CREATING A GUIDE TO MODERN GIRLHOOD	❖	❖	❖
HOW TO WRITE A HOW-TO		❖	❖
TALKING TRASH!		❖	❖
SPY SCHOOL		❖	❖
LITERARY MASH-UPS			❖
BRAIN SPELUNKING			❖
ANY WHICH WAY			❖
LIFE-SIZE BOARD GAME!			❖
HOW TO WRITE A COMIC			❖
THE MEANING OF LIFE	❖	❖	❖
HOW TO SURVIVE ANYTHING		❖	❖
ALL-STAR SPORTS STORIES			❖
I WROTE A GUIDEBOOK	❖	❖	❖
MADDENING MAD LIBS			
IF I WERE A KING OR QUEEN	❖	❖	❖

	Produce clear and coherent writing in which the development, organization, and style are appropriate to task, purpose, and audience. (Grade-specific expectations for writing types are defined in standards 1–3 above.)	With some guidance and support from peers and adults, develop and strengthen writing as needed by planning, revising, editing, rewriting, or trying a new approach, focusing on how well purpose and audience have been addressed.	Use technology, including the Internet, to produce and publish writing and link to and cite sources as well as to interact and collaborate with others, including linking to and citing sources.
MAGIC REALISM	❖	❖	
RECYCLED ELVES	❖	❖	
CREATING A GUIDE TO MODERN GIRLHOOD	❖	❖	
HOW TO WRITE A HOW-TO	❖	❖	
TALKING TRASH!	❖	❖	❖
SPY SCHOOL	❖	❖	
LITERARY MASH-UPS	❖	❖	
BRAIN SPELUNKING	❖	❖	
ANY WHICH WAY	❖	❖	
LIFE-SIZE BOARD GAME!	❖	❖	
HOW TO WRITE A COMIC	❖	❖	
THE MEANING OF LIFE	❖	❖	
HOW TO SURVIVE ANYTHING	❖	❖	
ALL-STAR SPORTS STORIES	❖	❖	
I WROTE A GUIDEBOOK	❖	❖	❖
MADDENING MAD LIBS	❖	❖	
IF I WERE A KING OR QUEEN	❖	❖	

Seventh Grade	Research to Build and Present Knowledge			Range of Writing
	Conduct short research projects to answer a question, drawing on several sources and refocusing the inquiry when appropriate.	Gather relevant information from multiple print and digital sources; assess the credibility of each source; and quote or paraphrase the data and conclusions of others while avoiding plagiarism and providing basic bibliographic information for sources.	Draw evidence from literary or informational texts to support analysis, reflection, and research. Apply grade 6 reading standards to literature (e.g., "Compare and contrast texts in different forms or genres [e.g., stories and poems; historical novels and fantasy stories] in terms of their approaches to similar themes and topics"). Apply grade 6 reading standards to literary nonfiction (e.g., "Trace and evaluate the argument and specific claims in a text, distinguishing claims that are supported by reasons and evidence from claims that are not").	Write routinely over extended time frames (time for research, reflection, and revision) and shorter time frames (a single sitting or a day or two) for a range of discipline-specific tasks, purposes, and audiences.
Magic Realism		✦	✦	✦
Recycled Elves		✦	✦	✦
Creating a Guide to Modern Girlhood	✦	✦	✦	✦
How to Write a How-To		✦	✦	✦
Talking Trash!	✦	✦	✦	✦
Spy School	✦	✦	✦	✦
Literary Mash-Ups		✦	✦	✦
Brain Spelunking		✦	✦	✦
Any Which Way	✦	✦	✦	✦
Life-Size Board Game!		✦	✦	✦
How to Write a Comic	✦	✦	✦	✦
The Meaning of Life	✦	✦	✦	✦
How to Survive Anything	✦	✦	✦	✦
All-Star Sports Stories	✦	✦	✦	✦
I Wrote a Guidebook	✦	✦	✦	✦
Maddening Mad Libs		✦		✦
If I Were a King or Queen	✦	✦	✦	✦

	Write arguments to support claims with clear reasons and relevant evidence. Introduce claim(s), acknowledge alternate or opposing claims, and organize the reasons and evidence logically. Support claim(s) with logical reasoning and relevant evidence, using accurate, credible sources and demonstrating an understanding of the topic or text. Use words, phrases, and clauses to create cohesion and clarify the relationships among claim(s), reasons, and evidence. Establish and maintain a formal style. Provide a concluding statement or section that follows from and supports the argument presented.	Write informative/explanatory texts to examine a topic and convey ideas, concepts, and information through the selection, organization, and analysis of relevant content. Introduce a topic clearly, previewing what is to follow; organize ideas, concepts, and information, using strategies such as definition, classification, comparison/contrast, and cause/effect; include formatting (e.g., headings), graphics (e.g., charts, tables), and multimedia when useful to aiding comprehension. Develop the topic with relevant facts, definitions, concrete details, quotations, or other information and examples. Use appropriate transitions to create cohesion and clarify the relationships among ideas and concepts. Use precise language and domain-specific vocabulary to inform about or explain the topic. Establish and maintain a formal style. Provide a concluding statement or section that follows from and supports the information or explanation presented.	Write narratives to develop real or imagined experiences or events using effective technique, relevant descriptive details, and well-structured event sequences. Engage and orient the reader by establishing a context and point of view and introducing a narrator and/or characters; organize an event sequence that unfolds naturally and logically. Use narrative techniques, such as dialogue, pacing, and description, to develop experiences, events, and/or characters. Use a variety of transition words, phrases, and clauses to convey sequence and signal shifts from one time frame or setting to another. Use precise words and phrases, relevant descriptive details, and sensory language to capture the action and convey experiences and events. Provide a conclusion that follows from and reflects on the narrated experiences or events.
HOW TO BE A DETECTIVE		♦	♦
HARRY POTTER SPIDER-MAN VS. THE EVIL ZOMBIE NINJAS		♦	♦
OUT THERE	♦	♦	♦
WHINING EFFECTIVELY	♦	♦	♦
THERE'S POETRY IN AN ATOM	♦	♦	♦
GUERRILLA POETRY			
FRANKENFILMS			♦
THE RULES OF MAGIC			♦
AND NOW I WILL PERFORM AN INTERPRETIVE DANCE		♦	♦
NOTE TO SELF	♦	♦	♦
SMELL THIS STORY, TASTE THIS POEM		♦	♦
GRAMMARAMA			
HOW TO BE THE NEXT PRESIDENT OF THE UNITED STATES!	♦	♦	♦
CHARACTER ASSASSINATION!			♦
SONNETS WITH SUPERPOWERS			
WHAT'S THE SCOOP?	♦	♦	♦
THE ILLUSTRATED BOOK REPORT			♦

	Produce clear and coherent writing in which the development, organization, and style are appropriate to task, purpose, and audience. (Grade-specific expectations for writing types are defined in standards 1–3 above.)	With some guidance and support from peers and adults, develop and strengthen writing as needed by planning, revising, editing, rewriting, or trying a new approach, focusing on how well purpose and audience have been addressed.	Use technology, including the Internet, to produce and publish writing and link to and cite sources as well as to interact and collaborate with others, including linking to and citing sources.
HOW TO BE A DETECTIVE	✦	✦	
HARRY POTTER SPIDER-MAN VS. THE EVIL ZOMBIE NINJAS	✦	✦	✦
OUT THERE	✦	✦	
WHINING EFFECTIVELY	✦	✦	✦
THERE'S POETRY IN AN ATOM	✦	✦	✦
GUERRILLA POETRY	✦	✦	
FRANKENFILMS	✦	✦	
THE RULES OF MAGIC	✦	✦	
AND NOW I WILL PERFORM AN INTERPRETIVE DANCE	✦	✦	
NOTE TO SELF	✦	✦	
SMELL THIS STORY, TASTE THIS POEM	✦	✦	
GRAMMARAMA	✦	✦	
HOW TO BE THE NEXT PRESIDENT OF THE UNITED STATES!	✦	✦	
CHARACTER ASSASSINATION!	✦	✦	
SONNETS WITH SUPERPOWERS	✦	✦	
WHAT'S THE SCOOP?	✦		
THE ILLUSTRATED BOOK REPORT	✦	✦	✦

	Conduct short research projects to answer a question, drawing on several sources and refocusing the inquiry when appropriate.	Gather relevant information from multiple print and digital sources; assess the credibility of each source; and quote or paraphrase the data and conclusions of others while avoiding plagiarism and providing basic bibliographic information for sources.	Draw evidence from literary or informational texts to support analysis, reflection, and research. Apply grade 6 reading standards to literature (e.g., "Compare and contrast texts in different forms or genres [e.g., stories and poems; historical novels and fantasy stories] in terms of their approaches to similar themes and topics"). Apply grade 6 reading standards to literary nonfiction (e.g., "Trace and evaluate the argument and specific claims in a text, distinguishing claims that are supported by reasons and evidence from claims that are not").	Write routinely over extended time frames (time for research, reflection, and revision) and shorter time frames (a single sitting or a day or two) for a range of discipline-specific tasks, purposes, and audiences.
HOW TO BE A DETECTIVE	✦	✦	✦	✦
HARRY POTTER SPIDER-MAN VS. THE EVIL ZOMBIE NINJAS			✦	✦
OUT THERE	✦	✦	✦	✦
WHINING EFFECTIVELY	✦	✦	✦	✦
THERE'S POETRY IN AN ATOM	✦	✦	✦	✦
GUERRILLA POETRY		✦		✦
FRANKENFILMS	✦	✦	✦	✦
THE RULES OF MAGIC		✦	✦	✦
AND NOW I WILL PERFORM AN INTERPRETIVE DANCE			✦	✦
NOTE TO SELF	✦	✦	✦	✦
SMELL THIS STORY, TASTE THIS POEM	✦	✦	✦	✦
GRAMMARAMA		✦		✦
HOW TO BE THE NEXT PRESIDENT OF THE UNITED STATES!	✦	✦	✦	✦
CHARACTER ASSASSINATION!		✦	✦	✦
SONNETS WITH SUPERPOWERS		✦		✦
WHAT'S THE SCOOP?	✦	✦	✦	✦
THE ILLUSTRATED BOOK REPORT	✦	✦	✦	✦

826 Centers and Staff

826 National
44 Gough Street, Suite 206
San Francisco, CA 94103
(415)864-2098

Staff: Gerald Richards, Erin Archuleta, Jen Benka, Ryan Lewis, Mariama Lockington

Board of Directors: Joel Arquillos, Jennifer Bunshoft, Howard Cutler, Jonathan Dearman, Dave Eggers, Brian Gray, Reece Hirsch, Daniel Kuruna, Pam McEwan, Tynnetta McIntosh, Amir Mokari, Scott Seeley, Amanda Uhle, Kevin Whalen

—————

826 Valencia
826 Valencia Street
San Francisco, CA 94110
(415) 642–5905
www.826valencia.org

Staff: Leigh Lehman, Raúl Alcantar, Justin Carder, Emilie Coulson, Anne Farrah, Margaret McCarthy, María Inés Montes, Cherylle Taylor, Miranda Tsang, Vickie Vertiz

Board of Directors: Barb Bersche, Nínive Calegari, Dave Eggers, Brian Gray, Thomas Mike, Abner Morales, Bita Nazarian, Alexandra Quinn, Mary Schaefer, Vendela Vida, Richard Wolfgram

—————

826NYC
372 Fifth Avenue
Brooklyn, NY 11215
(718) 499–9884
www.826nyc.org

Staff: Scott Seeley, Kate Ackerman, Joan Kim, Joshua Martin, Anthony Mascorro, Sarah Pollock, Chris Roberti

Board of Directors: Nínive Calegari, Brenda Chan Casimir, Dave Eggers, Bill Heinzen, Jeanette Lee, Tynnetta McIntosh, Jon Scieszka, Sarah Vowell, Sean Wilsey

—————

826LA

826LA East
1714 W. Sunset Blvd.
Echo Park, CA 90026
(213) 413–3388

826LA West
SPARC Building
685 Venice Blvd.
Venice, CA 90291
(310) 305–8418

Staff: Joel Arquillos, Bonnie Chau, Christina Galante, Marisa Gedney, Danny Hom, Julius Diaz Panoriñgan

Board of Directors: Miguel Arteta, Mac Barnett, Joshuah Bearman, Nínive Calegari, Dave Eggers, Jodie Evans, John T. Gilbertson, Naomi Foner Gyllenhaal, Keith Knight, Melissa Mathison, Salvador Plascencia, Sally Willcox

———⇒·⇐———

826CHI
1331 N. Milwaukee Avenue
Chicago, IL 60622
(773) 772–8108
www.826chi.org

Staff: Mara Fuller O'Brien, Zach Duffy, Patrick Shaffner, Kait Steele

Board of Directors: Stephanie D'Alessandro, Staci Davidson, Monica Eng, Larry Feinberg, Ira Glass, Justine Jentes, Trista Hertz, Dan Kuruna, Kyra Kyles, Mara O'Brien, Matt Schrecengost, Jan Zasowski

———⇒·⇐———

826 Seattle
8414 Greenwood Avenue North
Seattle, Washington 98103
(206) 725–2625
www.826seattle.org

Staff: Teri Hein, Samar Abulhassan, Justin Allan, Alex Allred, Toffer Lehnherr, Sarah Beecroft

Board of Directors: Sherman Alexie, David Brotherton, Elizabeth Duffell, Teri Hein, Pam MacEwan, Shawn Rediger, Ann Senechal, Joan Hiller, Matthew Leavenworth

———⇒·⇐———

826michigan
115 East Liberty Street
Ann Arbor, MI 48104
(734) 761–3463
www.826michigan.org

Staff: Amanda Uhle, Amy Sumerto, Catherine Calabro

Board of Directors: Vicky Henry, Keith Hood, Angela Kujava, Laura London, Jeff Meyers, Jeremy Peters, Jacqui Robbins, Julia Sheill, Christopher Taylor, Jennifer Traig, Laura Wagner, Richard Weise

---

826 Boston
3035 Washington St.
Roxbury, MA 02119
(617) 442–5400
www.826boston.org

Staff: Daniel Johnson, Lindsey Plait Jones, Karen Sama, Ryan Smith

Board of Directors: Kevin Feeney, Jon Fullerton, John Giordano, Helen Jacobson, Paul Oh, Junia Yearwood

---

826DC
3233 14th St., NW
Washington, D.C. 20010
(202) 525–1074
www.826dc.org

Staff: Joe Callahan, Mariam Al-Shawaf, Kira Wisniewski

Board of Directors: Holly Jones, Matthew Klam, Steven Oxman, Marcela Sanchez, David Wakelyn